Acclaim for Striving

"Who knew that invisibility is a superpower? Jo Thomas, of course, in this compelling story of a life doing work that men considered "not for a woman." That work, as Thomas describes it with equal doses of honesty, horror, and humor, was journalism: the art and craft of being in the wrong places at the right times and using common sense, courage, and compassion to better understand what folks are saying. The result is more than a memoir for women. It's for anyone looking for a good read."

—Margot Slade, Co-Founder/Deputy Editor, Special Sections for *The New York Times,* where she worked for 22 years

"The story of how Jo Thomas broke into the traditionally male province of newspapering and became one of the country's leading investigative journalists is the subject of her utterly engrossing memoir, *Striving.* A journalist at *The New York Times* for over twenty years, Thomas brings to her memoir—whether she's recounting the Timothy McVeigh trial or the age-old conflict between Protestant and Catholics in Northern Ireland—a rare capacity for analysis and a writer's eye for the telling detail."

—John Rosenthal, photographer and memoirist, author of *After: the Silence of the Lower 9th Ward*, and author of *Searching for Amylu Danzer.*

D1601041

Jo Thomas
STRIVING

Jo Thomas wrote for *The New York Times* over a period of 26 years, as an investigative reporter based in Washington, D.C; chief of the Miami/Caribbean Bureau, a London correspondent, national correspondent, and an assistant national editor, writing for every section of the newspaper: science, business, travel, style, sports, *The New York Times Magazine*, and the Book Review.

Earlier in her career, she reported for the *Detroit Free Press* and the *Cincinnati Post and Times-Star*, where she was the first woman hired in the newsroom in 20 years. She started out as a college graduate and housewife who wanted to write. By 1970, she was the youngest Nieman Fellow accepted at Harvard and one of the first women. In 1974 she was a co-recipient of the Robert F. Kennedy Award for a series "Psychosurgery on Trial."

Jo spent two years investigating the far right in America after the 1995 bombing of the Murrah Federal Building in Oklahoma City. In 1997, judges in the American Society of Newspaper Editors' Wire Content Committee reviewed the all the stories filed on the day of the verdict in the trial of the bomber, Timothy J. McVeigh, and singled out Jo's story as a "standout" for the "depth of reporting and level of detail." In 2002, she worked on *The New York Times* national staff that won the Pulitzer Prize for Public Service for "A Nation Challenged."

She is a *summa cum laude* graduate of Wake Forest University, which gave her a Distinguished Service Citation in 1983. The Society of Professional Journalists in Cincinnati inducted her into their Hall of Fame in 2014, the same year the Irish American Unity Conference established the Jo Thomas Award for Courage in Journalism based on her coverage of events in Northern Ireland. Jo is the mother of two daughters and has three grandchildren

STRIVING

Book Description of

Striving:
Adventures of a Female Journalist
in a Man's World, A True Story

By Jo Thomas

Readers who loved the fictional Jo March in *Little Women* will love this thrilling memoir by New York Times journalist Jo Thomas, a real-life Jo March who refused to give up when men said journalism was not for a woman. Jo was a young housewife when she first went to work for an Ohio newspaper that had not hired a woman in 20 years. The men shunned her, but she discovered people and issues they ignored and wrote about them. Follow her through ruined neighborhoods in Cincinnati, the underworld of Detroit, the office of a scientist who did covert experiments for the CIA, the admiral responsible for finding survivors of America's nuclear tests, the Cuban side of the Mariel boatlift, Northern Ireland during the Troubles, and the white right-wing enclaves in the American heartland after the Oklahoma City bombing. At home, Jo loses and gains a family. At work, she never becomes "One of the boys." Her story speaks to the struggles of women of all ages. Come along for the journey.

STRIVING

*Adventures of
a Female Journalist in
a Man's World,
a True Story*

by Jo Thomas

99 Cups of Coffee Publishing Company
Chicago, Illinois

This book is dedicated to my daughters,

Susan and Kathleen,

and to all women everywhere

Table of Contents

PREFACE:
TWA FLIGHT 128

It's November 1967, three days before Thanksgiving. In an apple orchard just beyond the bluffs overlooking the Ohio River, a light snow has begun to fall. Nothing much happens around here. A local fireworks factory will blow up, and the wags across the river in Cincinnati will say the whole town is gone, and the damage was five dollars.

No one will notice the apple orchard until three minutes to nine on the night of November 20, when its bare branches turn red in the light of a fireball. An airliner diving toward River Road hits the trees, ploughs up the land, and breaks apart. It's the end of TWA Flight 128 from Los Angeles to Boston, nearly two miles short of its scheduled stop at the Greater Cincinnati Airport in Northern Kentucky.

A farmer sees a lone passenger leaning over a fence, calling out to anyone left alive in the world. "My eyeballs are burned. Don't leave me here."

I'm in my car, on a last-minute trip to the grocery store, when I hear a bulletin on the radio.

"A plane is down near the airport."

I'm on the other side of the river, certain I am not far away. I stop at a pay phone to call my office. The night man at

1

the *Post and Times-Star* puts me on hold to ring the city editor, Leo Hirtl, at home. Quickly, the night man is back on the line.

"Leo says go to St. Elizabeth Hospital in Covington. They'll bring the survivors there."

"But I'm in my car. I can get to the scene."

"No. Leo says the hospital. Go!"

I phone my husband.

"I'm not going to the store." I tell him about the plane.

"Be careful."

Instead of sending me to the crash site, the editor rousts a veteran reporter. He's a man in his forties with a heart condition. By the time he gets near, the police have blocked off the roads, so he must hike across fields, break through hedges, and climb fences. It damn near killed him, he tells me the next day. "I thought my heart would explode."

When I arrive at the hospital and step into the lobby, I find a mob just arrived from the airport, where they expected to meet the flight at its scheduled stop in Cincinnati. Disoriented, they do not expect a long wait. Many still wear their coats. A few have come from parties. I see a man in a black tie, a woman in a sequined dress. They are dazed, weeping, walking around, generating a lot of body heat. The room smells of perfume, cigarette smoke, sweat, and fear. No one is allowed near the emergency room, where ambulances are pulling in.

A man appears to shout over the commotion, "No press!" Several photographers are coming into the room, their bulky cameras giving them away. A hospital official stiff-arms the photographers out the doors, where another crowd is gathering. I peek out from behind him, In the half-light, I recognize a few veteran reporters struggling to get in. I want to stay, so I step back into the room, out of view.

In the crush of people, I notice a woman in a camel hair coat, standing apart. Her back is to me, so it is just her stillness that makes me think she may give me a passenger's name. This is my first plane crash and the first time I have needed to interview someone without revealing I am a reporter. I walk over to her and ask, "Who are you waiting for?"

My voice is so calm it scares her. Perhaps I am about to bring her the worst news she will ever hear.

"Who are you!" she yells and backs away.

Oh no! What do I say?

I freeze. But the noise is so loud no one has heard. I try to look confused, as if I've just made a mistake. Then I step away, out of her sight, and keep going.

The hospital official reappears, and the crowd falls silent. He looks past us at the reporters and photographers pressing against the closed glass doors. He assures us no press will get in.

Now the woman in the camel hair coat is going to cry out, going to say he is mistaken! Now she is going to point to me!

But she does not. The crowd is pleading loudly for more information, for names of anyone left alive.

"We're asking you to wait," the man says, refusing to address rumors everyone on the plane is dead. "Be patient. Our doctors and nurses are doing everything possible, and our staff is talking to the airline, the firefighters, and the police. We'll tell you as soon as we know."

"Soon" is not soon. I sit down, trying to avoid the restless herd of people as they become more afraid. An hour goes by. I wait and squirm, hoping for news and dreading being unmasked. Ninety minutes. *Nothing.* I watch and listen. *Nothing.*

I get up and walk around, afraid to approach anyone else. I'm just hoping not to be discovered and thrown out. I have no information yet. I haven't found a single survivor.

I'm failing. I stare with envy at the photographers and reporters stuck outside.

They have nothing, but at least they have an excuse.

Then I see him coming through the door. A young priest I interviewed just this week for a high school story for my newspaper's "Youth Page." In this whole room, he is now the only one who knows who I am. He stops to talk with the hospital exec, and I wait for him to turn me in.

Instead, he walks over to me and smiles.

"Hi, Jo."

Before I can say anything, he says he has come to counsel a patient who is Catholic. I assume it's a routine visit. I walk him to the elevator. As he steps in, he invites me to come along. I go with him. I'm desperate to escape the scene of my failure and my shame. Only when the priest asks me to keep quiet do I feel a flicker of hope.

The small figure in the white hospital bed is Robert Deters, a survivor from TWA Flight 128. The staff makes a path to let the priest come to his bedside. Before I can say anything, Deters starts telling the priest what happened. The words rush out of him.

He was holding his wife Edith's hand when the airplane collapsed on top of her and broke open in front of him.

"I couldn't get her out," he says in anguish. "I couldn't get her out." He let go and stepped outside. Then he was running, and the plane exploded.

"I had her hand," he says, a man in a nightmare. "I let go."

Deters, a savings and loan executive, was returning with his wife from a bankers' convention in LA. He is humble, a man of great faith, and he will need it again. Twenty-five years from now, a tornado will flatten the barns and trees on his farm and knock him down as he runs into the house, but again he will be spared. He will lose a son to cancer, bury another wife, and live to be ninety-four years old.[i]

Before they pray together, the priest introduces me.

"I'm a reporter for the *Cincinnati Post*," I tell him. "I'm so terribly sorry to hear what's happened to you and your wife. Would you give me permission to tell people about it in the newspaper?"

"Yes."

It's so simple. I go downstairs alone.

In the lobby, I find Gordon Baer, a photographer from my newspaper who has managed to get in because he is a pro and a Kentuckian and has connections. I know it will be impossible without the priest to get Baer upstairs to photograph Deters, but before I can even mention this, he takes my arm and tells me to hush.

"I've been looking for you," he whispers. "We've got a chance to talk to the doctors in the emergency room. My friend here will help us."

A hospital orderly takes us through some halls and slips us into a room that is completely dark. On the other side, and down a long hallway, I can see an open door, see doctors and nurses in a brightly lit room.

"Wait here," the man says.

Not wanting to be discovered, we stand without moving, not even whispering. Long minutes pass. Then someone comes in from the other side of the room and turns on the light. We have been standing in the dark with the bodies of passengers who did not survive. Instantly, we are rushed out of this makeshift morgue and out of the hospital.

We do not talk about it. From outdoors, I can see the crowd back in the lobby, still clamoring for information, not knowing the dead are nearby. Outdoors, the reporters and photographers still wait for news. I get in my car and rush back to my office to give them Robert Deters.

I still believe the announcement in the lobby that everything will soon be revealed. I ask myself, as I drive across the bridge to Cincinnati, if my small part of the story is worth the pain I caused the woman in the lobby. Was I wrong to stay where I was not allowed? Are reporters necessary? Do we torment people?

I have some answers to these questions now. First, the crash. The airline will release a partial passenger list in a few hours, but it will take investigators years to learn exactly what has happened. The Deters story is an initial piece of the puzzle, so it is a valuable piece of a horrific picture.

On this snowy night, the airport's runway approach lights were shut down for construction and not working. The pilot and the crew knew this, however, and they were not concerned. The airliner and its instruments performed flawlessly until the end. The pilot was experienced. He had landed successfully at Greater Cincinnati fifty-nine times until this night, when he struck a tree 9,357 feet short of North-South Runway 18 and struggled to pull up, begging, "Come on, you!" in the last instant of his life.[ii]

The tree and the orchard were hidden in the darkness and lightly falling snow. After striking them, the airplane plowed into the next field and broke apart. In these moments, a very few were spared. Then the plane became a giant fireball.

Only two of the seven crew members live. Of the seventy-five passengers, only ten survive, including three children whose escape seems miraculous. One is an infant, whose grandmother did not survive. Two small children live, but their parents are killed. One of the two is a five-year-old boy. The other is his sister, who is two years old. A rescue worker found her wandering the orchard on two broken legs, calling "Daddy, I want my blanket!"

The National Transportation Safety Board will analyze the flight data recorder and the weather. They will talk to air traffic controllers and other flight crews in the area. They will interview all the surviving adult passengers and crew. One of these, a flight attendant, tells TIME magazine she remembers saying, "I sure hate to land in Cincinnati" just before the crash. The Safety Board will conclude that the pilot and crew of Flight 128 were deceived by an optical illusion created in the darkness by the lights along the river.[iii]

The sudden, shocking image of the dead in the makeshift morgue vanished as I was hustled out of the room. My memory stops with the doctors and nurses moving in the brightly lit room at the end of the hall. As time passes, I persuade myself I imagined everything else I saw there. I also forget anyone was with me.

But the photographer Gordon Baer remembers. More than thirty years later, driving across the country, he calls me from a coffee shop along the interstate and comes over to visit. After we catch up. He asks me – out of the blue – if I remember the crash, remember the hospital, remember the room with the bodies.

"You were there?" I ask, recalling the sight of the doctors and nurses working in the lighted room, "Did we see the bodies? Is it true?"

"Yes," he says. "I was there."

To this day, I cannot see the dead and do not want them in my dreams. With Gordon, I change the subject and accept the evidence of a dark void in my memory, one of many.

Addressing my doubts as I left the hospital, I wish I could tell my younger self, yes, journalists sometimes hurt people, although we try not to, but we are essential. Democracy and justice require us because they can only exist with the truth. The words "fake" and "news" do not belong together. Anything fake is a lie and not news. Is the truth worth it? It has been worth the lives of many journalists. I have been willing to risk my life but never had to pay the ultimate price.

Years after the night of the crash, I will have a chance to ask Hirtl, the man who let me into the all-male club of journalism, why he refused to send me to the scene.

"I was twenty-three years old," I will say, "I was in my car and just minutes away."

"It was not for a woman," he will answer. "What would the police and firemen say if I sent a woman to something like that?"

I wish I could tell my younger self, so riddled with guilt and doubt, how important women are to journalism. We are more than half the world's population, and we are skilled at dealing with men more powerful than we are. We bring different eyes, empathy, and something of particular value to investigators: invisibility.

These abilities enabled women to become the first investigative reporters, back in the late nineteenth century, when they exposed terrible abuses in mental institutions, laundries, and factories and had newspaper readerships in the thousands. Nellie Bly, Ida B. Wells, Eva McDonald, Elizabeth Banks. They were scorned as muckrakers, written out of history, and their work condemned as yellow journalism, as if it were not true. I will make my own path without knowing about them. I will read their histories in Kim Todd's groundbreaking book *Sensational: The Hidden History of America's Girl Stunt Reporters*, published in 2021, long after I have retired. [iv]

People in power are often men who consider women unimportant. When they do, we can venture where a man cannot. In danger, we may be safer than men, as we rarely present a physical threat. A man reluctant to speak with other men may talk with us because we are beautiful or remind him of his daughter or a sister.

In a distant future, when I list such advantages to an older friend at a college reunion in the South, she will dismiss me as "sly." No. Sly implies a predator. I try *not* to hurt people.

I do what I can to discover the truth. At the hospital on the night of the plane crash, I learn what an advantage invisibility can be, especially to those of us perceived to have no assets at all.

This is the story of a woman, a journalist making her way without maps through the life and fractured landscapes of the middle 20th and early 21st centuries, doing work men often thought and said was not for a woman.

As a journalist, I was a witness and an investigator while also a curious, anxious, and sometimes terrified human being who never apologized for being a woman.

My role as participant as well as observer has shaped my memories. My lens is deeply personal. I must begin by confessing that my story, like many movies and novels, is only based on a true story, as true as I can make it.

CHAPTER ONE:
CINCINNATI, 1966

Why am I here?

It's a Spring morning, blazing hot. We've just arrived in Cincinnati, Ohio. Our new car, covered in tar and bugs from the trip from North Carolina, is roasting outside on the street. My husband and I are drinking iced tea with his new boss and his wife in their living room.

Our host runs the factory where my husband will begin work as a junior manager, the first rung on the corporate ladder that runs from the shop to the top. My husband will start off making toothpaste, and I will make a real home, not the starter apartment we've had in grad school. So why do I want to disappear?

I'm with the wrong people in the wrong place at the wrong time.

I lean back and observe the room, the polished brass lamps, the brilliant, fringed rug, the art, the greenery. The manager's wife writes a decorating column for the morning newspaper. It shows.

Why did I sign up for this?

I'm in a panic I can't understand. This is the day I've been hoping for, the "happily ever after" I always wanted.

I grew up in a military family, the oldest of six children who moved around the country and the world. Our mother, a housewife, doted on us. Our father, a career Army colonel, tolerated us.

He was a war hero who saw combat in World War II when I was a baby and the Korean War when I was eight years old. Each time he came home from war he was more troubled. In those days, no one understood post-traumatic stress, and no one treated it.

He hid the pain well. He never missed work. His soldiers loved him, and so did his close friends. He could be the life of the party if you got him talking about drinking with Ernest Hemingway after the liberation of Paris. He never mentioned the war itself, not the landing on the beach at Normandy, not the battle in the Hürtgen forest, where huge numbers of infantry died. He only once mentioned the Nazi concentration camp at Dachau, where he was among the first Americans to arrive. His wartime letters home from Korea, where his headquarters was overrun by enemy troops, spoke only of the dreadful cold.

For as long as I can remember, on weekends and many nights, he drank. By the time I reached high school, and he was stationed at the Pentagon, his unpredictable outbursts of anger made me afraid to invite friends into our house.

I grew up in the 1940s and early 1950s without TV, which was in its infancy. I was a shy, bookish girl imagining a fairy tale life, trying to please my parents and stay clear of my dad's bad moods. I helped my mother with babysitting, ironing, and mountains of laundry. We were a big family without much money, so my mother made my clothes and taught me to sew. I dreamed of a prince who would rescue me.

Meanwhile, I studied hard so I could escape my family if no rescuer showed up.

By the time I got to high school, we were living in Northern Virginia, and no princes were available. I decided on a kind, handsome, smart football player I met as a sophomore. I pursued him all through our college years, and we married a few days after my graduation from Wake Forest College.

A princess is untouchable, and so were many young women in those days. We were taught that a girl who had sex before marriage was ruined, and no one would want her. I was a virgin when I married and knew nothing about sex. He knew I was a "good girl," but I never told him I imagined myself a princess. I never told him he was my prince. Without realizing it, I placed him in an impossible situation. It was profoundly unfair.

In the months that followed our wedding, we lived in a tiny apartment in Durham, North Carolina. I packed away my Phi Beta Kappa key and worked on a master's in literature at the University of North Carolina while my new husband finished his studies in mechanical engineering at Duke University. As soon as he graduated, he had a job offer.

Until today, sitting in this Cincinnati living room, it has never seemed real that my life's work will be marriage.

Our hosts laugh as my husband describes our trip through Ohio, encountering for the first time the orange barrels that inhabit the interstate highways here. We plan to rent an apartment and buy furniture this afternoon, so the manager and his wife suggest neighborhoods to explore and shops we might like. I pull a piece of paper out of my purse and start a list. My pen moves slowly, as if stuck to the surface.

Then, casually, the wife asks how I'll be spending my time.

Housewife. I can't say the word.

Just to be clear, I can do anything around a house – in high school, I was even the Betty Crocker Homemaker of Tomorrow for the state of Virginia – but suddenly I can't tell this woman my husband is my only blueprint for life.

"I'm finishing a master's degree," I say and change the subject.

We rent a small apartment on a wooded hillside in St. Bernard, a neighborhood close to my husband's factory but upwind from the smokestacks. We buy furniture and unload our belongings: books, wedding presents, a small TV, my typewriter, and a stack of new car payment coupons.

In the next weeks, my husband takes the car to work. I walk places or take the bus. Mostly, I write, eager to finish my thesis and move on – I'm not sure to what. For as long as I can remember, I have been heading toward the goal I have been conditioned to want: marriage. I have ignored any hazards or consequences, as if time would run both ways for me.

Elsie Story, my high school history teacher, tried to warn me, but I did not understand. One hot Virginia afternoon, when the windows were open and we girls were wearing sleeveless dresses, the boy who later became my husband distracted me. He yanked a lock of my short, curly hair. We were sitting in the back row, but this did not escape the hawk eyes of Miss Story. She came striding back to us, leveled one bare upper arm, and shook it six inches from my face. She was a heavyset woman, and her flesh jiggled.

"You'll look like this too, someday," she hissed as the class laughed and I turned red. I was sixteen and slender. I had never given a thought to the shape of my arm. As far as I knew, it would never change.

A more explicit warning came during my last semester in college from a junior member of the English department faculty, a man I knew only slightly. I was about to graduate *summa cum laude* at the top of my college class, and I had developed a passion for novels and poetry.

"Some women weren't cut out for marriage," he said, interrupting our conversation. His remark startled me because it seemed so random. Afterwards, I realized I had been twisting the small diamond engagement ring on my left hand as we talked, and he had noticed. It's possible he did not want one of his best students to spend her life at the kitchen sink. In the moment, I pretended not to hear him, excused myself, and walked away.

Now as we get settled in Cincinnati, my husband returns home for dinner with tales of the women in the factory, the "girls" who make toothpaste on his assembly line.

"I can't believe they use the stuff for bug bites!" he says. He jokes with them, and things go well for him. To his credit, he says nothing about his hopes for me. But our dreams are starting to move in different directions.

I begin to dread social events with the other junior managers and their wives. Many have children and often ask in a friendly way if I am pregnant or planning to be.

"No," I say, each time a little more sharply.

These women are not threats, but I don't see them as kindred spirits. They're like the girls who were going to fraternity parties when I was in the library, who flew to Florida on Spring Break when I took the Greyhound bus home, who played bridge in the parlor in the dorm while I studied in the luggage room to get away from the chatter.

Marriage hasn't changed me, nor has the prospect of moving up the social ladder. I was born into a family that was once in Baltimore high society – my great-great grandmother was a favorite cousin of Johns Hopkins, and her husband was the first treasurer of Johns Hopkins Hospital – but my grandmother married for love, and the family money disappeared. I've asked my parents to take my name out of the Social Register. It's this rebel streak that makes me cringe at deferring to the senior wives in my husband's company. Social climbing is not for me.

When someone asks if I want to join the Junior League, I panic. In two months, I finish my master's thesis and mail it off. Then I tell my husband I am getting a job, any job. Immediately. The next day at breakfast, I see an ad for a science writer in the classified section of the *Cincinnati Enquirer* and make an appointment for an interview right away.

As I am getting dressed, I look in the mirror and take a deep breath.

My freakish hair! Can I really apply for a job with hair like this?

Back at the beginning of grad school, I renounced my long brown hair. I never liked it – my sister and a brother got the blonde hair in the family – and I did not want to look like every other grad student at Carolina. I walked into a Chapel Hill beauty salon and asked them to "make me look like Marilyn Monroe."

"Not a good idea," they said. "Your hair's too dark. You can't go all blonde." They frosted it instead.

"Just sit still," the beauty operator said as she tugged a tight rubber cap full of holes over my head. Using a hook, she fished a strand of hair out of each hole and lathered them with bleach and then toner. The rest of my hair lay protected under the cap. When she pulled off the cap and shampooed and dried everything, the result was a cloud of light and dark hair.

I loved the look but learned to my dismay there was a catch. My hair grew fast, and the frosting needed touching up, even though the same strands of hair could not be found to pull through the cap again. By the time I moved to Ohio, so much hair had been bleached, I was mostly blonde with dark roots of varying depths. My hair looked dirty.

Trying to fix it, I went to a beauty salon that just put peroxide on everything. This turned the roots of my hair bright orange because my natural color has lots of red in it.

"Can you bleach it again?" I asked. The orange color was frightful.

"Don't know. It's risky. Might be able to. Might break it off."

"Go ahead."

The result was a little less orange and slightly blonder, but hunks of my hair broke off at the scalp after the shampoo. First, I laughed, and then I cried.

"Can you cut it a little?"

The mirror reflects my orange chicken/clown hairdo. Patches of short hair stick straight up in unlikely places, including the crown of my head.

It's my hair, my face, my life.

I turn around and walk out the door.

The ad for a science writer was placed by the Excel Personnel agency, with an office downtown on the 13th floor of the Enquirer Building. It has a small door, the kind you see in old black and white detective films, with its name on the frosted glass window. The proprietor is Georgia A. Waite, who describes herself as a "specialist in advertising personnel." She's wearing a snappy suit, and I can just imagine her as a Madison Avenue executive.

I make a fast-paced, breathless pitch for the science writing job, saying, "I studied physics and mathematics for two and a half years before I decided to major in English, and I've just finished my master's degree."

I graduated with high honors, I say, and I wrote articles for my college newspaper, and edited the college magazine. I have brought along some of my old college clips. I do not say my only job experience is two summers as a clerk typist for the Army, one summer at Cameron Station and one at the Pentagon.

Ms. Waite doesn't say who's hiring a science writer or what the work entails. She looks me over and seems doubtful.

I do not – cannot – explain about my weird hair.

Is she looking at my hair? Is she taking me seriously? Will anyone ever take me seriously again?

Ms. Waite rejects me for the science writer job but says she has a friend, Charles Hubbs, who is the managing editor of the *Cincinnati Enquirer*, the respectable and conservative morning newspaper in town. It carries the decorating column written by my husband's boss's wife. Ms. Waite makes a call and sends me downstairs to Hubbs.

I don't dare think about how weak my bid for a reporting job is.

I can't do it. I'm too shy.

Back in high school, looking for an elective, I took a class in journalism. With the encouragement of a magnificent teacher, Elizabeth Rion, who gave me the only formal training in journalism I ever had, I ended up as co-editor of the high school newspaper. I could do it during the school day. I had chores to do at home, so I was not allowed to stay after school.

At Wake Forest, I wrote articles for the college newspaper, the *Old Gold and Black*, but I lacked the confidence to study journalism, even though the professor was kind and encouraging. In 1964, the beginning of my senior year, everyone on campus wanted a comeback for *the student* magazine, shut down my freshman year for publishing a satire of the Rev. Billy Graham.ᵛ It couldn't be controversial. I was calm and a good writer, so I was chosen as editor.

My contemporaries on Pub Row, headquarters for all student publications, were real journalists: lively, strong, and self-confident, everything I was not.

Am not.

But now, sitting in Ms. Waite's office, I am desperate enough to consider asking for a job in journalism.

Those other wives! The Junior League! If Miss Waite thinks I can be a reporter, I can be.

I take the elevator downstairs and present myself to Hubbs, who is a gentleman and cordial. I tell him about myself, my academic credentials, and my student publications. Then he is inching away from me.

He's looking at my hair!

"What could you do for us, Mrs. Thomas?"

"Anything. Anything at all. I can report and write stories."

He's still moving away from me.

 I scale back my ask.

"Or if you want me to, I can get coffee, sharpen pencils, anything at all, just to start."

"We have copy boys who do that," he says. "We have nothing here for you. Thank you for coming." And that is that.

Crushed, I take the elevator back up to the employment agency. Ms. Waite is dauntless and tells me not to worry. She makes another call and sends me scurrying down the street to the *Cincinnati Post & Times-Star*, the afternoon Scripps-Howard newspaper, for an interview with the city editor, Leo Hirtl.

Unknown to me, the Cincinnati Strangler, who has terrorized the city since December, has just left his fourth victim dying on a manhole cover. The Strangler targets women who are middle aged and poor. He has beaten, raped, and strangled his victims in their homes and in a city park. The city is in a panic. The sales of weapons and locks have skyrocketed. This time, the Strangler changed his method, stabbing a woman seven times in the throat before making his escape in a taxi. [vi]

Hirtl is under extreme stress today because his newsroom is short staffed. When I walk in, I see a harried middle-aged man who is losing his dark hair. He doesn't look up, just hands me a writing test and motions to an empty desk behind a glass partition in a vacant office. The test is easy. It asks me to make up a story from a few facts. I whip it out in no time.

Hirtl reads it and says, "You can write. Can you come to work tomorrow?"

"Yes. Of course!"

He's offering a chance to start at the bottom, as a cub reporter, a union job that pays $68 a week, barely above the Federal minimum wage of $50. I'm stunned. I'm thrilled.

I'm about to take off! Like a feather!

I float out of the city room.

I am unaware that Hirtl's job offer on this day in August 1966 has turned a twenty-year tide in the newsroom, where I have become the first woman reporter hired since 1946, the end of World War II.

I am also unaware that Leo Hirtl has just changed the path of my entire life. Becoming a journalist will introduce me to the world and the woman I was meant to be.

CHAPTER TWO:
THE INVISIBLE WOMAN

The *Post* is an afternoon newspaper, so it has early morning deadlines. When I arrive at 7 a.m. the next day, many reporters in the city room are already on the phone or banging away on typewriters. Cigarette smoke hovers in a cloud at chest level, and the place is black with ink and dirt. As I wait to be assigned a desk, something dashes by my feet. Something else follows in an instant.

"Rat," says a man behind me. "Ferret."

The vermin come from the composing room. It's a vast industrial space connected to the city room. Rats are an annoyance in both places, so ferrets seem like a reasonable solution.

The composing room is where the miracle of producing a daily newspaper begins. I go there for a tour while I'm waiting for a desk. Linotype machines dominate the room. Even with these machines, so much printing is done by hand, Benjamin Franklin would feel at home.

Each newspaper story is written on a typewriter, edited by pencil, and then sent to a linotype machine to be typed again by hand into letters made of lead. These are arranged into words, sentences, and paragraphs of lead that are fitted into a metal column. The columns go into a frame the exact size of a page of the day's newspaper, allowing space for headlines, photographs, and advertisements. The frame is a complicated puzzle, changing until it is locked shut. The metal page is stamped onto a mat that becomes a curved metal plate affixed to the rolling presses.

The linotype operators, who have vats of liquid lead, also make sharp metal spikes about twelve inches high, each anchored in a heavy ball of lead. Editors and reporters use these spikes to hold the sea of paperwork that rolls over them every day. Spikes hold papers you need to find quickly. Other people, working different shifts, may use your desk, so desk drawers are used for office supplies, liquor bottles and junk.

There are mountains of paper. Every story is typed in triple copies, white paper with carbon paper sandwiched in between. News from the Associated Press, United Press International, and the Scripps-Howard newswire chatters off the teletype machines in wide continuous sheets. Copyboys — no girls here —rip off the breaking news as it arrives and run it to the editors. When the news is urgent, bells ring on these machines. The routine wire copy gets walked around newsroom.

Along one wall of the newsroom is an array of police and fire radios. One reporter is always assigned to monitor them. Their squawks and alarms give the city room the atmosphere of a permanent emergency.

On my third day at the *Cincinnati Post and Times-Star*, I know I was born to be here. I have never loved any place so much. On Thursday, September 8, 1966, I get my first press pass.

Ms. Waite mails me a bill for $115.34 from her employment agency. She congratulates me and adds that Hubbs of the *Cincinnati Enquirer* asked her about me. "I told him you already had won a byline or two at the *Post,* which unsettled him considerably."

"Nobody who is any good ever just walks in off the street," Hirtl tells me later, when we are friends. "And nobody ever hires a reporter from a personnel agency."

"Why did you?" I ask.

"Great legs," he says. "And you can write." I can laugh this off because I know Leo is not a ladies' man. He barely glanced up the day he hired me. I'm just thankful he took me seriously, even though I'm not one of his boys. He's someone to whom I owe everything. Leo Hirtl. And Elizabeth Rion, the high school teacher who taught my only journalism class.

I begin to move between worlds that do not know each other, sometimes by the day and sometimes by the hour, starting with the simple act of going to work.

Before dawn, I leave the sweet air on our hilltop and walk down to the bus stop. It's under the interstate highway. High above us, the traffic roars south toward downtown. The smog drifts down, wrapping around our shoulders. It mingles with the sharp smell of soap-making nearby.

Once the bus leaves my stop, it ventures into territory as unknown as Antarctica to most white Cincinnatians. The bus travels Reading Road, the main artery through Avondale, a former Jewish neighborhood now the heart of Black Cincinnati. Absentee owners collect the rent and don't worry about the upkeep. It's a journey of about seven miles and takes less than half an hour. The city bus is full every morning with Black passengers of all ages and a few older white people.

My first week on the bus, a white woman wearing a thin sweater sits down beside me and introduces herself. Her name is Mary, she says, and she is on her way to work. She looks to me to be about 50 years old.

"My husband's disabled," she says in a long rush of words, as if apologizing. "*He* can't work. He needs me to take care of him, but someone must work. He has to wait until I get home. It's hard for him. It's hard for me."

But that isn't the worst, she says. Her work is getting impossible. She needs new glasses and can't afford them. Her vision has gotten so bad she can't even read the signs on the buses.

"What's your job?" I ask.

"Sorting mail."

She is my mother's age. I am sure she will lose her job. I can't imagine her life. No words come to me. It doesn't occur to me I could simply give her the money I have in my purse today. Instead, I give her a sad nod and a sigh. I miss my one chance to help because I never see her again. But I think of her over the years.

When the bus gets downtown, my stop is across the street from the newspaper, near the House of Morgan, a dimly lit bar open for breakfast, ham and eggs, and a shot of booze. It caters to printers. Shortly after I start work, Bob Stigers, a photographer, invites me there for lunch.

Stigers is a big guy with legendary appetites and habits. He chews tobacco, and he may forget to roll down the window of the company car when he needs to spit out a chaw.

He looks ancient to me, but he's just losing his hair. He specializes in scenes of violence and prides himself on being the first photographer at every accident, fire, and shooting. He's best friends with all the cops.

As Stigers walks me into the House of Morgan, I can see in the dim light that the cook's apron is black with grease and dirt. I scan the menu on the chalk board for something that will not make me sick.

A fried egg sandwich: there isn't much he can do to an egg.

Then I watch as the cook reaches over the griddle and breaks the yolk with a filthy thumbnail. I look at my watch as if I have forgotten something important, apologize to Stigers, and ask the cook to wrap my sandwich to go. As soon as I am out of sight, I throw it away. Somehow, Stigers knows. He does not invite me again.

To learn the ropes, I am sent to the Federal Building my first Friday on the job to shadow Bob Stevens, another old stalwart. He calls his wife "Mom" and most other women "honey." The exception is the judge's secretary. He calls her "Missus." Nine months before my visit, he broke his ribs and leg in an auto accident. He still has trouble walking and tells me he drives only "to church and the liquor store."

Stevens has the white hair and geniality of a grandfather, so I am shocked when I walk into the courthouse press room, a men-only enclave for the last twenty years. Stevens' locker is plastered with nude photographs of 'playgirls," many of them women about my age. I feel sick. Then I pull myself together and decide to ignore them and try to look for Stevens' strong points. I learn by the end of our day together that he knows the first name of every secretary, clerk, officer, and judge in the Federal Building, as well as every attorney we encounter.

I'll need a memory at least as good as his.

The newsroom is my classroom, too, with instruction delivered at high volume. The assistant city editor, Eddie Halloran, shouts as I make one mistake after another, although not the same one twice. What looks easy is not, and the details matter.

"No! You cannot have the wrong house number!"

"You cannot misspell the name of the street!"

"It doesn't matter if the police report doesn't say if the burglar's home address is a street or an avenue. Find out! Lawsuits are filed on less!"

My inexperience is noticed. I hear muttering, half-joking, about "the good old days when there were no women in the newsroom, and men kept whiskey in their desks." But they are still short-handed, so they need me for the scut work, and the men still have their whiskey bottles.

Women did work in the city room during World War II, but when the veterans returned in 1946, all but two women were fired. Those two rarely come into the city room now. A few women remain on the copy desk, but they may as well be on another planet. The city room is a men's club. I have gained admission only because Hirtl was desperate for extra help, and I asked on the right day at the right time.

After I've been in the office for a few days, someone tells me the story of the fashion writer who was assigned to help out and write obituaries one day when the Hirtl was short-handed.

"She cried every time she talked with a funeral director," one colleague says gleefully. "It took her more than an hour to write a three-paragraph obit. They finally sent her back to the Women's Department. Useless!" It's clear that's what they think of women in general and me in particular.

I have no female fashion media role models. The male reporters wear suits or sport coats, awful neckties, and long-sleeved white dress shirts with the cuffs rolled up, so they do not blacken from carbon paper and ink. Rolled up cuffs will persist into the computer age, long after the death of the typewriter. For years, it will be a badge of honor that the journalist is the worst dressed man in the room.

I decide to dress like the women in my office, the secretaries. I wear heels, suits with skirts, and dresses. No trousers, ever. This is a mistake. High heels are fine for trips to city hall or the courthouse, but not practical for climbing out on a roof or walking around the scene of an accident or a murder.

Dressing up gives me no cultural protection either, as I learn the day I am covering a peaceful protest of the Vietnam War by students from Antioch College. Most are white, look to be my age, and have long hair. It's clear the police despise them. They shout at the students to keep moving. If the students hesitate, the officers grab them and drag them into paddy wagons. The officers are rough, too rough.

I am standing nearby, taking notes, wearing high heels and a business suit. I am clearly a spectator. It does me no good. The police officers grab both my arms and start pushing me toward the paddy wagon.

"I'm a reporter!" I tell them. They don't listen, so I start to shout. "I'm a reporter for the *Cincinnati Post*." They ignore me. I have a police press pass in my purse, but I can't reach it. This is before anyone uses lanyards.

The officers shove me, not too gently, into the police wagon. I am saved from being hauled away when another reporter from the *Post*, who knows the police officers and is also covering the demonstration, hears my cries. He calls off the police. With apologies, they release me.

Afterwards, when the other reporter files his story, he describes the Antioch demonstrators as "dirty" and "smelly."

"That isn't true," I tell Hirtl. "They were clean. I was in the paddy wagon with them." Hirtl shrugs it off. The story is already in the newspaper, and he is not going to get into an argument between two of his reporters. The other reporter is an old hand, and nobody likes hippies and demonstrators.

My looks also get me demoted, or at least that's how it seems to me. Hirtl appoints me Youth Editor of the *Post*, responsible for a flock of local high school and college journalists reporting to us. This job was last held by Jerry Rubin, who left the newspaper, grew his hair, and went to California to organize the radical group the Yippies. This should key me in that my new assignment will not be dull. Youth culture is about to swamp the nation and take me with it. I have no clue.

Several months after hiring me, Hirtl takes on another new reporter, a graduate of Yale – no matter how nice they are, they immediately tell you they're from Yale – at a salary of $105 a week, much more than my $68, even with no more experience than me and one less academic degree. When I ask

Hirtl about the pay difference, he says the new man has a wife to support.

When I meet the wife, I ask if she has a job.

"Yes," she says, "with IBM."

This is my first encounter with gender-based pay discrimination, and it hurts. Over the years, I will work for three different metropolitan daily newspapers, all of them union shops, and the gender pay gap never improves. Men less experienced than me, men I can write circles around, men who are afraid to go where I go, are paid more simply because they are men.

I decide not to take the pay gap personally. I do not want to be bitter and mad at the new guy in Cincinnati. He is a good person. Resenting him would crush my heart. But it's hard on some occasions to control my feelings on the subject.

One day I am walking down the sidewalk with Woody Sudhoff, the managing editor of the *Post*. He is taking me to lunch as a reward for a successful run of stories I'm having. He asks what I want to be doing in twenty years.

"Running the paper," I say.

He gives me a tight smile. "Women don't have the temperament for that."

Eventually, the grumbling among the men, about "the good old days when there were no women in the city room," runs out of steam. Then I just become invisible, especially at lunch time. I eat alone or walk around downtown. Other reporters depart in groups of two or three. I'm afraid to ask to join them because I do not want to be turned down.

CHAPTER THREE:
A LITTLE SOUL, BROTHER

In June 1967, less than a year after I become a reporter, racial tensions in Cincinnati explode at the intersection of Reading and Rockdale Roads in Avondale. A Black man has been convicted as the Cincinnati Strangler. His cousin protests the conviction, and the violence begins after the cousin is arrested for loitering. The *Post* goes into overdrive, and I beg to be sent to the scene.

"A riot is no job for a woman," Halloran tells me.

"But I take the bus through there every day. The people from that neighborhood ride with me."

"It's too dangerous." Hirtl backs him up. "You're staying here."

When the city is calm again, trash and glass cover Reading Road, and the shops I can see from my bus windows are ruins covered with wooden boards. The staff at the *Post* is exhausted. Stigers shows me a brick thrown through his car window. He's a white Southerner, and the experience has left him angrier and more afraid of Black people than ever.

We are printing stories about the arrests, with a heavy emphasis on law and order. Dozens of cities have been going up in flames, starting with Watts in Los Angeles, and white people are paranoid about "outside agitators"— In fact, Congress is proposing a bill to make it a crime to travel between states to incite riots.

Hirtl, who doubts Cincinnati needed input from outsiders, finds himself short-handed, and I am the only fresh person he has. He assigns me to go out and ask around about what caused the trouble. He is looking for a spot story, a couple of quotes from local ministers or spokespeople in the Black community.

I pass through Avondale every day on the bus, so it does not occur to me, as it has to my editors, I should be afraid because I am white or a woman. As I walk past the burnt-out stores on Reading Road, I feel invisible, just the way I feel on the bus and in the office. Most people on the sidewalk ignore me.

When I stop to ask a question or two, people are surprised, then interested and helpful when I identify myself as a reporter. They want to talk. No reporters have interviewed the young people who took part in the violence. I am on deadline, without much time, but I want to talk with them, and the rioters are easy to find. I wait on the sidewalk as their mothers, their uncles, and their friends walk down a few doors or up some stairs to find them and bring them outside. Most are just out of jail.

The violence has everything to do with race, they say, their voices full of pain, but it is about more than Black people against whites. They never touched some of the shops owned by white people. They say they hit the stores with owners who are "cheats, gougers, and destroyers of human dignity."

"There's a market across from my house," one kid says. "You're supposed to get two cents for a pop bottle. But when Black kids bring their bottles in, the guy that runs it cheats us. We hit his place every night."

Most store owners are white. Some returned after the riots to find their stores intact, with "Soul Brother" signs on their windows. Avondale was once a Jewish neighborhood, and Jews still own many stores. Some had their stores burned. Others did not. It was a Passover of sorts, based on their customers' perceptions of fairness.

In 1967, Cincinnati's Black ghettos are at a tipping point. Their citizens have the epic Voting Rights Law and other civil rights legislation, but they want justice on the ground. The unemployment among Black people in Cincinnati is 250 percent that of whites, greater than during the 1930s. The city's economy is booming, but Black Cincinnatians are having their very own Great Depression.

"I see advertisements for jobs in your newspaper. But when I go for an interview, they tell me the job is filled." The speaker is a young Black man, who just made bail after an arrest for disorderly conduct. "The ad keeps running, but when I go back, the job is always filled."

They feel like prisoners in their own communities, they say. Just step outside to see some friends, and here come the police. They're standing on their own sidewalks. They want the city's anti-loitering ordinance thrown out.

"People who have to live in crowded conditions don't have air conditioners," the Rev. T. X. Graham tells me. "On these hot days, they just can't stay in the house. They come to the street for a breath of fresh air. The street is a meeting place. The police officer doesn't know what's happening. When he tells them to move, he is trying to do a job. The law permits him to move anyone, but where can these people move? They live there. They have no recreational facilities, no funds to go someplace else."

"Cincinnati is spending a fortune on a football stadium," State Representative William Bowen tells me. "Will kids be able to play *there*?"

The riots have put the city's civil rights veterans in a bind, bringing into question their insistence on non-violent tactics. "We did it the peaceful way," Dr. Bruce Green, the president of the NAACP in Cincinnati, tells me when I find him in his office. "What happened? Nothing. We had to move aside. Unfortunately, and I stress the word 'unfortunately,' some cities will respond after a riot."

The Rev. Fred L. Shuttlesworth, secretary of the Southern Christian Leadership Conference, happens to be in town, and Dr. Green puts me in touch with him. He tells me his message of nonviolent resistance is facing increased opposition.

"Young people tell me, 'Reverend, you keep on praying. We appreciate your praying – but you let us handle it.'"

When I file my story, I conclude with my own personal observation. I am sure it will be deleted by my editors: "In the confusion of picking up the pieces this week, in the secret meetings, rumors, demands and partial explanations, the one thing that every Negro leader seemed to be asking of the city went unwritten in any of their formal demands: a little Soul, brother."

Hirtl looks at my finished story for a long time. "We've never published anything like this," he says. I think he is going to discard it. Instead, he puts my story on the front page. The copy editors take a phrase I think they will cut, "a little Soul, brother," and put it in the headline.[vii]

An avalanche of letters arrives. So do telephone calls about terrible conditions in Avondale and other Black communities, ghost neighborhoods invisible to our newspaper, politicians, or anyone in power. Although I am still the Youth Editor, I read the letters, answer the calls, and plead for permission to follow up on them. No one else wants to, so sometimes the editors say yes.

My newspaper has no Black reporters or editors. This is a problem I can't fix. As a white Southerner raised in the land of Jim Crow, I always assumed Northern whites were different, that they were not racial bigots. The riots in Cincinnati shock me, catch me up short.

I do not know Cincinnati's history. I am unaware its culture is Southern – not Northern. My newspaper colleagues give me no guidance. I am still invisible to them, and this is fortunate, because no one stops my efforts to write about the problems in Avondale and other Black neighborhoods. I proceed in radical innocence, the dangerous kind that questions everything.

As I do, I begin to see the value of journalism. The Scripps-Howard motto on our front page is: "Give Light, and the People Will Find Their Own Way." When there is no light, citizens are left in the dark, unable to make informed decisions about critical matters of public life. For an individual or family affected by these issues, they can be matters of life and death.

One day, I am out in the streets to report on a demonstration by teenagers and adults demanding the city provide recreation facilities for inner city children and teens. The mayor is there, and a Black woman engages him in a heated debate. She is on fire, and she has him on the defensive. Her name is Cheryl Grant, and she's a social worker for Memorial Community Center in Mt. Auburn, a neighborhood next to Avondale. I can't say just why, maybe just the tough time she gives the mayor, but I feel a real connection with her and seek her out after the mayor leaves.

"Can we talk?"

I quote her in that day's story, then go to see her. Over the next few days and then weeks, we get to know each other. In age, we are less than a month apart. Like me, she comes from a large, churchgoing family and has married young. Her husband is in the army, just back from Vietnam. She's a University of Cincinnati graduate and has more books than I.

We both like music, so I invite her downtown to a Janis Joplin concert. In a huge audience of whites, Cheryl is one of the few Black people. When the singing starts, Cheryl recognizes Janis's voice from hearing her on the radio and shouts, "Oh my goodness, I thought she was one of US!"

The tables are turned when Cheryl invites me to a party at a friend's house where I am the only white person, and they dance to music I know from white fraternity parties down South, but this time it's Black people dancing to Black music, and they dance better.

Cheryl and her husband follow up with an invitation to my husband and me to go dancing at a club across the river in

Covington, Kentucky. We take two cars, as they bring along two of Cheryl's best friends, both Black people, both schoolteachers and so stylish they could be from Beverly Hills. We leave our cars near the club entrance and start to go in. Laughing and joking, we are stopped at the door.

"This club is for members only."

We look around for a sign. Seeing none, we start to go in again. The door attendant stops us again.

"Members only, please."

As we step aside and try to figure out what to do, other couples arrive and just walk in. No one is asked for a membership card. I walk back up to the door attendant and start to argue.

"This can't be a club! Nobody else has a membership card. Why can't we go in?" I do not realize the membership card is white skin.

Within minutes, a sheriff's deputy arrives. He is stuffed into a tight uniform, and he is not friendly.

"Y'all have to leave," he says, looking at the license plates of our cars, "and I'm going to escort you back to the bridge to make sure you know the way to Ohio."

I am so angry and stunned I can hardly breathe, but we get back in our cars and follow him. Somehow, this racist and deeply personal insult is even more outrageous because we are up North, next to Ohio. A Southern white like me does not expect this here.

Furious, I go to Hirtl on the city desk the next day. He passes me along to Vance Trimble, editor of our sister newspaper, the *Northern Kentucky Post*.

"Their town, their story," Hirtl says.

I go back across the river, still angry and believing someone will be assigned to this story as soon as I can tell my tale.

"No," Trimble says when I finish. "Not a story."

Trimble has come to the *Northern Kentucky Post* with a Pulitzer Prize in his pocket, and he is starting a seventeen-year career he will describe at the end as "aggressive, hard-driving, and effective." On his 100th birthday in 2011, he will tell television station WCPO his editorial philosophy is "to uncover, expose and hold people accountable" so "anybody can get in the paper, and nobody can stay out," including him. When the police pull him over on suspicion of drunk driving in his wife's car in 1977, long after I meet him, he orders a staff photographer to hurry down to the Kenton County Jail to photograph him for the next edition. A photo of Trimble smiling next to the deputy jailer runs on the front page above the fold. [viii]

When I meet him, I know nothing of the cozy relations between newspapers and the citizens of their small cities – or who might or might not count as a citizen. I also do not know the codes of newsroom language. When an editor tells you something is not a story, it means you should give up. I just think Trimble does not understand me, so I rush on with more information.

"We were well-dressed," I say, "well-mannered, with plenty of money. It can't be a club because nobody had a membership card to get in." He listens, impassively, until I finish. Then he repeats himself, slowly, as if to a child or someone who does not speak English as a first language.

"It… is …not…a…story." Then he adds, "The mob runs those joints. Write something about them, and you'll get acid in your face."

Baffled, stunned, I blurt out the first question that comes to mind: "If this is true, if these clubs are run by criminals, why haven't you assigned someone to expose them?" Trimble takes this as a wisecrack, and things deteriorate when I volunteer to help him work on such a story.

"Don't tell me how to run my newspaper!" he shouts, getting up from his chair to show me out. "And another thing —" He waves in the general direction of the Ohio River and the city of Cincinnati, and his voice turns mean.

"I'm the top candidate for editor-in-chief of your paper. If I get it, I promise you'll be writing obits for the rest of your life."

He will live to the age of 107, but fortunately for me, our paths will not cross again.

CHAPTER FOUR:
ALL FALL DOWN

Hours after the assassination in Memphis of the Rev. Dr. Martin Luther King Jr. on April 4, 1968, a riot begins in Avondale and spreads quickly. The Ohio National Guard is sent to Cincinnati.

This is two years before national guard members gun down the students at Kent State University. We don't know that the guardsmen are young and jittery. We don't know that they can be lethal. It does not register with me they are the army. To me, they are just cops with different uniforms.

Hirtl needs more staff, so he relents and dispatches me to Avondale with a photographer much older than me. Everything is looking great until we reach a roadblock where two national guardsmen say we can't go on. Without thinking, I get out of the car, duck under the arm of the guardsman on my side and run ahead down the road. The other guardsman detains the photographer and the car.

Fire. Black smoke, firefighters with their hoses. Police, soldiers, the sound of breaking glass. In the chaos, I do not see anyone I recognize. I stand there confused, not knowing what to do, until the photographer drives up. He is in a rage.

"You idiot! You almost got yourself shot! We could have both been arrested!" He has spoken with the city desk on his car radio. They ordered him to put me in the passenger seat while he gets some photographs, then bring me back to the office. I must stay in the car. In a community I am just beginning to understand, I am grounded.

CHAPTER FIVE:
CHANGING THE JUGGERNAUT

In May of 1968, a month after the riots, teen-agers from the ghetto begin to show me how hard it is for poor people, especially people of color, to change the juggernaut of an all-white city bureaucracy.

After last year's riots, social workers urged teens in riot-torn communities to organize into councils and make lists of things they needed so they could negotiate with city officials. The teens did this. In February, they invited the mayor to meet with them. He waited until now, a month after the second riots. The teens have invited me to cover the meeting for my newspaper. It's in Over-the-Rhine.

Over-the-Rhine is a dilapidated neighborhood spreading over a hill that begins downtown and rises at a steep angle. It is a warren of brick row houses and narrow streets with dead ends. Black people and poor Appalachian whites live here.

I'm trying to find the meeting spot, a gymnasium. At last, I admit to myself I'm lost and decide to walk. I park my car and ask directions of a small child sitting in a doorway. I'm in luck. The gym is just around the corner. The child escorts me through an alley to one of the entrances.

Some forty teenagers are sitting quietly on folding chairs, dressed up as if for church in the suffocating heat. Giant electric fans labor to move the sweltering air, but there's barely a draft. Inside, it's hard to breathe.

The mayor arrives with his entourage, and Roger Owensby, the teen chairing the meeting, reads them a long welcome. The microphone quits, so he struggles to be heard. He tells the mayor the teen councils have gone to their neighborhood churches, a local electrical company, the transit company, and other groups, to ask for any unused space they can use for recreation. They've had some success, and now they need the city's help to transform these vacant spaces into recreation centers.

One by one, as Owensby introduces them, teenagers step up to ask the mayor for specific items so they can create a wood shop, a study room, gyms, and places to dance. They want paint, lights, pool tables, and a record player, things to make life a little bit better.

It's merciful no one in this room, especially young Owensby, can see into the future. In just three years, Owensby will become the father of a son, Roger Owensby, Jr. He will grow up, join the U.S. Army, and be promoted to the rank of sergeant. He will also become a father. Then he will die in one of fifteen police shootings that will ignite the next great riot in Cincinnati.

On November 7, 2000, Sergeant Owensby will walk out of a Sunoco Mini-Mart in Bond Hill, a nicer neighborhood than Over-the-Rhine. Two white Cincinnati police officers will stop and search him for fifteen minutes before he runs away.

They will chase him, tackle him, and put him in a police car, where he will die in their custody.[ix]

But in 1968, his father is a Black teen-aged leader with great hopes, finishing the meeting with three questions for the mayor: "Why has the city given us no recreational facilities in the past? When is the city going to ask for recreation for these teens? And what are they going to receive?"

The mayor, Eugene Ruehlmann, tells his audience he remembers suggesting they take the initiative and "by golly, you've taken us up on it." His response now is to ask them to put their requests in writing. He will return in a month. Then, ominously, he says, "All of the funds that were available have been earmarked."

This is a vast understatement of a huge injustice. As I tell my readers, Over-the Rhine has the city's highest population density, lowest income, highest rate of child abuse, and worst juvenile delinquency. It has 14,000 children with no playgrounds and no safe places to play, not even front yards. Cars kill the children who play in the streets.

Over-the-Rhine once had ballfields. The city sold them to make way for Interstate 71. City officials then spent this windfall on recreation projects all over the city, including tennis courts in three wealthy neighborhoods. Over-the-Rhine got nothing. What's left is earmarked for the new stadium downtown. In Cincinnati, the rich have robbed the poor.

Some readers respond to my stories right away. Suburban volunteers and church groups begin coming into Over-the-Rhine and other beleaguered neighborhoods. They offer buses to take city kids to summer programs in the suburbs.

In June, when the mayor makes his promised return, he brings his recreation superintendent, who tells the kids the city has no pool tables or ping pong tables to give them, only small items like ping pong balls that must be handed out by recreation coordinators.

"Can the coordinators be hired from the neighborhood?" one teen asks.

"No. They must be people who have passed the civil service exam. We can't hand out these items to just anyone."

My stories in the newspapers point out that the city recently paid a thousand dollars for a new table and four chairs for the mayor's office. The city also furnished his office with a new chandelier, new paneling, a new sofa, and a new door.

The city manager holds a press conference to justify these expenditures. When he uses the word "idealist" as an epithet to describe me, I am happy.

My newspaper is conservative politically, so I am surprised at the end of August when the editorial page weighs in on recreation for inner city children:

"Golf courses are enjoyable. The stadium is a good thing. So are remodeled tennis courts in Western Hills and Pleasant Ridge. But the children with the greatest need are low on the priority list. The budget is now under consideration. As citizens we have a duty to see that the city doesn't come up with another summer of empty promises."

Then a miracle of sorts happens. The Federal government announces grants to acquire land for seven new playgrounds in Cincinnati, all with swimming pools. The uproar over recreation, the demands of the teenagers reported in my stories and relayed to Washington by concerned citizens and community advocates has moved some money to the right place. President Lyndon Johnson is still in the White House, still talking about a Great Society, and the riots have given his administration a strong incentive to do something.

I view the creation of these playgrounds as evidence of what can happen when people who are excluded are finally seen and heard by the press, and someone in power listens. It strengthens my calling to be a public witness. I can't prove I have played a role in this victory, but over many years, few announcements will ever bring me such joy.

Other things are much harder to change, like the plight of the man I meet while he is lying on the floor in the Chitwood Apartments. His neighbors take me down a dimly lit hall. Before they knock on his door, they say they visit every day to bring food, help him get to the bathroom, and do what they can. They are all poor.

He has congestive heart failure. His legs are gigantic, so swollen from edema he is unable to get into his bed. He is a great wedge of a man, and the floor is the only place that can accommodate him. It takes him a few moments to work up the energy to speak with a stranger.

"This is what happens if you don't have insurance, don't have money, don't have a family to take care of you," he gasps. "Thank God for my friends."

I ask the city desk for permission to report a story about our two-tier health care system, one for the poor, and one for everyone else. In the basement corridors of Cincinnati General Hospital, I see patients parked on gurneys under filthy pipes with peeling insulation. It's the teaching hospital of the

University of Cincinnati medical school, the hospital that's willing to care for Black people and poor white people. It has some of the best doctors and some of the worst conditions. In 1968, the system is unfair.

CHAPTER SIX:
ONE COUPLE, TWO CITIES

At the end of August 1968, I sit on my living room floor, crying and watching the police beat the demonstrators to the ground on live television at the Democratic National Convention in Chicago. I can't believe what I am seeing. To me, the country is falling apart.

My husband doesn't understand my distress. He knows about my run-ins with the Cincinnati police officers and the national guard and remembers our face-off with the sheriff in Covington, but he does not understand why tears are running down my face about something happening in Chicago.

His Cincinnati is still okay. I can't explain that my city is not the city he knows. In Cincinnati, as in Chicago, things are not all right. He listens patiently, but he thinks I'm overwrought. He's right, but I'm more upset than he knows. Night after night, my feet drag more slowly on the walk home from the bus stop.

To relax on weekends, we drive out to the country and look at the mansions in Indian Hill and the other grand suburbs. This has been a tradition for us. As teenagers, when Northern Virginia was still countryside, we'd go driving through pastures and lanes of honeysuckle on Sunday afternoons.

I enjoy seeing the gardens and the trees in the green suburbs of Cincinnati.

"We'll live out here someday," my husband says.

I cringe and keep looking out the car window as the mansions slide by.

We also shop for groceries together, falling into the same pattern every week. My husband pushes the cart and pays the bill – he earns most of our money. When we get home, I put the food away because I cook and want to know where things are. I do the cooking because it's my job, not because I'm good at it or enjoy it. My menu is dull. I never suggest that my husband and I try cooking together or even take turns. My stereotypes – men don't cook! – limit my imagination.

We are not as easygoing now as we were during our first year of marriage because the ground has shifted under us. I am not sure I want children, and I do not want to run a household. I can, of course.

My mother taught me how to sew, make a bed with hospital corners, iron like a professional, and make an apple pie. I could change my baby brothers' cloth diapers, using those big metal pins, so smoothly they barely knew what was happening. I love my mother. I just don't want to become her.

Long after my mother dies, I will walk past the open door of a department store beauty parlor where someone is getting a permanent wave, and the pungent smell will bring me to my knees in tears. Instantly, it is fifty years before, and I am standing in our Virginia kitchen while she is giving a home permanent to our neighbor. In that moment, my longing for her will be unbearable.

But I'm 24 years old, and marriage seems like a cage to me. I have signed up to be a wife – in fact, rushed for the safety of being a wife! – but now I do not want to be caged. I can see how large the world is and how much it needs people who care. I am one of those people.

I don't know how to talk to my husband about it. I am afraid we will fight. I learned from my parents how dangerous arguments can get and how fast. So, I am quiet and polite. We survive on small talk, going through the motions of marriage. I have learned a lot about sex but nothing about intimacy, and I do not know there is a difference. We talk about work, but we work on different planets.

On Halloween, we dress up like hippies. I'm surprised, standing among the pirates and clowns, to find myself wishing my costume were for real. I would like to be goofy or silly just for once. For years, I have been sweet, serious, attentive, dutiful. Other feelings too dangerous to show linger below the surface: boredom, anxiety, hurt, defiance, anger. I say nothing to my husband, to my family, even to my one friend, Cheryl. Nothing at all. But a battle has begun within me. There's only one outward sign: I can't eat.

I keep cooking, but I don't take care of myself. I lose a great deal of weight and ignore a minor burning sensation until it becomes a major kidney infection. I end up in Christ Hospital with a raging fever and an IV.

One day, when I am alone in my hospital room and my husband is at work, a doctor stops by.

"No reason for a young, healthy woman like you to be taking up space here," he says. "You have done this to yourself. You need to start eating, start taking care of yourself. Stop the nonsense. Fix whatever is wrong in your life. There are people who really need this bed."

Here I am in my clean bed, much less sick than the man I met lying on the floor, taking advantage of my husband's expensive health insurance.

I look around my plain, but infinitely better private hospital room.

Oh, those people on the gurneys in the basement!

I am disgusted with myself.

The doctor is right. I need to do something. I don't know what.

I pick up the phone next to my bed and call my husband. I tell him I need to get out of the hospital, come home, and go back to work.

I feel caught between two worlds grinding against each other, and I am comfortable only in the noise of the newsroom, where I am still largely ignored, although more women are slowly joining the staff. It is less male but still all white. I am not sure who I am as a person, but I am starting to understand who I am as a journalist.

CHAPTER SEVEN:
HOUSE TROUBLE

In the winter, I get a call from a widow who is having big problems with her house. It's late in the afternoon.

"Please come to see me," she says. "I just need you to see it."

From the outside, her house looks okay. Three stories, wood, upright. It has an average roof and a new coat of paint. I walk up the porch steps and knock. When she opens the front door, the stink hits me like a fist. I take a couple of steps back.

The basement flooded weeks ago, she explains, and she can't afford a plumber.

It's cold standing out on the porch, so I go with in with her. It's cold in the house, too. The furnace has quit. In the light of her one table lamp in the living room, I can see children wearing their coats. This is her dream home, she says, at least it was. Now it's her nightmare.

"We've been living on my money from baby-sitting," she says, "and the children get Social Security."

So, they're poor. Extremely poor. They are the victims of structural violence, a concept I do not yet understand, inflicted on Black families here in several ways. Urban renewal and highway clearance have uprooted them. Property owners have refused to rent to them. They say they don't want large families. Lending institutions have redlined the city and refused to lend to them.

The widow needed a place to live. When she was offered a chance to "rent-to-own" a house, it sounded like a godsend. But this arrangement, legally called a land contract, was a deal with the devil. It hid a world of harm.

The widow agreed to make a small down payment and then small payments every month to the seller until she could convert to a real mortgage. From the beginning, there was trouble. A land contract does not require a home inspection, and she did not ask for one.

"Three months after we moved in, along comes a building inspector. He tells me my house is a death trap. It must be rewired." She didn't have the money. Then her basement flooded.

I walk through the house with her. A horrible smell of sewage reaches all the way up to the third floor.

Overwhelmed financially, she has stopped paying for the house. The seller is suing her, and the Legal Aid Society attorney has advised her to move out. She'll lose everything she has paid so far.

As I investigate her case and others, I find that land contracts have many pitfalls. They require no appraisal of the property, so the buyer may pay far too much. There is no title search, so the seller of the house may not actually own the property. The deed is not recorded, so the seller can borrow money on the property or even sell it while the new buyer is still living there. The tax bills go to the seller, who may not pay them, so buyers are always at risk of losing the home. This is a huge problem in Cincinnati.

The *Post* persuades a local legislator to introduce a state law regulating the sale of homes on land contract in Ohio. It takes many months, but in August 1969 the bill passes, and the governor signs it. The new law requires disclosures to buyers about the condition of the houses. It also requires the recording of deeds from these sales. But the law is toothless because it has no sanctions. If sellers break the law, home buyers must sue in civil court. Most are too poor to litigate.

Half a century later, *The New York Times* will report this "mirage of home ownership," the purchase of homes on land contracts, has returned to hurt families across the nation, including some in Cincinnati, where the Ohio law is still on the books. In 2023 the city of Chicago will file a civil suit against a property management firm alleging the identical abuses I have found in Cincinnati. The lawsuit will put a price tag on losses in wealth to Black families in Chicago from contract sales in the 1950s and 60s: somewhere between $3.2 billion and $4 billion. [x]

While I am investigating land contracts, I stumble across the footprints of a different real estate monster, one that will devour thousands of homes in Detroit and devastate cities across the nation. The first alarm comes in phone calls from home buyers in the prosperous neighborhoods of Price Hill and Westwood.

I go out to meet Harry F. Klenk, who bought a home on Cora Avenue in Westwood. It's a tidy, appealing, two-story brick house with a front porch and stone foundation, set slightly up from the street, with a small front yard.

Klenk is disabled, and he used a small inheritance from his father to make a down payment, He got an FHA-insured mortgage with modest monthly payments and hoped to rent out the upstairs apartment. His income is less than my $68 a week.

As soon as he and his wife moved in, they discovered that cracks in the pipes in the basement had been covered with plaster and painted. Contractors told him 75 percent of the plumbing in the house needed replacing.

"The estimated cost is $2000," he says with a sigh, "and there's more."

"The electric wiring needs to be replaced, and the gas pipes are not hooked up correctly. To make this place livable, it'll cost more than $5000."

He can't afford the repairs.

We are standing in his living room, and the smell from the basement is awful. The drinking water from the tap tastes bad, too, he tells me.

He can't rent the apartment upstairs.

He has tried to sell the house to investors, but he has no takers.

"Our only alternative will be to vacate this house and file for bankruptcy," he says. "It is our opinion that we have been victimized. They have laws about labels on cans, boxes, weights, and measures. Where are laws of any protection in housing?"

Another home buyer says the seller told him the FHA mortgage meant the house would require "no repairs for six years." The plumbing doesn't work, the wiring is inadequate, and water runs into the house when it rains. The new owner can't afford the repairs.

"It's a used product," the seller tells me, "And when you buy a used product, you can expect something will need repair." He denies saying the FHA mortgage meant the house would require no repairs for six years.

A third couple who bought a house with an FHA-insured mortgage were so convinced that anything associated with the federal government had to be in undamaged shape they didn't believe the tenants who told them the furnace was defective. But three days after they moved in, the gas company refused to turn on the furnace until it was repaired.

The FHA director for the region tells me "Let the buyer beware" applies to most of the homes his office handles. The only exceptions are the houses FHA owns and sells. These have a six-month warranty. The director says Milwaukee has also started seeing problems like Cincinnati's. Buyers misunderstand that the FHA guarantees the mortgage, not the condition of the house.

My stories in the *Cincinnati Post*, which appear in 1969, are among the first in the nation to report problems with FHA mortgages. Shortly after they appear, I get a call from the office of Congressman Wright Patman, Chairman of the House Committee on Banking and Currency. He's concerned about abuses in the FHA program. The committee wants me to come to Washington to testify about my findings.

I am thrilled until Dick Thornburg, editor-in-chief of the *Post*, calls me into his office and tells me that squeaky clean corporations such as IT&T are involved with the FHA loans, and they would never participate in anything dishonest. He tells me I am not going to Washington, and I am not going to be writing anything more about FHA loans. Period. End of story. I feel crushed.

This is only a few years before IT&T becomes a household word for scandal as allegations surface the corporation has tried to bribe the Republican Party in exchange for help from the Nixon Administration's Justice Department. An investigation by Special Prosecutor Leon Jaworski subsequently clears the company of criminal activity. Not until 2000 will CIA documents reveal the corporation financially supported the 1973 coup that overthrew the democratic government of Chile, where IT&T owned a majority share of the telephone company.

Now and then, I can help someone quickly. One Monday in November, I learn that a boy who is just 19 has been sentenced to five years in the Workhouse for loitering after leaving a religion class at a church near downtown. The boy, who is poor and white, did not move fast enough when a policeman told him to clear the area in five minutes. Five years in the Workhouse! I can't believe it.

The next day, I go to the neighborhood. The sidewalks are full of trash and leaves. It is a downtrodden white ghetto with so little commerce that the proprietress of one store is working a giant jigsaw puzzle between customers. She says kids sometimes interfere with her deliveries. She has often threatened to call the police, she says, but she never has. The cashier in a small grocery store tells me kids steal from the store, pester and badmouth her. Accordingly, they are banned from the premises. The bartender at a nearby establishment looks out of the dark and says the kids shake down his customers for quarters and fifty cent pieces after they leave his place.

I pound on the door of the church rectory. The priest is not thrilled to see a reporter. He tells me he asked the police to keep the kids away from the church after they carved their names in stone there. Still, he wants to be on good terms with the boys. When they asked permission to be on the property, he granted it, knowing the police would run them off. As we speak, the Father tells me about a police/community relations meeting tonight at a church nearby, so I attend and take notes. I am amazed by the venom I hear from the adults at the meeting, and I write it all up.

Two days later, the judge in the boy's loitering case, who is sensitive to publicity, suspends the boy's Workhouse sentence. I am happy, and the boy never knows a thing about me.

At about this time, I am pulled off inner city stories to work on a big story for a special section of the paper to commemorate the 150th birthday of the University of Cincinnati. Suddenly, I am on campus at the high tide of the 1960s. I sit on the grass for lunch. I listen to endless speeches about the failings of the faculty and higher education. The war in Vietnam is growing bloodier and more unpopular, and dozens of students speak out against it.

I interview the most outspoken of the radicals, Joe Herring and his friend Jim Finger. I can't get over their appearance. I've known my husband since high school, but he has always cut his hair so short I can't say exactly what shade of brown it is. Jim Finger has long, dark curls below his shoulders, and Joe Herring's hair is almost black, frizzy, long, and sticks out as if struck by lightning. The women students have long, loose hair, scarves, and fanciful clothes, costumes, like nothing I've seen.

I'm only a few years older than they are, but compared to them, I was never young. It's not the marijuana or other drugs – my family's hellish experiences with alcohol have turned me off drugs – it's everything I have missed. Everything I want. The music, the hair, the passion, the euphoria.

It's late spring 1969, and all the feelings I've shoved aside in my unexamined life fuse together and ignite one Saturday afternoon after my husband decides to reorganize my kitchen. He means well, but he delivers a fatal blow to our marriage. He stands a foot taller than me, and when he's done, everything in the kitchen is out of my reach. Our small kitchen is the only place in our apartment that belongs to me. Suddenly, it does not.

I do not yell, scream, or cry. I wait one day. Two. Late one afternoon, when we are both home from work, I tell him I'm leaving. He can have everything we own except my books, my mother's silver, and my blue Wedgewood dishes. I don't want to talk about it. I refuse to argue. He leaves the apartment first, taking the car. He's certain I'm not serious.

I pack some clothes in a bag and, on impulse, call a guy I've met who owns a blue Mustang convertible. To my surprise, he comes to get me. For the first time in my life, I feel free.

CHAPTER EIGHT:
STARTING OVER

It's my second effort to run away from home. The first time, I was eighteen months old and on a railroad train. My mother and I had traveled from my grandparents' home in Long Beach, California, to meet my father's ship in Seattle. World War II had ended in Europe, and he was coming home. The year was 1945.

He was a young infantry officer. After the Normandy invasion, he was promoted rapidly to lieutenant colonel. He fought throughout Western Europe, including the Battle of the Bulge, and was a much-decorated hero. He was desperate to see my mother, a gorgeous blue-eyed brunette who adored him.

I have no idea why she took me along. I was a toddler. He was a stranger to me, and I was afraid of him.

The night he arrived, they got a hotel room and a crib for me. I wailed when they put me in it. I wanted my mother. This set him off. He did not want a crying brat. In the rural Georgia, where he grew up, disobedient children were punished severely. He spanked me, and I messed my pants.

My mother tried to stop him because I was so little, and no one had ever hit me. He ordered her not to comfort me or clean me up. I finally stopped crying and fell asleep. I remember nothing about this night – I got the story from my mother, who blamed herself for ruining my father's homecoming.

But we learned in the years to come that, when my father came home from the war, the war came home with him.

As I grew up with my dad's drinking and unpredictable outbursts, I mastered ways to defend myself. Some of my coping skills hurt me: silence, obedience, denial, and dreams of rescue. Others ended up being helpful: I was always on the lookout for danger when my father was around. I learned to pay attention to the slightest change in his voice, the way he breathed, the look in his eyes, his smallest move. Now, when I interview most people, I can read them, and they know it. It's more than empathy. It's an extreme awareness of them. I try not to use this skill, which is very invasive, unless I must.

My father impressed on all his children the importance of honor, duty, courage, patriotism, and achievement. However, he rarely showed affection. He took me in his arms just once, when I was three years old and seriously injured. This void left me with a yearning for him no man can ever fill.

Still, I ran away from him after that night in Seattle.

I did this on the troop train home to Los Angeles the next day.

Our car was crowded, and my parents, wrapped up in each other, forgot me. As they both told the story, it was some time before they realized I was missing. Both panicked. My father ran through the train, cars swaying and open in between, imagining the worst, that I had fallen off.

The cars were segregated by race. My father ran through the white cars and kept going through the cars where the soldiers were Black. That's where he found me, sitting on the lap of a Black soldier who was playing poker. He looked up at my father and smiled.

"Don't take her, Colonel. She's bringing me luck."

My father occasionally told the story of my escape as a joke on himself, the senior white officer from the South who lost track of his daughter, only to find her among Black soldiers who snagged her during a card game. He never remarked on the grace and quick wit of the card player's greeting or the absolution it gave him.

In the far distant future, after my father retires, he will become the bedrock in the lives of my two youngest brothers. By the time he dies of cancer, he will love and be loved by his family and the school children who know him only as the kind old retiree who taught sixth grade science. He and I will forgive each other, but the clay of my character has been fired. I will have to accept what cannot be changed, only understood.

Back in Cincinnati, my flight from my husband will end my marriage, but this is the last time I will ever run away from anyone or anything. Instead of escape plans, I will look for answers, starting with new ways to confront pain, my own and the pain of others.

The guy with the blue Mustang convertible is the kid from campus, Joe Herring. I know little about him beyond what he said in our interview for the *Post:* he opposes the status quo in general and the Vietnam War in particular. He's a sociology major at the university, finishing his junior year. He has the top down on the Mustang.

It's late afternoon, but the sun is still hot, and I'm melting on the bucket seat as we roar up and down the hills of Cincinnati, our hair flying in the wind. To my surprise, people wave and yell at us. This guy is a lot younger than me, and I'm not sure what I'm doing. I feel delirious. It's the feeling I want, the sense of possibility I have missed.

Joe stops to buy us a couple of fiery Coney Island hot dogs before he asks what's going on.

"I'm leaving home," I tell him.

"I can't offer you a place to stay," he answers. "Not even overnight. I live with Bill, that's my older brother. He — my whole family — they're devout Roman Catholics. Couldn't bring anyone to stay the night."

My heart begins to sink. I have no plans. I am just running away.

"But no problem. Tonight, we can go camping!"

We buy soft drinks, stop by Joe's apartment to pick up sleeping bags, and drive out to a state park. From the front seat, we watch the day fade into a long twilight. Joe has brought his camera, and he shows me the small things in nature you can see through a telephoto lens. A leaf. A flower. Up close, they are transformed.

Night in a sleeping bag by myself on the ground is less than thrilling. It's still dark when the birds wake me up.

I'm soaking wet. And itching. Crap! I'm bitten all over by bugs!

I pull some clothes out of my bag, change in the park restroom, brush my teeth, and try to wash up. As I dry off with brown paper towels, nothing seems real. The sun is up by the time I get back to the car. Joe is throwing the sleeping bags into the trunk. He gives me a big smile.

"Good morning! I have class, but we have time for breakfast. There's a place near campus."

"Yes! Of course! Thanks!"

I'll be late for work - I can call the office. I wish Joe would skip his class - no, I don't. I'm crazy itching with these bug bites. I'm free.

I can't stop smiling.

Joe leaves me sitting in a coffee shop with the morning *Enquirer*, looking in the classified ads for an apartment and a new life.

I have no car and no furniture. I use the pay phone in the shop, walk to see a few apartments, and settle on a furnished place in the university area. It's on a bus line, so I can get to work. The rent is half my take home paycheck. I have never paid attention to money, so I do not know how long I can manage this, but the proprietor agrees to a month-to-month lease.

When I get back to my desk at the office, my husband is on the phone.

"What in the world are you doing? When are you coming home? Can we talk?"

"No," I say to everything. "I just want a divorce."

I do not want to talk. I want out.

I know I am being unreasonable and unfair, but the only thing I want is freedom. I do not want to be married. What I can't say to him is how much it will hurt to leave his parents. For years, they have treated me like a daughter, and I love them. I wish I could just stay in the family and be my husband's sister. But how can I say that?

My parents, who moved to San Francisco after my wedding, are now living in South Korea, where my father is stationed in Seoul. When I write to say I'm filing for divorce, my mother says little, but I'm certain she is shocked and sad. I keep thinking about the big wedding reception they staged at the officer's club. They are not wealthy and still have four kids to send to college. Our family has never had a divorce. I don't want to shame my parents. But when they finally call me long distance, I weep and say I cannot change my mind.

Joe Herring stops by to see my new apartment and eventually to welcome me to the new age of romance. I am baffled. Joe is thrilled to have a new best friend and lots of sex, but he does not want a girlfriend. I am still married, so we shouldn't be involved. Worse, even though I reject being a wife, I'm insecure, tempted to want an exclusive relationship. Joe does not want a commitment. Emotionally, I can't get my balance.

I keep my married name. Jo Thomas is my newspaper byline. Changing my byline back to Jo DeYoung will be a public announcement of my divorce, which is embarrassing enough already. Also, I am no longer the same person I was before I married.

As the summer moves along, I am divorced from a good man, just the wrong husband for me. Joe takes me with him to softball games with his brother and for beers afterwards at Fries Café with the rest of the team. Later, he takes me home to meet his parents and family.

Joe's mother, Louise McCarren Herring, has a legendary history. She will become known as the "Mother of the Credit Union Movement in America." As a young woman, she was arrested more than once for her organizing efforts – opposed by the banks – to get ordinary people, not just rich ones, access to consumer credit. Her better-known collaborator was the department store magnate and philanthropist Edward Filene. Louise is now a gray-haired matriarch and mother of five, still deeply involved with credit unions, including the one at my newspaper, where she knows everyone in the building – printers and janitors as well as reporters and editors.

One of Joe's sisters is a nun, and the whole family has a profound commitment to social justice, expressed in diverse ways. The conversations at their dinner table show me that families can disagree without screaming at each other. I am a divorced woman a few years older than their promising, unmarried son, and they are surely worried about our relationship. Still, they welcome me without judging me. Their kindness has no conditions because that's who they are.

As the months pass, I buy a car. With car payments, I can no longer afford my furnished apartment. I rent a tiny, unfurnished apartment on the ground floor of a building on Ravine Street in Over-the-Rhine. My new landlady is covered in tattoos – she's the first woman I've ever seen decorated this way – and my furniture, a step above ratty, comes from the Salvation Army.

One night when I'm alone in bed, I am startled awake at two a.m. by a funny scraping sound. It's my casement window, the one next to my bed, being forced open with a metal object.

Oh, my lord! What do I do now? I smash my fist into the metal blinds covering the window. This makes a tremendous noise, and I can hear something being dropped and someone running away. The next morning, I find a tire iron outside. I don't like this version of living on the edge and on my own.

Again, I am rescued, but not in the way I expect. Walter Friedenburg, the new editor of the *Post and Times-Star*, calls me into his office.

"Jo, your stories are making it hard for me to get a tennis game with anyone." He's smiling, but my stomach is churning.

He keeps smiling and tells me he has good news. The *Post* has nominated me for a Nieman Fellowship at Harvard, a chance to take an entire academic year off to study anything I want at the university's expense with a stipend large enough to support living in Cambridge or Boston. I have made the first cut in the selection process, and I'm invited to an interview in New York at the Algonquin Hotel.

That trip now seems like a dream: the cat in the hotel lobby, the wood paneling and the white tablecloths in the Oak Room, the lump in my throat. I tell the selection committee I need help in thinking about inner city problems in Cincinnati.

"I don't understand the politics of race," I say. "My academic background is in English. I never studied sociology or education. I want to read about justice. I want to study social sciences. It would also be good to understand statistics."

Back home, I can't stop thinking about my academic inadequacies and how poorly I understand the workings of cities. I discount what I've learned since coming to Cincinnati. I must do something about it, even if I don't make the cut at Harvard.

My divorce and the upcoming disappearance of Joe Herring – he plans to go the graduate school at Washington

University in St. Louis – will leave me no emotional roots in Cincinnati except for Cheryl, so I can go anywhere. For good measure, I apply to the new Stanford University Fellowship program for journalists. As a wild card, as I have none of the prerequisites, I also apply to the graduate program in urban planning at the University of California at Berkeley.

UC Berkeley, which once admitted me as an undergraduate and offered me a scholarship, turns me down, but Stanford and Harvard both say yes. I am thrilled. I decide on Harvard.

CHAPTER NINE:
A NEW EDUCATION

It's the summer of 1970. Joe and I are relocating in opposite directions, east and west. We decide to take six weeks, camp out, and move our possessions, mostly books, in two U-Haul trailers, heading east first. We grossly underestimate the distance and the difficulty of towing a trailer.

Packed full, it springs from side to side on the road, like a clumsy beast. It is impervious to slowing down, careful steering, everything but reloading. Just as we are considering pulling over and doing this, something shifts, and it settles down.

When we get to Massachusetts, we leave the trailer at a campground in Andover and go looking for an apartment. We get lost and can't find Cambridge. A gas station attendant looks at Joe's long hair and my sandals and tells us, "Throw away the map. You can't get there. Are you *sure* you even want to go there? Are they having a demonstration or something?"

When we finally arrive and see the price of rentals in Cambridge, I decide to look for a place across the Charles River in Boston's Back Bay neighborhood instead. I rent a tiny apartment on the third floor of a house on Marlborough

Street. When we return to unload the trailer, cars are triple parked at my front door and all along the block.

"The Kennedys are at Symphony Hall," a passerby explains, and I can see there will never be any place to park on Marlborough Street. I have just had several near-death experiences in Boston traffic, so I suggest sending my car to Missouri with Joe. I'll use public transportation here.

I've learned the Russell Sage Foundation liked my plan to study the social sciences so much they've endowed my fellowship at Harvard themselves. At the end of the summer, I stop by their offices in Manhattan to thank them. That's when I meet Phil Meyer, on leave from Knight Newspapers. He will play a key role in my career, which, at the age of twenty-six, I do not imagine as a career.

During my first week at Harvard, I accidentally lock myself out of my third-floor apartment in Boston, and none of the neighbors in my small building are home. Looking up at the façade, I see that my front window, which faces Marlborough Street, is open and connects to a fire escape that crosses over to window on the same floor in the building next door. I ring the bell for that apartment.

The occupant, a psychiatrist, answers. He and his wife invite me in for a cup of coffee. Once I explain my predicament, they let me crawl out their window, onto the fire escape, and into my own apartment.

Not long after, at one of the exquisite get-acquainted luncheons the Nieman Foundation hosts for incoming fellows, I am seated next to a woman whose name card tells me she is Mrs. George C. Lodge. He is a Harvard professor, former journalist, and the son of the former UN Ambassador Henry Cabot Lodge. *That* family, the Boston Brahmins.

When Mrs. Lodge asks how I like Boston, I think about my neighbors, the psychiatrist and his wife, and gush, "Very much! Coming here from the Midwest, I had no idea people would be so friendly!"

"Clearly," she says, without cracking a smile, "you aren't meeting the right sort of people."

Is she serious? Or is she kidding me? I am speechless.

I begin my Nieman year in 1970 as the second woman fellow since the 1940s. Catherine (Cassie) Mackin, the pioneering television journalist, came before me. She arrived in 1967 from Hearst Newspapers and went to NBC, where she will become the first woman to anchor a nightly evening network newscast.

The Nieman program is for mid-career journalists, and I am the youngest Nieman ever. Bob Manning, editor of *The Atlantic* and a member of the selection committee, has told me, "Most Niemans have accomplished a great deal. We think you *will* accomplish a great deal." So, they are taking a chance on me.

My classmates, all older men, welcome me and help when gender is an issue. Some of our Nieman dinners are held at the Locke-Ober Restaurant in Boston, which does not allow women, so a few of the other fellows just smuggle me under a coat to the private dining room upstairs.

As a fellow, I receive a ticket to the press box at Harvard Stadium stamped "Women and children not admitted." Harvard football does not thrill me – I saw enough college football watching my former husband play for Duke – but to prove a point, I show up anyway at the press entrance to the stadium. The security guard points to the "women and children not admitted" on my ticket.

"I'm a fellow, and it's my ticket."

He is not impressed, so I dodge past him as male reporters come in, and I run up the stairs. After a few seconds, I can hear the security guard calling and climbing up after me, not as fast. By the time I reach the top, he is well behind. I look around me and start shouting.

"Who's in charge here?"

When a staff member appears, I explain as fast as I can.

"I am a fellow, I have a ticket, and I intend to watch the game."

When the guard arrives, he is waved off.

"You're welcome here," the staffer says. "It's just that now we'll have *two* women here today, and it's very *distracting*. A woman from the *Boston Globe* is doing sketches."

The press box is a sea of men in white shirts eating hot dogs, no woman in sight. I get my hot dog and find a seat. I do enjoy the band — it announces itself as the "The Harvard University Salute to Rich Alumni Band" – and I stay for one quarter of the game before I leave without spotting the woman from the *Globe*. As far as I can tell, the only man I've distracted is the security guard.

Back in the early 1960s, as an undergraduate at Wake Forest, I often felt like an outsider. Campus rules in those days confined women to the dorms at night, so we spent evenings locked in together, but I spent the time studying, sometimes in my room and sometimes in the luggage room because it was quiet there. On weekends, when I could, I went from Winston-Salem to Durham, where I stayed at Miss Mary's boarding house and visited my boyfriend at Duke.

I never sought out other women to discuss the meaning of our lives, those we were living and those we planned. My roommate agreed to be my bridesmaid, and then she was gone. In those days, women expected to be friends with the wives of their husband's friends, something I failed to do in Cincinnati.

My friendship with Cheryl has shown me the importance of woman friends. And, as different as they are, Cheryl Grant and Joe Herring's mother, Louise, are both role models of the fearless, committed woman I want to be.

Louise is finishing middle age with many accomplishments, but Cheryl is young and just setting off on her journey. Life in social work has so made her so frustrated with the criminal justice system that she is joining the Cincinnati police as a rare Black woman officer, but that will not suffice. She will enroll in law school, open a private practice, and then serve on the bench as a Hamilton County municipal judge for many years. Over the lifetime in which we are friends, she will complete her studies at a seminary and become a Baptist minister. She will be the embodiment of courage, love, and justice.

At Harvard, I have new chances to connect with young women my own age who are preparing to face life on their own terms. Most are graduate students at Boston area universities. Notices on bulletin boards all over campus announce women's collectives organizing themselves, and the atmosphere is electric.

At Adams House on the Harvard campus, where I can attend meals, I meet Brenda Silver, a graduate student in English literature. She introduces me to her friend Helene Foley, a graduate student in classics, and we become friends. The two of them belong to a women's consciousness-raising group, one of many organizing on campus. They introduce me to women forming a new group, and I join.

We gather once a week at members' apartments in Cambridge, Somerville, and in my tiny place in Boston. We drink tea or coffee, and as we talk, a curtain seems to fall away from the world as I have seen it. We share a tremendous sense of possibility and excitement. When people speak of women's liberation, I think it's this intoxicating sense of being set free to care about the world and free to do something about it.

As Helene observes at the time, in an essay she will show me many years later, many of us have been caught between two worlds, the one we were brought up in and the one where we find ourselves. Some of us were the "bright girl," in high school, afraid of being socially unacceptable. We haven't been able to get beyond superficial feelings of rivalry, superiority, or inferiority with most other women. We've patterned our professional lives after men. If married, we've expected to make friends through our husbands, giving lower priority to our women friends. In these groups, for the first time, we discover a new women's culture of mutual respect, where we can trust each other, where we can find new strength. We will need it for the days ahead.

My friend Brenda Silver will join the English department faculty at Dartmouth College in 1972, the same year women students are first admitted to Dartmouth, where Brenda says she experiences a strong subculture of misogyny. Her struggle there is painful – she and I will exchange letters and telephone calls in the middle of the night – but she will triumph. She becomes admired and respected by her colleagues and loved by her students. She marries. Her scholarship on the work of Virginia Woolf is famous, and she establishes women and gender studies at Dartmouth. She will teach there for forty years.

Brenda's friend and mine, Helene, will become a specialist in ancient Greek literature and women and gender in antiquity, eventually becoming a professor of classical studies at Barnard College at Columbia University and a member of the university's Institute for Research on Women, Gender and Sexuality. When we meet, her husband, Duncan, is teaching at M.I.T.

Duncan, a Marxist economist, is on board with the women's movement from the start. But his attitude is rare. For many years, I have considered Helene one of the lucky ones who has not had to give up marriage for her career. Other women I meet in academia will either not marry or not have children. Most of us can fight just so many battles at once.

As things turn out, my year at Harvard will be the only year of my professional life I am free to say what I think about politics to anyone outside my family or my closest friends. In the future, I will have to keep my thoughts and feelings to myself. I cannot let them get in the way of my reporting.

Only this year, when I am a student and not a working journalist, can my opinions be out in the open. Dwight Sergeant, who administers the Nieman program, calls me "that woman who came here and raised hell about women's lib."

I join other women in campus sit-ins. Peacefully, we occupy a campus building, demanding day care for the children of women working at the university. We stay until the police turn off the power and water. We leave when the campus administration agrees to put the topic on the table for discussion.

On another occasion, we sit down on the floor outside the office of Francis Skiddy von Stade Jr., the Harvard dean of first year students. The press has quoted him as saying educated women contribute little to society. We want him to know his remarks disgust us. As we sit on the floor, a group of fashionably dressed visiting Radcliffe alumnae appear at the other end of the hall, and we send an emissary to explain our presence. They slip off their high heels, bring a bottle of sherry, and join us on the floor.

As a Nieman fellow, I have a membership in the Harvard Faculty Club, which has tables for faculty and guests and one section of tables reserved for male faculty who walk in solo. Other men may join them, but unescorted woman may not sit at these tables.

The women I know who have junior faculty positions are justifiably afraid to join me, but several graduate students are game, so we walk in and sit down at the forbidden tables as the waitress tries to wave us off. We look at our placemats and forks and knives for a long time, drawing angry stares and shaking heads from men and women alike as others finish their lunches and leave, and new arrivals take their places.

Finally, the uncle of one of my companions happens to walk in, spots us, and sits down with us. Ironically, this give us the required male companion to be served, and we are handed menus. We're hungry by now, so we are glad to eat despite the resentful looks. I do not know whether we have desegregated the faculty club with this lunch because I will not return there after this run-in.

Scorn for women knows no bounds. At one Nieman lunch, I find myself seated next to Daniel Patrick Moynihan, the sociologist whose controversial report on poverty blames ghetto culture. I try to start a conversation with him about racism, but he startles me by reaching over and patting me on the head.

"There, there," he says, apropos of nothing, "everything didn't start with Vietnam."

I do, in fact, spend a semester studying the history of Vietnam in a class taught by Alexander Woodside, a Canadian historian of China and East Asia. His scholarship brings new dimensions to the stories about the war I am reading in the newspapers. When Brenda and other members of Adams House take the bus to Washington, D. C., for a huge march to protest Nixon's bombing of Cambodia, I go along.

Pursuing my promise to the Nieman selection committee to learn more about cities and more about race, I take a class with the sociologist Thomas Pettigrew, a professor of social psychology and an expert on race relations.

I have been looking for ways to think about justice. The lack of justice for so many people in Cincinnati haunts me. I take a class with the philosopher Judith Shklar, who has her students read Hannah Arendt. I am stunned by the brilliance of Shklar and the writing of Arendt in addressing injustice and change.

Michael Useem, a sociology professor who will later teach at the Wharton School of Business, has us read Karl Marx. A lot of Karl Marx. For the first time, I can see other ways to analyze the social ills caused by capitalism. Harvard is not making me a Marxist, but it's making me think. Great institutions nurture ideas.

I cannot foresee that Mikhail Gorbachev, the future President of the Soviet Union, will make the same point when I meet him in London years from now. He will joke with the reporters gathered around him that Karl Marx studied at the British Museum reading room, and "If people don't like Marxism, they should blame the British Museum." Great institutions nurture ideas, but no one can predict what those ideas will be.

The ideas and the people I encounter during my Nieman year set me on fire.

I am, however, spending more time studying than networking or job hunting, and I do not want to return to work in Cincinnati when this is over. My editors have indicated they would be just as happy not to see me. When spring arrives, I get serious about finding something else because Harvard is not going to last forever.

I write letters to *The New York Times* and the *Washington Post* – nothing. The *Boston Globe* – nothing. A fellow Nieman arranges for me to meet a *Newsday* executive who happens to be in town. After we are introduced, my classmate leaves the two of us sitting in the lobby of the man's hotel.

The man invites me to his room to talk. As soon as the door is closed, he makes a lunge at me, then starts chasing me around the room. I start laughing because he is so old and disgusting, and I cannot believe this is happening. I dash into the hall and leave.

Is this my fault? Did I do something wrong? I blame myself and feel ashamed. I say nothing to the Nieman classmate who introduced us, nothing even to my women's group. The man is dead now, and fifty years later I wonder about naming him here. But I have waited too long. It would protect no one and only hurt his family. I am sure he is not thinking about his family when he tries to assault me. So, he gets away with it. It's enough to say that he expects no consequences. But I feel them. Based on this experience, I decide not to apply at *Newsday*.

It is Phil Meyer from Knight Newspapers and the Russell Sage Foundation who comes to the rescue and makes a connection for me with the *Detroit Free Press*. They are looking for a reporter, he says, and they will get in touch.

CHAPTER TEN:
WELCOME TO THE MURDER CITY

I'm afraid.

I am standing on the front porch, shivering.

It's an anonymous two-family house in a block of peeling look-alikes, a downriver neighborhood I don't know. Kerekes[xi], my guide to the Detroit underworld, brought me here last summer, but nothing looks the same. It's December 1973. I double check my notes. I have the right house number.

Kerekes. I look at the mailboxes, knowing I won't see his name. A Polish name is on the right. The mailbox on the left is blank, so I ring the bell on that side of the porch. No answer.

It is 1:30 in the afternoon. Kerekes sometimes jokes when we talk on the phone, but today he sounded like a stranger.

"Come alone. Be there at 1:30. Any sooner, it's off. Any later, we're gone."

I ring again and wait. Silence.

Something's wrong. I knock — softly at first, and then hard. Nothing.

They've left the door open for me.

I try the handle of the front door and push it open. I poke my head inside and call into the dark.

80

"Hello! Hello!"

No answer.

I should leave.

Instead, I step over a dusty pile of junk mail and walk down the hall to a first floor flat. It's empty and freezing cold. I keep my coat on and sit down to wait on a brown sofa. The room is just as I remember it, with bulky furniture, heavy red drapes, mirrors, and gold-framed landscapes. It could be a funeral parlor. In the shadows along the wall are a row of bar stools and a counter. I never want to see the other rooms. Kerekes told me he keeps this place for parties. His family lives in the suburbs.

My hands won't stop shaking.

It's the cold. It's just the cold.

No one knows I'm here. That's one of Kerekes' rules. No one can know about him or the friend he's promised to bring today.

If he doesn't back out again.

I've been working on a Mafia story. It has consumed me for months, and I need more sources. Kerekes says the friend can help me.

If everything's okay. If this isn't a set-up.

If Kerekes is someone I can trust, I'll talk to the friend, take notes, and go back to my office.

If everything's okay, nothing bad will happen.

If.

I have not come to Detroit to end up in such a room. When I arrived, my idea of danger was insisting on lunch in the section of the Harvard Faculty Club that did not serve women. But my editors weren't looking for courage. They wanted a behavioral science columnist, and I just needed any newspaper job.

Phil Meyer gave them my name, and they mailed me an application form. I filled out most of it, leaving blank the parts asking if I could type and take shorthand. I also refused to reveal my abysmal salary. I told them why: I was afraid they would follow the usual industry practice offering only fifteen dollars a week more, which would not be enough.

Before returning my application, some self-destructive impulse moved me to add: "I can take notes and type stories but asking a woman reporter if she can type and take shorthand in a business where most women are secretaries is like asking a Black applicant if she likes watermelon."

Kurt Luedtke, the executive editor, wrote back to invite me for an interview and observed, as an aside, I was a person who had trouble with authority, problems with my father. He was right, of course. I had grave doubts about my chances of success in Detroit, but since Luedtke invited me, I accepted and flew out.

Great crowds of people could still stand at the gate to greet an arriving flight, but no one waiting at Detroit Metro looked remotely like a newspaper editor. I was briefly engulfed by a sea of people wearing polyester United Auto Workers windbreakers, but then I was alone, uncertain, and disappointed.

So, my strange journey begins with the appearance of a woman wearing long, flowing white robes, as if she's dressed for Halloween.

"Hello," she says. "I'm Cleo. My friends at the *Free Press* asked me to pick you up."

Cleo is a huge local celebrity, the leading astrologer in Detroit. As we walk to her car, she hands me a horoscope she has prepared just for me. As we speed down Interstate 94 towards downtown, it's raining so hard the road is barely visible. I find myself clutching the handle of her passenger door.

I hope you can see the highway as well as my future. I can barely see a thing.

But I can't miss the giant Uniroyal tire on the side of the highway. It's eighty-six feet high, a former Ferris wheel at the 1964 World's Fair in New York. Jackie Kennedy and the Shah of Iran were among thousands who rode it before it was dismantled and transformed into a tire that never moves, a Motor City welcome sign.

Cleo drops me at the Pontchartrain Hotel, saying the editors will meet me in the bar after work. I cannot decipher the future she has prepared for me, so I leave it in my room and head for the bar. It is smoky and dark, with plush cushions, a jazz piano player, and a substantial afternoon crowd. I don't know it's a favorite rendezvous for prostitutes and their johns. The pianist will strike up "Strangers in the Night" at the first sight of the vice cops. I order a soda and wonder who the *Free Press* will send next.

Neal Shine, the managing editor, arrives. He is an older guy, gray-haired and wearing a suit. He is kind, funny and smart.

I may be okay here.

We have dinner at the Pontchartrain Wine Cellar across the street, and Shine makes no effort to psychoanalyze me. Then Luedtke, as dour as his letter to me, appears. He's a young man wearing an old man's pair of spectacles. Shine leaves shortly, and Luedtke and I go back to the Pontchartrain for drinks.

Unknown to us, the FBI has started to bug the tables at the Anchor Bar, a bookie hangout just down the road. To the dismay of the federal agents, many of the conversations they will capture on tape before the Anchor Bar burns down will not involve bookmakers. Instead, they record reporters complaining about their editors.

"Who the hell is this guy Luedtke?" one of the agents will ask me.

Luedtke is a man on the move. As an assistant city editor, just twenty-seven years old, he led the *Free Press* to a Pulitzer Prize during the Detroit riots. At the age of thirty-one, when I meet him, he is running the newsroom as assistant to the executive editor, an astonishing ascent in a business where promotions tend to be glacial. He dresses like a man of forty-five, in expensive suits, but he is a true *enfant terrible*, slim, with the grace and disposition of a cheetah. In the newsroom, he rarely smiles.

In a few years, he will surprise everyone else, leave journalism, and try his luck in Hollywood, where he has no experience and no connections. It will not matter. His immense drive and talent will carry him as a screenwriter, and he will win an Oscar nomination for the film *Absence of Malice* and the Oscar itself for *Out of Africa*, both projects propelled by him.

When we meet, he is drinking gin and tonics the way other people drink water. I don't drink alcohol, so I keep up with sodas. I have long blonde hair, and I am wearing a short skirt that passes for graduate school dress-up style in this era.

After several hours, Luedtke has drunk too much to drive himself home and suggests – purely in the interest of public safety – he spend the night in my room.

"Get your own room," I tell him quietly, but without a moment's hesitation, remembering the editor from *Newsday*. Then I walk out fast. By the time I reach the elevator, I'm sure I've ruined any possibility of a career in Detroit.

The next morning, it's still raining, and I feel hopeless. My itinerary from the *Free Press* lists a series of job interviews just a few blocks away.

What's the point? They'll never hire me. But I don't have anything else to do today. I might as well go.

The *Free Press* building exudes permanence and respectability, although I will learn it is often a stage for local drama. An insulted opera singer stands on a desk and insists the music critic re-evaluate her talent. A widow demands the newspaper's help in getting a funeral home to cremate her husband's remains a second time. In several years, two homeless women will come to live in the building's stairwells.

There is no "security," just a polite man who answers questions at a desk near the elevators in the lobby. Now and then someone on the staff speculates on the possibility a gunman will walk off the elevator and shoot us all, but no one thinks this could happen.

In a few years, in fact, a man does arrive and asks the man in the lobby where he can find the reporting staff.

Although he is carrying a large gun, he is directed straight to the third floor, where the elevators open directly into the city room. The reporters scatter when he comes out with his gun, shouting, "Where's Judy Diebolt? I kill all my own snakes!"

Diebolt is not there. She reports from Detroit Recorder's Court, the venue for criminal cases. The gunman is angry about a mention she has given him in a story. Little pieces of paper saying "I am not Judy Diebolt" begin appearing on shirts and blouses throughout the newsroom as people telephone the police. They arrive swiftly and remove him, no harm done.

My first job interviews at the *Free Press* go smoothly, as if I have not insulted the boss the night before, but there is a problem. I do not want the behavioral science columnist job they are offering. Now I'm here in person, I try to explain I've been studying the social sciences to become a better city reporter, not to write about the social sciences themselves.

This gets me nowhere. The *Free Press* has enough city reporters. They want a behavioral science columnist. By the end of the afternoon, I have persuaded myself I could do it. Anything is better than returning to Cincinnati. Then a secretary reminds me I'm dining with Luedtke.

I'm done. I have no hope.

All I can remember about my dinner with him is the napkin. When we finish our meal and order coffee, Luedtke picks up a cocktail napkin, writes something on it, and lays it face down on the table.

"You have a hostile, suspicious personality," he says, staring at me through his glasses. "You think we're going to underpay you, and I'm not going to pay you too much. I've written down the highest salary I'll pay. You tell me the lowest salary you'll take. I'll turn the napkin over, and if you're over my figure, we're done."

Visions of a life in the city of Detroit, still hidden in constant rain, begin to disappear. Groping for a figure, I add fifty percent to my fellowship at Harvard.

"Fifteen thousand dollars."

He looks pained and turns the napkin over.

"$15,000."

Neither of us smiles.

"If you want the job, it's yours," he says.

"Yes, I do."

Without another word, he drives me back to the hotel. When I take a cab to the airport the next day, the rain is still falling.

I return by car on a sweltering day in July 1971. The city is a vast panorama of factories wrapped in a dirty brown haze, chimneys puffing black or yellow smoke. It is the landscape of a bad mistake.

What have I done?

Detroit is fast becoming a city in flight. A million and a half people still live in the city, but four years after the riots, white neighborhoods are retreating like the tide, leaving behind rings of bad mortgages, decaying homes, and forty thousand stray dogs rounded up and killed every year.

As I can see from the interstate, the auto industry is still going full blast, and there is still money in the metro area. Some of the wealthy still live in the five Grosse Pointes, an easy bicycle ride from downtown, but these neighborhoods are in a different universe.

I rent a first floor flat on Van Dyke Street, a thoroughfare that begins at the Detroit River and runs past my building in a straight-line west. Over the miles, Van Dyke Street gradually becomes a broad and respectable suburban artery.

My neighborhood is a favorite with drug dealers, but it also sustains a surprising number of nursing homes, retirees, working families, journalists, urban pioneers, and some doctors who work downtown at Detroit General Hospital. Van Dyke Street marks "the demilitarized zone" for Indian Village, an enclave that once housed the city's elite and still accommodates middle class families.

I have chosen my flat for its location. I've learned from working in the grim, poor neighborhoods of Cincinnati that fear can paralyze a reporter. If I can live in one of Detroit's worst neighborhoods, I should have the confidence to go anywhere on a story.

At first, I don't think I'll be living alone. At the last minute, Joe Herring decides to stay in graduate school in St. Louis. So here I am, in a place too big for me, with almost no furniture until my father and brothers arrive for a visit. They buy sheets of lumber and build me a dining room table so large it will have to be cut apart when I move out. I fill the rest of the flat with bookcases, green plants, and wicker chairs. For company, I acquire a German shepherd puppy and name him "Kurt," although he will never meet Luedtke.

My bravado about living here lasts only until I visit the local vet for Kurt's puppy shots. The office is just a few blocks away, but I drive. The parking lot is awash in trash and flattened beer cans.

As we walk in the door, the vet is standing in the waiting room, listening to a woman in purple, who is yelling at him. She's slim and elegant, wearing makeup and high heels.

"No, indeed! Three hundred dollars? That's robbery! You keep the damn dog yourself!"

Nearby, an assistant holds a giant Doberman, head and chest swathed in bandages.

The woman walks past me and slams out the door. The dog whines and tries to follow her.

"Now I've seen everything," the vet says and leaves the room, stopping to take the dog with him. His assistant comes over to greet me and assure me this is an unusual case and not one of over-charging.

"We could have arranged payments," she says. "The dog saved her life. She went to bed with the window open, and a man climbed in and tried to rape her. He had a gun. The dog attacked the man and chased him out. But he shot the dog. The dog needed three surgeries. Now she won't pay."

The receptionist stares at the door, as if half-expecting the woman to return, but she does not. I look down at the puppy sitting at my feet, his tiny legs and huge paws aligned with my shoes.

I will never betray you. It is a promise I cannot keep. In a matter of weeks, I will run for my life and leave him to fend for himself. In two years, again for my own safety, I will give him away. It will be longer before I can entertain the possibility the woman in purple owns only the clothes she is wearing, that she cannot pay a fraction of the vet bill, and anger is one way, although not the best way, to hide shame and a broken heart.

Detroit is still the Motor City, still Motown. The music that captures its glamor and its dreams, loved by all the world, is still the beating heart of the city. In a year, however, Motown Records will move to LA, taking along the stars and the money.

In this summer of 1971, Detroit is becoming its own dangerous planet, with an atmosphere that is starting to paralyze, hurt, and hide the city from itself and from the world outside. Detroit is a Black city with a white mayor and a white police force, a city scared of itself and armed to the teeth. By the end of this year, the murder count will climb to 550 and keep rising for three more years.

Everyone in my neighborhood is either a potential criminal or victim, so the police are interested in all of us, even Remer Tyson, a white man, a Southerner, and the chief political writer of the *Free Press*. He lives a few blocks from me in Indian Village. He has a house with greenery and trees. One day he finishes building a tree house for his children in the back yard and climbs up to rest in it and enjoy a few beers. Immediately, the police raid him.

"What do you think you are?" they demand. "A squirrel?"

Black or white, if you live here, the cops know you are guilty of something. And if you are walking a dog, you are hustling something, because no honest person *ever* willingly walks down Van Dyke Street. If you are a woman of a certain age, a squad car will slow down, and a voice from the loudspeaker will give you a long, sexual critique.

You do not look. You do not stop. You just keep walking.

Police helicopters make regular appearances over our rooftops, their spotlights illuminating a porch, a back yard. We call it Vietnam. The only night we are sure we won't see them is New Year's Eve. Detroiters welcome the new year at midnight by firing as many guns as possible up into the sky. It is a deafening gun concerto that is also dangerous because no one considers the laws of gravity that make the bullets fall back to earth. The police stay out of the way, and the arsenal vanishes before daylight.

Several weeks after moving to the neighborhood, I am walking my puppy Kurt on a tree-lined street two blocks from home. A man runs out of a house about a hundred feet ahead of us, carrying a body. He drops it on the sidewalk, turns to face the house, and fires a handgun several times at the front door. I freeze. Then he turns, looks up and down the street, and sees me standing on the sidewalk. He raises the gun, and everything goes into slow motion.

Oh, Lord, I'm a witness to a murder. I need to hide.

Cars are parked next to me and on both sides of the street, but there is no point trying to hide behind one of them.

What will stop him from just walking over and shooting me?

In those seconds, a car comes down the street from behind me, and the man with the gun waves it over.

Run.

I run across the street before the car arrives. I dash between two houses, then across a field, zigzagging because I have read somewhere it is difficult to hit a moving target with a handgun. In my panic, I forget my dog until I reach Jefferson Avenue, which is several blocks away. When I stop and look back, the car and the man are gone. The puppy is with me, bouncing up and down and dragging his leash.

When I get to the office, I check with Mike Graham, our reporter in the cop shop, and learn I've witnessed a dope house robbery but not a murder. No one is injured. The dead body turns out to be a huge pile of designer suits. Later, on the neighborhood grapevine, I hear the drug dealers have moved out, and the house is vacant. I never take that route again to walk my dog.

The dog grows up to be huge and silent. He rarely barks, just lies on the window seat in my living room and looks out. The appearance of a big German shepherd in the front window is all the protection I need. In the two years I live in this first floor flat, it is never burglarized, although many homes on my block are.

On our walks, my dog introduces me to everyone in the neighborhood, including Larry, who lives across the street and kept pets before he got old and started drinking. As soon as we step out the door, Larry calls us from his front steps, ready with new stories about his days in the army, his former girlfriends, and —always — some new outrage committed by his landlord Louis, one of two people who will accompany me to Larry's funeral in a few years. My dog loves Larry. I believe the dog would love anyone. Fortunately, this is not true.

During our first winter, I am in a hurry one freezing morning before work and take the dog on a shortcut through an alley. A car comes speeding towards us and pins the dog and me between the side of the car and the wall of a building. When the driver starts to roll down his window, the dog launches himself at the glass, barking, snarling, and pawing.

The window rolls up, and the car backs away and squeals off. We are alone again in the quiet of an ordinary morning.

The city is doing its best to stop crime, but it isn't enough, and many anti-crime programs make things worse. One of these has a cruel but apt acronym, STRESS – Stop the Robberies, Enjoy Safe Streets. It is ending the lives of many young Black men.

On the surface, it sounds plausible enough. Specially trained policemen dress like old ladies or drunks and lure muggers, then arrest them on the spot. But it almost never works that way. Muggers or not, the young men are shot dead. Their families are devastated, their communities outraged, and the streets become more dangerous than ever. When reporters question one of these shootings, the police officers say it's drug-related, as if that explains it all, especially the worthlessness of the lives lost, in their view, and the futility of asking for more information.

I live on Van Dyke Street for four years, two in the first floor flat at the corner of Van Dyke and E. Lafayette, and the next two in a brick apartment building on Van Dyke on the other side of the corner with Lafayette. It has the advantage of a lighted parking lot. It's not much more secure, however. On the day two newlywed friends of mine move in, a bullet comes through their living room window. Another day, a motorist is shot dead at the corner. His fatal mistake is honking at the car in front of him for moving too slowly when the light turns green. In the 1970s, Detroit calls itself the Murder Capital of America, and it is.

During my first year at the *Free Press*, my perilous living arrangements contribute nothing to the effectiveness of my reporting. I gather the information for my columns in tame settings while other reporters cover my kinds of stories: arson for profit and the HUD mortgage fraud that is just starting to ravage the city. In a few years, thousands of houses will disappear, their owners ruined financially.

I approach the *Free Press* editor running the housing story to ask if I can join his reporting team. I tell him I wrote for several years about fraud in federal housing programs for the poor in Ohio, but he refuses.

"You're a columnist. We have everyone we need."

Even at the *Free Press*, which has more women reporters in one place than I will see again, this editor is a man's man, and he never changes. Years later, when I am briefly his editor at *The New York Times,* I will invite him for dinner with my family in New Jersey. He will spend the evening in a monologue about the great gang in Detroit, luminaries that include no women.

"Why did you invite him?" my husband will ask afterwards. "He doesn't even like you."

"I don't know," I will say. "For old times' sake, I guess."

My columns in the *Free Press* give me a place to address issues far more important than I know. Veterans returning from Vietnam need mental health care they are not getting. Working mothers are under tremendous pressure. A silent epidemic of depression is underway. It's growing, and few are talking about it. Boredom has become a dangerous problem for workers on the assembly line. But my colleagues on the reporting staff barely notice my stories, and it is their approval I want. My columns are not on the front page, and the larger spinoffs rarely make Page One either, so they count for little, even to me. As my first year passes, I miss every story I consider important, and I never grasp the significance of the stories I am writing .

I do realize we are witnessing the slow death of one of America's great cities, but Detroit's fate is one of many, and it is invisible to the rest of the nation, one island in the sea of tragedy and scandal washing over our cities during the wars in Southeast Asia. The next body blow to Detroit – the Arab oil embargo that will trigger the first collapse of the American automobile industry – is a few years away. None of us can imagine it.

I sit in the rear of the newsroom with the other specialty reporters: the business writer, labor writer, medical writer, education writer, and the religion writer. After a year as a columnist, I beg the city editor to let me join the reporting staff.

The city editor has not warmed up to me. He is a conservative family man who seems uncomfortable with slightly younger reporters he regards as cutups and drunks, although it was two older assistant city editors who arrived loaded at his annual Christmas party, stumbled while dancing, and fell into the family Christmas tree. I was not invited, so I have the story second-hand from gleeful eyewitnesses.

Some of my feature stories please the assistant city editors. I give them a story about a day in the life of a stray dog. Another highlights a day in the work of the city's rat patrol.

"People don't have rats," the members of the patrol assure me. "Their *neighbors* have rats." The story is easy to report, but the photographer on the story needs a photo of a rat. This is difficult. It's daytime, and rats are nocturnal.

The rat patrol finds a tunnel in the ground with two entrances. They stand at one entrance and tell the photographer and me to be ready at the other. They will blast some poison gas into the far entrance. They promise one rat, at least, will make an emergency exit near us.

In a few moments, a rat staggers out and collapses on the ground. This is not satisfactory, as we do not want a picture of a dead rat. A member of the city crew hastens to the rat's side and begins fanning its face to revive it. The rat jumps back to life and makes a fast escape as I shriek, and the photographer takes its picture.

The office grapevine reports that the city editor never wanted a behavioral science columnist in the first place. Later, I am frightened by a rumor that he cut a deal with Luedtke to put me on city reporting staff on the condition he can fire me – and fight the union – the first time I foul up. Whatever the arrangement – and I never learn whether this is true – my first city desk assignment does not look promising.

CHAPTER ELEVEN: DANGEROUS HIGHWAYS

Twelve freeway bridges are under repair, causing huge traffic jams on the city's expressways, and I am sent out with a map, a stopwatch, and a company car to find the quickest detours for commuters. By now, I know the city, so I am sure I can do this.

Although five years have elapsed since the riots, the city is still a war zone, alien and unfamiliar to many suburbanites who traverse it every day. If they come downtown for a game or a concert, they travel from door to door. They never take shortcuts on the side streets. One wrong turn, and you can find yourself in a no man's land of boarded-up houses, vacant lots, and streets traveled by tumbleweed, rats, junkies, and the occasional stray dog.

The Chrysler, the Fisher, the Lodge, and the Ford: the expressways are named for three automotive titans and a mayor of the city they created. The Lodge runs along the bottom of a trench between factories, shops, and homes. The others slice along at ground level or above, passing over bridges that are chipping, peeling, and popping their concrete surfaces.

As ugly as these superhighways are, they serve as freeways in many ways. They lead to freedom, safety, and a good life. With any luck, they get you there in a hurry. But this day in July 1972 is not lucky for anyone, me included.

I start well before rush hour, but I still end up among the hordes of drivers stuck like flies in glue on the eastbound Edsel Ford expressway, roasting in a hot, stinking cloud of exhaust fumes.

I'm driving a typical company car, notoriously uncomfortable, driven without mercy, and rarely repaired. Such cars are so unreliable they occasionally lose a wheel. Auto air conditioning is unknown, and sweat has plastered my nylon half-slip to my legs. A horrible aroma of half-eaten sandwiches and rotting fruit wafts from the back seat. In the rush to get stories and file on deadline, reporters and photographers often abandon their garbage.

As time passes, the traffic moves by inches, and I begin to worry about my deadline and my future at the *Free Press*. Why have I been given such an easy assignment? I have a graduate degree. I've worked for four years as a reporter and a year as a columnist.

Why am I the one sitting in the world's worst traffic jam with a clipboard, a map, and a stopwatch? And why am I alone?

When we can, most of us travel with photographers. They drive their personal cars, and they are good company if you do not refer to them as "my photographer," the way someone might say "my driver." This irritates some more than others.

Who built these crap bridges? Idiots? Crooks? And why are they falling apart?

When I finally return to the office, hours later, I have not found enough freeway detours. My failure is unforgiveable, and the easy story I scorned is handed to another reporter. I must produce something, so I suggest investigating why the freeway bridges failed. One of the assistant city editors says I might as well try, so I head out again the next morning.

A basic problem, I find, is the price of upkeep. The Federal government built the expressways, and only the Feds have the money to maintain them. Instead, the repair bills have gone to the state of Michigan, which has let the bridges deteriorate to the point of collapse.

I take a close look at them. The concrete on the roadways has eroded down to the steel reinforcing rods, inviting even more rust and decay. This process, called "spalling," began shortly after the bridges were repaved a couple of years ago. There are excuses and explanations. This time, my story makes the front page. Many readers write letters or call.

"Nice job," one of them says, "but you missed the problem that's right now. It's the overloaded trucks that break up the roads." Then he hangs up.

As I am telling this to an editor, the night man on the desk speaks up. He remembers another caller – back in April, as it turns out – who complained about overloaded trucks. The caller had offered to take a reporter around to see the problem. The night man, who is meticulous, made a note and stuck it in a file reserved for tips that are plausible but not urgent. After a few minutes, he finds the note, with a name and a phone number, and gives it to me. I call the number.

No one answers. I can't leave a message. Answering services exist, but home answering machines do not. So, I just keep calling. It's maddening. Sometimes, the line is busy for hours. Other times, it rings and rings. Then one night, a man picks up. When I explain who I am, he offers to meet me after work on a street near his trucking company.

It is just getting dark when I arrive. He's waiting in a huge black Cadillac with the engine running.

I don't know this man. Should I get in?

I hesitate for a moment. Then I park my car, walk over, introduce myself, and get in. The car suits him. He's big, an older man with graying hair. He starts talking before he even gives me his name. I'll call him Bruno because he asks to be anonymous. He works for a trucking company that carries freight.

His complaint is about the cartage companies that haul foreign steel off the docks for the auto companies.

"They're wrecking the roads. They pile on every pound they can and cut the rate."

Trucking companies get paid by the weight they carry. A company has a competitive advantage if it charges less per pound. To make a profit, each truck carries much more weight.

Truck overloading is dangerous and illegal. Roads and bridges aren't built for monster loads, and neither are trucks. It's nearly impossible to maneuver an overloaded truck in traffic or stop at red lights. Still, the drivers do it, the Teamsters go along with it, and the weighmasters don't stop it.

The more Bruno talks, the more indignant he becomes.

He's looking everywhere but the road!

I find myself gripping the handle of the passenger door, my futile gesture for riding with careless drivers. I listen as Bruno drives us downriver toward the docks.

The deep water of the Detroit River, which links the Great Lakes and the St. Lawrence Seaway, makes Detroit a fine port for the large freight terminals the automobile industry needs. Bruno parks his car in sight of one of these docks, and we watch a freighter unload huge coils of steel onto enormous tractor trailers with eleven axles.

We follow one truck to a steel warehouse, where it pulls inside to unload. Bruno follows, inching his Cadillac past the warehouse gate, on the lookout for security guards.

"If they stop us, tell 'em we're lost," Bruno says. Then he parks, and we watch a giant crane lift off the coils, one by one.

"Each truck is tens of thousands of pounds too heavy," he says, "but the truckers get away with it because they bribe the weighmasters who're supposed to catch them." Bruno ticks off the names of the worst offenders, and I take notes.

The coils are chained to the flatbed trailers in plain sight.

It should be easy to prove the trucks are overloaded. I just need to find out how much one coil weighs and then add them up.

We stop for a late supper at a trucker place on the east side. It has country music and two menus, one for breakfast and one for beef. Bruno calms down but seems pessimistic about my chances for success with a story.

"You'll never be able to do anything about this," he says as we finish our coffee.

Afterwards, he drops me back at my parked car. Despite his case of nerves, I don't think to ask if he has a reason other than his obligations at work to meet me so late in the day.

I go looking for weighmasters. The state of Michigan has some. So does Wayne County. I try the state weighmasters first. They are sympathetic but tell me their hands are tied. They've been told to stay out of the city of Detroit.

The county weighmasters are neither sympathetic nor helpful. With prodding, they agree to let me look through the records of tickets they have written for weight violations — no steel trucks — but they refuse to let me accompany them on their rounds or to weigh even one steel truck for me.

The head of the city's department of weights and measures has no budget and no staff. I find him in a second-floor office in Eastern Market. The cabinets there are filled with measuring devices and dust.

"I've seen the steel trucks," he says. "They can't even move sometimes. I can't do anything about it."

Then I try Teamsters Local 299, the union that represents the drivers and owner-operators. There I introduce myself to Hal DeLong, a nervous little man with one of the worst jobs in the world, press relations for Jimmy Hoffa's home local, an organization that detests the press. As he will explain to me many times, his job is to keep the Teamsters *out* of the news.

The only place a journalist can have an honest conversation with DeLong is outside his Teamsters office. Ralph Orr, the newspaper's veteran labor reporter and a generation older than me, teaches me this and many more things as he becomes my closest colleague in the newsroom and my friend.

Ralph and I find we can soothe DeLong's nerves with delectable lunches at an upscale local seafood restaurant. We follow the food with "flaming beauties," small glasses of Cointreau set alight. Ralph and I try not to drink too many.

"I'm a dead man," DeLong will say between sips.

On the day I meet DeLong for the first time, he introduces me to Dave Johnson, president of the local. Johnson is an old friend of Hoffa, who is still in prison. I ask Johnson if he knows anything about the overloading underway in the steel hauling business. The question surprises him.

"Officially, we're against overloading – it's unsafe, and it takes jobs," he replies. "But as sure as I complain about it, I'll have fifty guys at my door saying, 'What are you trying to do – ruin my business?'" He suggests contacting the Michigan Cartagemen's Association, an organization of trucking company owners, and gives me a telephone number.

I call them. The man who answers says everything is on the up and up, but if I want to pursue the matter, I can call the association's "Dock Committee." He gives me the names of three committee members.

Why would they admit to breaking the law? I'm not calling them. I'll go to the docks to see for myself. I can count the coils of steel going onto each of those trucks.

Getting permission turns out to be difficult. I am midway through my first call to a shipping terminal office, explaining I am a reporter looking to expose truck overloading, when the man hangs up on me.

That didn't work. I've got to try something else.

On my next call, I tell the shipping clerk who answers the phone that I am a reporter interested in the importation of Japanese steel.

"Can I come down to the docks to have a look the next time a ship comes in?"

He eventually says yes and promises to call me back. A few weeks later, he does. Several large ships are arriving.

Unknown to me, the terminal has new management. They think publicity in the *Free Press* is a wonderful idea. I congratulate myself on my approach, but the night before my appointment, I'm not so sure.

I'm scared. I don't want to be noticed there.

I mention my doubts to my roommate Jackie Lapin, a college intern from the University of Southern California who is staying with me for the summer. Her biggest worry is baseball and surviving in the *Free Press* sports department, where she is the first woman, and often the only female in the press box at the ball game. The major league baseball writers alternate between hostility and hospitality. She's young, but she will not back off. Compared with her struggles, my trucking story doesn't seem like a challenge.

Jackie's sportswriter wardrobe is more casual than mine, and I ask if I can borrow something to wear to the docks.

"I don't want them to remember me," I explain.

Jackie laughs and opens her closet door.

Nothing fits me, so I just borrow a scarf to cover up my hair. Then I decide to wear the only pantsuit I own with short sleeves. It's made of white seersucker, good for hot weather, but too dainty for any place but church. I'll wear it anyway.

The day is muggy, and Jackie's scarf is hot. I'm wearing it peasant style, tied tightly around my hair and fastened under my chin.

I'm sweating, and I look silly.

I take off the scarf and stuff it in my purse as soon as I arrive at the docks and get out of my car. My wardrobe worries have been pointless. Anonymity here would be impossible, especially for a woman in a puffy white suit. All the employees, even the secretaries, are men.

Chris LeFevre, a former sea captain with a faint French accent, meets me with a friendly smile at the gate of Detroit Harbor Terminals and introduces himself as the vice president. He leads me to a small office trailer where he gives me some fresh new brochures. Through a window, I can see a freighter, huge and black. We tour the terminal and then go on board the ship.

As if by magic, I am sitting next to the Japanese captain. He speaks English and offers me a beer. Normally, I would say no. I accept because I want him to keep talking as we watch cranes lift coil after giant coil of steel out of the hold and lower them to the pier below. Trucks idle in line, waiting to load up. I ask him about the steel trade, the shipping business, and the port, and then I point to the cargo.

"This is so fascinating, all the different kinds and sizes." I point to one coil and then to another. "How much does that one weigh? How about that one over there?"

The captain says it is hard to tell. They are all different. He suggests asking the truck drivers after we go out to lunch.

While we are dining, the captain himself brings up the subject
of overloading.

"I've seen them go out of here with 325,000 pounds,"
he says. The legal limit is 120,000 pounds.

I'm on to something. But don't act surprised.

When we return to the docks, the trucks are gone. I'm
relieved to learn they'll be back for more.

All I must do is wait.

It's hot in the sun, so I follow LeFevre back to the
trailer where someone produces a bag of peanuts and a bottle
of Cold Duck. Again, I should say no. But there is nothing else
to drink, and I'm thirsty, so I take a glass and then another. I
am starting to feel queasy and more than a little guilty about
misleading my hosts. At last, the trucks start to line up again.

I feel sick, but I can't let them know. Just let me not throw up.

LeFevre walks me over to the trucks, but the drivers
don't want to talk to me about weights. They do not tally up
poundage, they say. The dispatcher does that, writing the total
weight for each truck on slips they hand over at their
destination. The drivers say they hardly see the paperwork.

I investigate the darkness of the dispatcher's shack. It's
empty, but there is a desk with a big stack of papers. Fueled by
courage that is sheer alcohol, I step inside. The papers are
copies of weight slips. I flip through them and see a weight
slip for 341,000 pounds – almost triple the legal limit.

Oh, crap, the dispatcher is back!

A man takes my shoulders and pushes me back out into
sunlight so bright I am momentarily blinded. Standing there is
a burly man with dark hair I haven't seen before. He's wearing
black sunglasses and directing the loading of a truck. LeFevre

is there, too. He gives me a disapproving look and takes my arm. He starts to walk me past the man with the sunglasses, then stops and introduces me to Jack Russo.

Oh no! That Jack Russo.

The name is familiar because he is a member of the Dock Committee I never called.

"Well, you certainly do get around," Russo says. Even though he surely saw me flipping through the weight slips, I give him my phony line about writing a feature story about imported steel.

He listens and then asks lightly, as if making a joke, "How would you like to have a load of steel fall on you?"

I've got to say something.

"I don't suppose it would be any worse than some other ways you could die."

LeFevre is there, getting between us and trying to lead me away. "Don't get involved with Russo," he whispers. "You get involved with him, and you get involved with the Mafia. You don't need him. He's trouble."

"I'm okay," I say. The Cold Duck hasn't worn off. I disentangle myself and walk over to Russo, who starts to rant.

"Detroit needs heavy trucks to keep the rates down," he says, gesturing at the dereliction of the city around us. "Without the cheap rates, all the warehouses would move to the suburbs, where the neighbors don't beat up the secretaries in the parking lots."

This is ridiculous, wrecking the highways and bridges and justifying it to shore up the city. Now I've heard everything.

Russo's hot temper seems to cool when the truck finishes loading. He turns to me and asks, as if it has just occurred to him, "Would you like a ride?"

"Yes," I say, curious and reckless. I let him pick me up and lift me high into the cab. When he does, I see he is wearing a shoulder holster and a handgun.

Tony, the driver, is a big guy. I have put him at risk and sense his fear, but I smile and pretend not to know. He tries to signal the danger we are in by showing me pictures of his wife and children before he even turns the key in the ignition. Slowly, he starts to pull the truck away from the dock. LeFevre seems bewildered but waves an optimistic goodbye. Russo gets into a large black Lincoln Mark IV and follows us, talking with Tony on the radio.

I can't believe I'm doing this, going for a ride with these people. Oh, Mama.

The steel truck is new, air conditioned, with a stereo. Tony doesn't want to talk about his cargo.

"I just get it where it's going, safe and on time."

But it is clearly not safe, even at a crawl. Tony cannot stop the truck for red lights. We roll slowly through them, massive and inexorable, up to the freeway and over the remaining bridges. Eventually, we arrive at a Chrysler warehouse on the east side.

After the truck is unloaded, Russo is gone. I ride with Tony back to the docks, where he insists on walking me to the parking lot. My own car is there. It's new, and he makes a note, aloud, that it's a 1972 Olds Cutlass.

Why is he doing this? Will he tell Russo about my car?

Because I have no copy of the weight slip I saw at the dock, or any of the others, I still cannot document the overloading. I go back to the *Free Press* and call the newspaper's bureau in Lansing. They call the governor's office. The state weighmasters do not believe any truck would or could carry 341,000 pounds, but the governor sends weighmasters to Detroit anyway on a confidential assignment to scout for overloaded steel trucks. They find nothing.

The steel haulers knew about the weighing team before they arrived. "They must have some good friends," one of the governor's aides tells me.

I start to worry about Russo's gun and his remark about falling steel. Memories of LeFevre's warning about the Mafia and Tony's close observation of my Oldsmobile rachet up my anxiety. I call my colleague Mike Graham at the cop shop and ask him to introduce me to the organized crime unit at the police headquarters. It's my first visit there.

The headquarters is situated a few blocks from Greektown, a neighborhood known for great dining late at night and known as a favorite hangout for the mob. Sgt. Joe O'Hare, the head of the organized crime unit, is an old hand and can do a roll call of the Mafia in Detroit. I'm impressed by the scope of what he knows but not reassured when he says he's never heard of Jack Russo. When I walk out of his office, I'm still afraid.

So, I agree when Graham suggests we take a walk down the hall and visit the bomb squad.

"Just as a hypothetical," I ask them, "if you wanted to look for a bomb in your car, where would you look, and what would you look for?"

"Underneath," they say, not hiding their smiles.

No help from them. And I've embarrassed myself and the newspaper.

In four years, Don Bolles, a reporter for the *Arizona Republic*, will be assassinated in a car bombing. But now, as far as the police officers are concerned, a mob attack on a journalist is unthinkable. Not to me. I'm still worried. But I decide to ignore the Mafia angle and write a simple story about truck overloading. It makes the front page on September 11, 1972.

The governor sends in a permanent truck weighing team, and I get a lot of telephone calls. LeFevre is one of the first.

"You're not very popular with the truckers anymore," he says.

"You should burn your notes," another caller says.

Caller ID does not exist, and no one will say who they are, so these conversations leave me in the dark, even about the person on the line. One regular caller finally reveals that he's injured and can no longer drive, which may explain why he sounds drunk when I hear from him.

"Do you know why this is going on?" he asks at last.

"Sure. To make more money."

"You're wrong. To take over the trucking business. Check out the owners."

I make a list of the steel cartage companies and check city and state registrations for their owners and stockholders. None has ever made the news. I make the rounds of investigators in the city, in Lansing, and a couple of federal agencies.

Nothing.

Other callers say the weighmasters are being paid off, as well as some auto company executives. One man promises to come to the newspaper but never shows up.

"Forget it," the city editor says. "There's a lot of whiskey courage in Detroit. You'll never prove any of this." In a strange way, I feel relieved.

Summer ends, and I don't like living alone. Jackie has returned to school. Despite the coaching in self-reliance from my women friends in Boston, I have been raised to believe I need a man in my life to make it worth living. I can't shake this feeling, and I can't find the right man.

A series of losers present themselves: men just looking for a fun time, men who hate women, men who hate themselves. It's an odd assortment – an editor who is always stoned, a deejay, a physician, a beer salesman, a professor, a real estate developer. I should give up on lovers and look for male friends, but they are scarce, usually married, and short on time.

Ralph Orr, my colleague, and a father figure to me, says his wife has her doubts about me. She's friendly the few times I meet her, but Orr says never to call him at home, no matter what. When I need to get in touch urgently about a story, he tells me to get someone else to call him.

Isolated and full of nervous energy, I call LeFevre. He doesn't want to hear from me and says I should forget the trucking story. I want to continue, but I'm still worried about the mob. I check again with the Feds, this time with someone Orr knows, a federal agent who works for the Department of Labor. He knows the Teamsters. He puts his head in his hands when I mention Russo.

"Why didn't you ask someone before you went to talk to him? If I were you, I'd get rid of my car and move."

"Why? What do you mean?"

He will not explain.

This same afternoon, another voice is mumbling on my office telephone.

"Jack Russo? You're writing about *him*? He works with Vince Meli. He's a man with a lot of friends – like Tony Jack." He hangs up.

I call Sgt. O'Hare at the organized crime unit and find out that Tony Jack is the street name for Anthony Giacalone,[xii] who is feared as an enforcer. The names Meli and Giacalone are both new to me, but our newspaper library has clippings of stories about both. Meli's name has appeared in Congressional testimony, the gold standard for identifying who is in the Mafia. (As protected speech, Congressional testimony can be cited by newspapers without risk of libel, but libel is the least of my worries.)

The *Free Press* has covered the Mafia before, but the usual pattern is a press release from the police or the feds about an arrest, an indictment, or a murder, with background and some details, all from law enforcement. No one interviews the bad guys or their victims. Even so, when one of these stories is published, the reporter is usually treated to drinks and lots of praise at the Press Club for daring to put the details in print. It is understood the reporter is always a man. This is true at my newspaper and every other, except for a few columnists who can draw upon their familiarity with the boys in the old neighborhood, and they are out for nostalgia, not to nail anyone for a crime.

I'm out on a limb here, all on my own. The cops and the feds don't seem to know anything about the truckers, and I can find no official investigation underway.

What should I do?

I am so frightened that I take the advice from Orr's man. I park my car in a downtown garage and check into a hotel, feeling like a character in a bad movie. But each passing hour makes me more afraid. And I cannot afford to stay there. After three days, I go home.

I feel ridiculous.

This is how terror works. Trivial things frighten you into believing terrible things can happen at any minute. When they don't, you feel absurd. Ordinary life goes on as before.

In my case, the everyday routine and my office are real. Meli and Giacalone are phantoms. I decide to forget them and give up on the trucking story. The city editor is fed up with my costing the newspaper money and time and coming up with nothing. The truth is, I am out of leads. But Meli and Giacalone are real. I will meet them both. And dreadful things will happen. Just not right away and not what I expect.

CHAPTER TWELVE:
DROWNING

At Christmas, my younger brother Willis calls me with sad news.

"The cancer has come back. I don't have long. Will you come home with me to tell Mom? I'm not as worried about myself as I am about her."

He is the darling of her life, and he senses correctly that she will never recover from his death. He is twenty-six years old, just married, a West Point graduate, and a captain in the army. He was diagnosed in Germany two years ago, when the army doctors finally stopped sending him to psychiatrists for his headaches and ordered blood tests. He had acute leukemia.

I got this news while I was at Harvard. My mother called me, crying so hard I could barely understand her. I have forgiven what she said, but I cannot forget.

"Why can't it be *you*? *You* are the one with the messed-up life. *He* has done everything right. It isn't *fair*!"

Willis was sent from Germany to Letterman Army Hospital at the Presidio of San Francisco, where our dad was the post commander. Our family had a home there, overlooking San Francisco Bay, and we all came for Christmas that year. It was such a sad affair that I still find it painful to look at the photographs: Willis's bloated torso, my mother and sister trying to decorate Christmas cookies, my brother Andy's baseball cap lying on the ground at our feet in our group picture.

The family group picture was always an agonizing affair at Christmas, when my dad would be drinking and trying to get just the right lighting as we stood attention, six siblings separated in age by a span of nineteen years. That Christmas, with Willis's illness, my dad was drinking more than usual, and decided to photograph us outdoors. At the last minute, he spotted the baseball cap on Andy's head, and tore off the cap in a fit of rage, and thew it on the ground. It lies there in defeat as we force smiles in the last photo of all six of us, separated afterwards by distance and by death.

Willis's cancer went into remission for a while. My sister got married. My father retired from the army and moved my mother and three youngest brothers to El Paso, Texas. Willis was stationed at Fort Hood, near Killeen, Texas. He is calling me from there.

Willis is two years younger than me, and he is the son my parents wanted in the first place. Yes, I've felt jealous, but never for long. He is too sweet, too generous. As a child, he was my best friend.

Fully grown, he's short like my dad and tough. His perfect nose was rearranged playing football in high school, where he was one of the smaller players. At West Point, he did not make the downhill ski team— the others had learned to ski as children — so he joined the ski team that jumped. "It just takes guts," he explained. His teammates called him "the barrel."

Now, in the last stages of leukemia, he has come to sit with me in our parents' living room in El Paso. We talk about preparing our parents for his death. When he asks what I'm up to, I tell him about the truckers and the Mafia.

"Tell them they'd better not lay a hand on you," he says. He is frail and thin, his face puffy from his medications. "Tell them you have a brother in the army."

Back in Detroit, I am afraid to call my sister-in-law to ask how Willis is doing. When I finally do, no one answers. He is back in the hospital, in an era before the bone marrow transplants that might have saved him or at least given him more time. Willis calls me once from a pay phone in the hospital while my parents are on the way to Killeen to see him. They take charge of his phone calls then, and I never speak with him again.

I dream of him.

Snakes are attacking him. He is drowning in water, and I can't reach him.

My waking life is like trying to live in that ocean, shipwrecked and strapped to a raft. The sea produces things, some of them heartbreaking and some of them strange, calling for help. I can do nothing to rescue my brother, so I try to help others that come floating my way.

The baby chimpanzees are the first, John and Lisa, named before their keepers know they are both males. An engineering professor at Wayne State University is researching air bag damage to young children, and he wants to use the chimps to see how bad the injuries can be. A group calling itself the Zoological Action Program (ZAP), backed by the Audubon Society and others, objects.

"It's a foregone conclusion that injuries will occur," George Campbell, the ZAP director, tells the university's committee for protection of human and animal subjects. He urges them to use pediatric dummies and cadavers of both children and chimpanzees instead. Members of ZAP offer to help the university acquire them. Some offer to have air bags, not then in widespread use, installed in their family cars for testing, too.

John and Lisa have come from Sierra Leone, where their mothers were shot, and they were captured for sale. ZAP says six babies and their mothers are killed for each baby captured alive. ZAP wants the chimps to be relocated to a research facility that will allow them to live a semblance of their normal lives. The engineering professor objects. He does not think the air bags will injure the chimpanzees severely. Researchers say the young male baboon that died last year was improperly strapped in.

My editor wants to accompany my story with a photo of the chimps, but they are locked in a lab in a locked building. I knock on an outside door until two men in white coats show up. I finally talk them into letting me into the building, but when I turn around, the photographer has disappeared. I hold the door open and shout for him, thankful that he turns up instead of the campus police.

We make it inside and persuade the attendants to open the door to the chimps' room. We find them playing ball. They are nice little animals, and smart. Earlier, they learned to unscrew the knob to their door. I am hoping they will do it again and unscrew the knob to the door of the building, too. Although I never learn of their fate, there's no telling what they can do. I've done the best I can to tell their story.

On the day the chimpanzee story appears in the newspaper, I get a call from Gabe Kaimowitz, a lawyer who lives in Ann Arbor and takes hopeless cases. There are rumors of an upcoming experiment to give a group of patients psychosurgery – brain surgery to change their mental health – in this case, their violent behavior.

"Do you know anyone from your days with the column who can tell you what's going on?" he asks me.

I rummage through my old business cards and start calling people. A man I met at a conference knows about the experiment and has deep misgivings about it. Male patients from Ionia State Hospital are involved, all of them "criminal sexual psychopaths," he says. The state is paying for it, and the first inmate is already in Detroit awaiting surgery.

"Do you have a name?" I ask.

"No."

"Can you get it?"

"I don't know. Patient files are confidential."

"Sounds like he could be a victim as well as a patient."

I hear a sigh.

"I'll see what I can do."

In a few hours, he calls back with the inmate's name.

"I can't give you the file," he says, "but there were stories about him in the newspaper."

I look up the name, and there he is, the son of a Kalamazoo paper worker. When he was a child, he'd recovered from a severe case of measles but began throwing violent temper tantrums. As a teen-ager, he'd committed juvenile sex crimes, including breaking into a girl's home, and terrifying her until her parents captured him. When he was seventeen, his parents asked the court to commit him to Kalamazoo State Hospital. Nine months later, he confessed to luring a student nurse to the basement, strangling her with his necktie, then sexually assaulting her dead body.

"I don't know why I did it," he told the police. "It was an impulse, I guess. But she was awful pretty. I wish I were dead."

He was charged with first-degree murder but never put on trial. Instead, On January 11, 1955, under a Michigan law that was later repealed, a court declared him a "criminal sexual psychopath." On the advice of three court-appointed psychiatrists, the court ordered him confined to Ionia "until such time as he is proven not to be a danger to society." He is the kind of person we all fear.

I go for help, first to the city desk and then to the *Free Press* medical writer, Dolores Katz. She calls doctors. I call the man's mother.

When I ask whether it is true her son is getting surgery, she starts to cry.

"We've gone to see him every week for eighteen years," she says. "After seventeen years, we got to take him out to lunch – once. And now he has a chance to get well and get out, and you're calling me?"

"It's important," I say. "We need to know."

"Do you know what you're doing? You'll ruin everything. How can you do this to us? Please don't." Her voice is full of pain and desperation. "Please."

"There's a lot we don't know," I say, trying to get off the phone. "But it doesn't sound right. We're still trying to find out what's going on." Telling her I'll stay in touch, I hang up.

I feel like a monster.

For a moment, only a moment, pity makes me consider dropping the story.

To spare his family, I decide not to use his real name. Our story refers to him only as "John Doe," a practice that will continue when his case makes its way into the courts and, eventually, into what will become a landmark legal decision.

Katz confirms that an experiment is ready to begin. It involves surgery to remove the amygdala, a part of the brain believed responsible for controlling fear and aggression as well as playing a role in sexual libido. Katz arranges for the two of us to interview the doctors at Lafayette Clinic who are running the experiment, Dr. Ernst A. Rodin and Dr. Jacques Gottlieb. They are furious with us for questioning them.

Dr. Rodin, a neurologist, tells us twenty-four Ionia inmates have agreed to take part. Half will get surgery, and half will get drugs. Both treatments have drawbacks.

"The problem with taking drugs is that if he stops taking them, he reverts to his merry old self," Dr. Rodin says. "The problem with surgery is that it's permanent. If it works, he's cured for the rest of his life. If it doesn't work, he has a problem for the rest of his life."

There are other huge problems. Oversight has been poor, and it is far from clear the participants understand the experimental nature of the surgery.

As soon as our story appears, Kaimowitz files a complaint for a writ of habeas corpus on behalf of John Doe, alleging that Doe is being illegally detained in the Lafayette Clinic for the purpose of experimental psychosurgery. The operation is postponed, and funds for the research project are stopped by the director of the Michigan Department of Mental Health.

After the publicity, Doe changes his mind about participating. So do the rest of the inmates, who write a letter to thank Dolores and me, saying they had not understood the risk.

A panel of three county judges is set up to hear the case, and Dean Francis A Allen and Professor Robert A Burt of the University of Michigan Law School serve as counsel for John Doe. The American Orthopsychiatric Society enters the case as *amicus curiae*. I cover the hearings.

As a first step, the court takes up the issue of the constitutionality of Doe's detention. On March 3, 1973, the judges rule it unconstitutional. Dr. Andrew Watson testifies that Doe can be safely released to society, and the court releases him. Has he hurt anyone since? I don't know. There is no record.

At this point, some argue that Doe's case is moot, but the judges decide to take up the fundamental issues the case has raised about the way the psychosurgery experiment was set up. Four months later, they issue a landmark ruling that becomes known as *Kaimowitz v Department of Mental Health for The State of Michigan.*

"Psychosurgery should never be undertaken upon involuntarily committed populations, when there is a high-risk, low benefits ratio as demonstrated this case," they rule. "This is because of the impossibility of obtaining truly informed consent from such populations."

Some people praise the decision. Others call it tragic.

Later this year, Katz and I receive the Robert F. Kennedy Award for these stories. The Kennedy family invites the winners to attend a reception at their home in Virginia after the ceremony. I ask my dad to accompany me. During the party, I am amazed to find my father out in the kitchen, talking and laughing with Ethel Kennedy, who is recovering from an accident. In the usual course of things, the Kennedy family's liberal politics are anathema to him.

I even persuade my dad to carry my award, a heavy bronze bust of Robert Kennedy, home to El Paso with him on the airplane. In a way, it's penance for a terrible act of his earlier in the year.

My father called me in February to tell me my brother Willis had died. I arranged to join my parents and three younger brothers in Killeen, Texas, and accompany them home and then to the funeral.

Shortly before this, I had discovered that the owner of the flat I was renting had ties to an investigation of mine. I needed to move out and could not take my dog Kurt with me. I had placed a classified ad in the newspaper to find him a loving home. The calls from people wanting to adopt my dog

were coming in just as my family was calling about the funeral.
I rehomed Kurt as I packed my suitcase to go to Texas.

When I arrived in Killeen, my parents were wild with
grief, arguing and drinking heavily. Willis was to be buried at
the military academy at West Point, New York. First, the
family had to drive their old Ford Country Squire station
wagon from Killeen to my parents' home in El Paso, a journey
of some six hundred miles. We needed to leave at once, but
my parents were too drunk to drive.

I was never allowed to drive their car when one of them
was present, but I insisted, and they let me. Then, late at night
in the no man's land of west Texas, my father's sodden grief
rekindled into a red-hot rage at cancer, at Willis's death, and at
me for being alive. Also, for presuming to drive his car. He
reached over from the front passenger seat and, at seventy
miles an hour, yanked the keys out of the ignition. I don't
know whether this turned off the engine, but the power
steering and the power brakes cut off. As we hurtled along the
highway, I could barely steer the car, could not slow it down. I
prayed and kept my foot off the gas pedal. At last, the car
came to a stop on the side of the highway.

"Dad, please. Please. Give me back the keys."

He said nothing, just handed them back to me, and I
began to breathe again. Since then, I have known exactly what
takes place in the split seconds when anger and grief cause
someone to try to kill themselves and their whole family.

CHAPTER THIRTEEN:
IN THE SHADOWS

It's the middle of June 1973, and the phone is ringing as I walk in the door from work. Chuckie O'Brien, a Teamster and protege of Jimmy Hoffa, is on the line. I met him months ago at the Teamsters Local 299 hall when talking with PR man, Hal DeLong. Afterwards, O'Brien surprised me with an invitation to coffee. I surprised myself by saying yes.

I've seen him off and on since then but know little about him, only that he lives somewhere in Detroit. He is divorced, with kids. Although his looks are intimidating – he is short, wide, and tough looking – he has a great laugh. He is also close to the Mafia figures in the trucking story I am pursuing, or so he says.

He calls the reputed mob enforcer Anthony Giacalone "Uncle Tony," and once casually mentioned that Vincent Meli, the Mafia don, is godfather to one of his children. I should run from him. Instead, I have a notion that Chuckie can be a barometer for the danger I am facing. If not, he may see me as a human being who should not be killed. I have no idea how wrong I am on both counts. I am a rabbit among wolves.

Looking back today, I do not know why I am still alive. It's possible the angel who saved me as a toddler on the train has kept protecting me.

My acquaintance with Chuckie is episodic. I will not see or hear from him for months, and then he will turn up and call me for dinner or a movie. I have taken him to a couple of foreign films. He does not like the ones by Ingmar Bergman.

At this time in Detroit, I am in love with another man, so there is no question of a romance with Chuckie, at least not for me, but I am naive. Seeing him at all is dangerous for me, but also bad for my reputation. I'm sure the police are watching him.

The last time I saw Chuckie before this call in June was on the TV news, fighting the organizing efforts of Cesar Chavez and the farmworkers in the fields of California. The Teamsters are cozy with the growers who employ the farmworkers. Their efforts to drive off Chavez and his organizers are often violent and deeply repugnant to me.

On this call, O'Brien tells me he's just returned from the docks in Cleveland.

"Be careful," he says. "There are a thousand Sicilians out to get you." He laughs. "Watch your head. It's the only way to watch your ass."

He says he is taking a plane to Toronto and will call me later. "Be careful," he repeats.

Even on major metropolitan newspapers, few reporters can spend all their time on a single investigation. Most days, we work on other assignments. Investigations can linger for months while we fight for the time to work on them or wait for a break in the investigation itself. In the summer of 1973, I get my first chance to have a close look at the engine of Detroit, the automobile industry.

I join Ralph Orr, the *Free Press* labor writer, on a team covering the national negotiations between the United Autoworkers and the Big Three auto companies. I'm the first woman to cover the talks for a major newspaper. The negotiations take place simultaneously at the Detroit headquarters of all three companies. Chrysler is the weakest and the least likely to be the union's strike target. As the new person on the team, I am assigned to Chrysler.

I encounter a big problem on the first day. The talks have no scheduled briefings, so reporters wait for updates that can come at any time in the press room. You can play poker or spend time any way you want, but you must be there. As no women have covered the talks before, there is no women's rest room. The nearest one is on another floor. I don't want to miss anything, so furious negotiations take place. Then a new handwritten sign goes onto the men's room door. It says "Persons." Anyone who wants to use the bathroom must knock. My male colleagues are shocked. First, they laugh. Then they get mad. Then they get used to it.

My second problem, a journalistic one, is more challenging. Most of my competitors have years of experience covering labor, with inside sources at the automobile companies and the union. My colleague Ralph Orr, who is covering the talks at General Motors, has sources he can meet in the parking lot between sessions for inside information about the negotiations. I don't know anyone. When I first get this assignment, I decide to ask the workers themselves what

issues they consider most important on the bargaining table. I
choose the Good Time Bar, across the street from the Ford
transmission plant in Livonia. It's a place for men, where the
waitresses will smile and tolerate customers who stuff tips
down the front of their blouses.

I arrive with a photographer at 2:30 in the afternoon.
We identify ourselves to Opal, the manager. She and the
waitresses are only other women in the place. After three
hours, the photographer leaves, and the auto workers still have
a lot to say. First, they want the right to refuse to work
overtime. They work so many hours; they never see their
families.

"I'm working seven days a week, from four in the
morning to four in the afternoon," says John, who operates a
machine called a bore, which enlarges a hole in metal. "My kid
is three years old. He always asks if I'm going to stay home. I
can't get the kid off me. He follows me around like a tail. I
went up to work on my roof once, and he followed me right
up the ladder."

It's a delicate balance, says Ron. If a few workers refuse
overtime, they derail the gravy train for everyone else. "We've
only got seventeen guys," he says. "Four or five could shut
down our department and the others. That isn't fair if other
people want to work."

On the other side of the bar, painters say overtime pay
is essential to them.

"You get no luxuries on forty hours a week," says one.
He has worked at Ford for more than twenty years. "If you
work extra, you can buy the color TV and that washer and
dryer." He sips his beer, then asks the others, "Did you see

that show about Germany on TV? It said they close up shop at 6:30. Those people aren't *living* though. They got no color TV, no car, one suit."

"They are living on what they got," another replies. "You know what Americans do – work, work, and work."

After my visit to the bar, I speak with workers wherever I can. Some say they work so much overtime they are too tired to work safely. Some confess to taking dangerous shortcuts. Safety is a huge issue and difficult to measure with statistics.

Ford's Cleveland Casting Company had 1.76 million hours without a disabling injury, then had five deaths within a year. One of these workers was electrocuted. Another was burned to death, and a maintenance foreman fell through a roof to his death. Do the fatalities mean the plant is unsafe? Does the long accident-free period mean it is safe? Both things can be true at the same time.

Melvin Glasser, head of the UAW's Social Security department, tells me there's often a conflict if a dangerous machine may be malfunctioning, but the foreman is trying to meet a quota.

"Recently, a machine that was bolted overhead started to creep. The bolts were loose. The workers told the foreman to check it, and the foreman said, 'Keep working. We'll check it this weekend. The machine fell on the worker and crushed him to death."

My reports of these conversations upset both the management and the union, but voluntary overtime and safety both turn out to be huge issues in the negotiations. In fact, workers take over Chrysler's giant Mack Avenue Stamping

Plant in a protest over poor working conditions. When they refuse to come out, they end up in a standoff with the police.

The police threaten to storm the factory, and a crowd begins to grow. I wait all day and into the night to see what will happen next. Among the press corps, no one has been expecting this, and it's hard to tell who's who. We started the day dressed for Chrysler headquarters.

"See that guy who looks like a banker?" the *Free Press* photographer asks me, pointing to a man in an expensive suit. He's the reporter for the *Daily World*, the communist paper. And that guy with the beard in a tee shirt? He's the reporter for *The New York Times*." In the stifling heat, the second man has shed his suit coat and dress shirt. With his glasses and neat beard, he could be V. Lenin.

I am wearing my dainty white seersucker pantsuit and high heels, so by nightfall, my feet ache from standing on the sidewalk. I sit down on the curb, amid the accumulated sea of paper cups, bottles, and trash, to rub my toes, and the *Free Press* photographer takes my picture.

In the background, the local pushers and pimps are looking on. The photo certainly seems to bear out the prediction of my former husband, that I will "end up like Ratso Rizzo," the ailing con man in the movie *Midnight Cowboy*. Years from now, when I do a stint as a university professor, the picture will hang next to my academic degrees, and I hope someone will ask about it. But no one ever does.

The Mack Avenue siege ends peacefully. The workers surrender, the police leave, and the negotiations resume. But workplace issues rise to the top of the bargaining agenda. Despite predictions, Chrysler ends up being the UAW's strike target. Ralph Orr takes over the main story, but I stay there to help. Other women arrive from broadcast outlets, now that the national focus is on Chrysler, and they thank me for the "persons" room. The talks conclude September 28, and a tongue-in-cheek booklet about the talks, published by the Chrysler public relations office, features the "Persons" room sign on the cover.

In a matter of weeks, the Arab Oil embargo of October 1973 will mark the first stage of failure for the domestic automobile industry as we know it. Gasoline prices will spike, long lines will appear at gas stations for the first time, and the appeal of enormous American cars will begin to fall in favor of smaller, more fuel efficient foreign-made cars. The need for auto worker overtime will disappear, along with union jobs and pay. Much of the automobile industry in Detroit and other northern cities will move South and then abroad. We cannot imagine.

In September, there is a new anonymous voice on the phone. "On the trucking," a man says, "check out Kerekes." He gives me a street address and hangs up.

It's an address for a trucking company, a freight carrier, not one of the steel haulers I am investigating. I call them and ask for Kerekes. I have no first name or gender.

"Not here," a man answers. "He doesn't work here anymore."

"Do you know where he is now? I really need to talk to him." I realize my voice sounds like a desperate woman, not a newspaper reporter, but I do not explain. In a way, I am desperate.

"Lemme see." There is a long pause while he asks around. "Try Murphy Freight."

I call. Kerekes is there. When he picks up, I tell him who I am and ask if he's seen my stories about truck overloading.

"Yes."

"Would you...would you talk to me about it? Well, not exactly that, but I'd rather explain in person."

"You can meet me here."

It is early November 1973, cold and muddy, and it is getting dark. I walk through the trucking company yard and go into the office. Kerekes is a middle-aged businessman, with short, dark hair, neat and conventional. I wouldn't notice him if we were the only two waiting for a bus. He suggests I accompany him to a nearby restaurant, and I make small talk as he drives. He is polite but seems puzzled.

I've made another mistake. I'll ask him just a few questions. Then I'll apologize, and we can leave.

We order coffee, and then I mention Al, the automobile company executive I'm told is taking payoffs from the truckers. I don't say who Al is or what he does.

Kerekes smiles. "What do you want to know about him?"

In the interview that follows, Kerekes confirms everything I've heard and more about the takeover of the steel hauling business off the docks, including rate-cutting, overloading, bribes to the weighmasters, help from the Teamsters, and oversight from the Mafia. Payoffs to auto company traffic managers may be part of it. Honest companies can't compete.

As we speak, I become so nervous that my voice falls to a croak, and Kerekes can't hear me over the noise of the music and the cocktail crowd that has come in after work. So, we go out in the parking lot and sit in his car.

"Can anyone corroborate what you're saying?" I ask him.

"One person, but he'd never talk to you. He's a friend of mine. He might do it if I was there."

"Could you – could you ask him?"

Kerekes has told me he's a family man. On the surface, from his quiet manner and his dress, he lives in a world a million miles away from the docks and a man like Russo. Then Kerekes turns toward me in the front seat and gives me a long look.

"Do you know what can happen to you?"

I shake my head. "No."

"They're going to hurt you and humiliate you because you're a woman," he says. "They probably wouldn't kill you at first, just humiliate you. Like strip you naked, cut off a breast, and throw you in Kennedy Square."

His tone of voice hasn't changed, nor has his face. He could be talking about sports or the weather.

I can't breathe.

"Gotta go," he says. "My daughter's in a concert at school tonight."

After he drops me off at his trucking company parking lot, I feel as if I have been pushed through a wall.

Is he telling the truth? Is he showing off? Is he threatening me? Why would he?

He isn't trying to sell me a story – I called him, not the other way around. If he's trying to scare me, why talk to me? Should I run from him or thank him? Why risk helping me? His calm manner is so at odds with what he says.

I sit in my car in the parking lot and put my head on the steering wheel, trying to gather my wits. I want the story badly enough to play along with Kerekes and see where we go.

Days pass. Then he calls to say his friend Rocco will talk, but not in public.

"I'll pick you up in half an hour," he says, giving me the name of a restaurant and telling me to look for his car in the parking lot. "I have an apartment. I'll take you there to meet him."

"Can't you just give me the address?"

"No. You won't find it soon enough. This is safe. You can meet me – and come alone or forget it. Rocco doesn't want anyone else to know."

I'm not sure how just how safe this arrangement is, but my editor is out. I call Sgt. O'Hare, hoping for advice. But he is out, too. So, I go to meet Kerekes.

When I see him in the parking lot, I suggest following him, thinking my parked car will mark my last location in case I disappear. But Kerekes tells me to leave the car.

"Get in," he says, opening his passenger door.

Suddenly, I am terrified.

I'm about to jump blindfolded off a high dive.

But after all these months, I really want this story. I'm a journalist and a soldier's daughter. I get in. We drive downriver to an older house and walk into a first floor flat. Kerekes gets out some glasses and ice and mixes us drinks.

"I keep the place for parties," he says, "but I don't use it often."

We wait. I try not to look nervous. Rocco doesn't show, and I find myself holding my breath. I hope Kerekes doesn't notice I'm not drinking.

The curtains are drawn. I want them open, but I can't think of any reason that will not insult Kerekes. An hour passes. Then Rocco calls the apartment. He can't make it.

In the days that follow, we arrange other meetings, but Rocco always has a last-minute excuse to cancel. I mention his name, as an aside, to Ron, one of the Federal investigators I have gotten to know by this time, an expert on labor racketeering. He says never to try to meet with Rocco.

"He's involved in every racket there is. If he ever said he'd help you, he'd probably be trying to set you up." In the mob, Rocco's specialty is robbery. One of his sidelines is prostitution.

On the day I get this advice, I call Kerekes again, and he agrees to try one more time. I hear nothing until December, the day before my birthday. Kerekes calls to say the meeting is off and will be off for good. By now, I know Kerekes has been trying to help me because he wants to settle an old score. I do not know what that is.

"Are *you* willing to call things off?" I ask. It's the right question.

Five minutes later, he calls back and tells me to be at the flat that afternoon at 1:30.

∞

The two men arrive only minutes after me. Rocco looks as if he's just stepped off the plane from Vegas or Miami. He is a big man with a golden suntan, a rare sight in winter in Detroit. He is wearing a pastel pink shirt. He pours himself a beer.

He doesn't want to talk to me. He mumbles and talks in riddles. A man on trial for murdering his grandmother would say more. Kerekes has something on him, something Rocco does not want known, but Kerekes never says.

Rocco wants the curtains open. My hands are frosty, but he is sweating. He keeps getting up to check the window and the lock on the door. Then he sits down again and looks at the beer. He never touches it.

"Some people would consider me bad company," he says at last. He goes on to explain he can never escape his life but does not want it for his children. He also makes it clear he is not among the Mafia elite.

"When the door is closed, I am on the outside of the room," he says. Then he adds, "But I am still in the house, and I keep my eyes and ears open."

From his expression, I begin to suspect he is more frightened than I am. I know this is true when he asks, "How much would you take for my name? How much?"

"Nothing," I say. "I won't give up your name."

"No more meetings," he says. "And I'll swear we didn't meet this time."

Then he tells me what he has seen. He gives me the name and unlisted telephone number of the bag man who collects the weighmaster payoffs from the drivers. He confirms many details of the takeover of the steel hauling business, from the docks to the warehouses and auto companies, as well as the conspiracy with the Teamsters. We talk for several hours.

I walk out alone, feeling both thrilled and numb. My sense of relief at being alive is so great that my birthday the following day seems like a victory, not just an annual event.

The dangerous nature of my investigation is underscored a week later when the corpse of a well-known mob enforcer is discovered in the trunk of his own car. He is not one of my sources, but I hesitate before calling Tony, the Mafia bagman who collects the weighmaster payoffs. Calling his unlisted number catches his attention.

He listens long enough for me to explain that I am working on a story about steel hauling and to ask him for an interview.

"I have no reason to talk to you," he says.

He's right, and I can't think of any way to argue with this, so a line from my mother comes to mind.

"You'd *better* talk to me," I say.

Tony waits a moment. Then, astoundingly, he says, "All right."

(You never know what will work in impossible situations. Once when I try to talk with a Justice Department lawyer, his secretary will tell me, "He doesn't take calls from reporters." I ask her to ask him, "Do you take calls from taxpayers?" After he stops laughing, he does.)

I suggest meeting Tony in a coffee shop, but the name makes him sputter that it will not do at all. Later I learn it's a mob joint. Tony says he'll meet me instead at ten that night at the Interlude East lounge on Eight Mile Road.

This time I am truly afraid to go alone. Tony is deeply involved with the Mafia, and I have no idea who he'll bring with him or have waiting for me. I call my friend and colleague, Mike Graham, again. Not only is he the *Free Press* police reporter, but he is also a Vietnam vet and a tough guy. I ask if he can do me a big favor and get to the bar that night before I do and keep an eye on me during the interview. If things go wrong, he can call the police.

I mention this plan to another friend of mine, John Weisman, who is the rock and roll music critic at the *Free Press*. John has a flair for the dramatic and loves adventure, so he insists on coming, too. Weisman has brought me with him to dozens of rock concerts, ending up afterwards in Greektown with the singers and musicians for long after-concert interviews and drinks. I haven't been on John's A-list since the night I passed out, face down, in a salad, but I owe him.

Graham calls back to say we should take a third person, someone who can carry a gun. A friend of his, another Vietnam vet and former homicide detective, will join Weisman and Graham at the bar.

We take two cars and set out early. Ice storms earlier in the day have turned the streets into skating rinks. I can't find the Interlude East. I drive back and forth on Eight Mile Road, Weisman and Graham following, until I realize the name has changed. It's now Scotty's Interlude, and it is poorly marked.

Graham and Weisman go inside. I don't want to wait at the curb, so I drive over to Biff's for a cup of coffee and a piece of day-old blueberry pie that curdles in my stomach as I watch the cook polishing the coffee urns and cleaning the grill. We are in the same place, different worlds.

When I drive back to Scotty's, there are no parking spots on the street. I pull into the lot and find a space in the back. It's dark, and as I walk toward the entrance, I see a car sitting at the front of the lot with its lights out and motor running. Then the car backs up toward me.

Oh, my God. Everyone who can help me is already inside.

It's Tony. He has been watching for my car, he says, because he realized he forgot to give me the new name of the bar. He pulls into a space I missed, gets out, and walks with me toward the door. He looks inside, then turns around.

"I can't go in," he says. "It's too crowded. The wrong people are there." He wants to go somewhere else. I get a bad feeling.

This is looking more like a setup, and I'm not going anywhere with him.

I try to argue, but he is adamant.

"The weather's so bad," I say as we walk towards our cars. There is a bar and restaurant adjacent to the parking lot on the other side.

"We shouldn't drive," I say, "Why not just go next door?" To my surprise, he agrees.

The pavement is like glass.

I'm gonna fall. But I'm not letting him touch me.

I don't grab his arm, just go flailing along. The place next door is almost empty. We go in and sit down.

In the light, Tony turns out to be young and handsome. "If anyone finds out I met you, I'm a dead man," he says. He seems so worried that I start to feel a little safer, a little less concerned about being a target myself.

He orders drinks and tells me the story of his life, about not having a formal education and learning everything the hard way. The implication is that I am someone who's had everything, which is true. For a moment, I am tempted to feel sorry for him.

Then my guardian angels walk in. When I did not arrive, they went outside, saw my car in the lot, and went back inside to have another drink and talk things over. Eventually, one of them thought to check next door. They sit down at a table across the room, order drinks, and start telling cop jokes in loud voices. An hour earlier, I had been frantic with fear, wondering if they would find me in time. Now I am worried they will ruin my interview. Tony notices my anxiety.

"You look tired and nervous," he says.

It's now-or-never time to bring up steel hauling. As I do, I watch his anxiety level rise.

"You know too much," he says, like a line from a bad movie. We spar verbally for the next two hours, drinking and scaring each other.

"Everyone has his hand out," he says, rationalizing the payoffs. "Even the sweeper. He says, 'You're buying coffee tonight.' If you say, 'No, I don't need you,' he tells the man on the dock, 'Let him sit four hours.' There's larceny in everyone."

The county weighmasters, too, he says. "A man making $100 a week can kill you on weights. Say he makes $10,000 a year. We add $12,000. You're not getting me to hang myself — but there was a collection every month."

I ask him about Al, the automobile company traffic manager also rumored to be on the payroll.

"You know too much."

When I turn to the Mafia, he cuts me off. "Look, we all grew up poor and Italian and had to work hard. Why take anything away from us?"

When we finally get up to leave, my friends walk out behind us and follow my car home. As easy as that.

My list of sources grows longer, and I go to see them one by one, working to confirm my story. One man who reluctantly speaks with me on the phone says he's already been threatened with having his legs broken on another case.

"You start asking questions and get nosy, and you cut your own throat," he advises. He gives me more names to call.

That same day, I visit the owner of a competing steel hauling company at his home after dinner. We sit stiffly in the living room at first – the man, his wife, and me – but we end up eating chocolate cake and drinking tea at the kitchen table while the children run around in their pajamas. They give me the same scenario and more names. In passing, I mention Kerekes' friend Rocco.

"He would know," the trucking company owner says, "but he would never talk to you."

Several days later, I call Al, the crooked automobile company traffic manager at his home. I tell him a little of what I know.

"You have a great imagination," Al says.

"But is it true?"

"I'm not going to deny it," he says, "and I'm not going to say it's true." I stay on the phone for an hour with him as he tries to figure out what I know.

The next day I get a furious telephone call from the only public relations man I know at the auto company; a buttoned-down type I met while covering the auto talks.

"What is this – calling up our employees and talking about the Mafia?" he snaps. Then he launches into a tirade about lawsuits for libel and slander. "How in the hell would *you* know anything about the Mafia?"

"From talking to them."

"Oh, sure. They call *you* up and tell you their life story."

"I'll call you back," I tell him.

Then I call his boss, who ends our conversation with an invitation to lunch in the auto company's executive dining room, where I am the only woman not waiting tables.

"You're too intense," the boss tells me over lunch. "You look like you need a good night's sleep and a decent meal."

I ask him if his company has ever investigated allegations that some of its employees are on the mob payroll. He acts as if I've slapped him. Here in a room full of expensive suits, with well-modulated conversations, it does seem preposterous. I start to wonder about myself.

A few days later, he calls me. There was an investigation, he says. When do I want to come out and talk about it? I do not want to talk with any of the bosses at his company until I've had another run at getting the real story out of the traffic manager, so I stall him.

"When I have more proof."

One of the men involved in the trucking scheme had an ex-girlfriend. Kerekes met her in a bar a couple of years back when she was lonely and in a bad mood. He remembers her first name and what she looks like, but he can't recall more. I call around and find her name and address.

It takes me a week to get the courage to knock on her door. The woman who answers says the former tenant has moved away, and she does not know where. I go to the post office, pay a dollar, and buy her forwarding address. It turns out to be an apartment building. I do not have her apartment number.

I go there the next Sunday and ring buzzers in the vestibule at random. A woman is still asking "Who?" when a boy sweeping the hall decides I have an honest face and lets me in. He recognizes the name of the ex-girlfriend and tells me her apartment number.

Kerekes's description of the woman is accurate – she is exceptionally beautiful – and she is terrified. "How did you find me?" she keeps asking.

"I'm sorry to come in like some gangster movie –" I say, then want to kick myself. "I know I should have called ahead, but you have an unlisted phone number, and…" The woman is backing away from me.

I explain as fast as I can that I am writing a newspaper story and wonder if she can help me with information about some of the people who are involved. I give her some names. "Are you acquainted with them? Could you tell me anything about them?"

The woman shakes her head, mute.

"If you ever found anyone who wanted to talk to me, would you give them my card?" I ask.

The woman takes it and motions with her chin toward her front door.

"Please, do me a favor," I ask as I start to leave. "Please don't tell anyone I came to see you."

"Are you kidding?" she says. "Tell *them*?"

I want to interview a few people who have left town. One is living in Las Vegas. When I call him, he agrees to talk, but only in person. He will meet me at the airport. I like this arrangement because he cannot bring a gun there.

The connecting flight from Phoenix is filled with vacationers. The weather is beautiful, and my reason for the trip seems surreal. When I get off the plane, my contact is not there. I call his house, and his wife answers.

"He had the wrong arrival time," she says. "He was there two hours ago." She tells me he is back at work.

"He wants you to meet him in one of the hotels downtown."

No way.

I call him, and he agrees to come out to the airport, "but meet me at the ticket counter. I don't want to go through security again."

Should I just leave?

I want to refuse, but it has been a long trip and a huge item on the expense account. The city desk is out of patience, and my editors say I am out of time. Reluctantly, I agree.

When the man I want to interview arrives, he looks ancient and friendly enough, but I know better. One harmless-looking old gangster I interviewed at his home in Detroit was arrested shortly afterwards for murdering someone with an ice pick.

The man in Las Vegas drives me to a casino, where we eat lunch by the pool and watch people toast in the sun. I gradually realize this man has agreed to see me only because he wants to find out what I know. He has nothing to add but an apology and an excuse.

"I'm fifty-eight years old," he says, "and I've still got my health. What can a little guy do about this?"

It is an expensive, useless trip, a complete failure. It's February, so it's snowing when I arrive back in Detroit. I still do not have enough corroboration to draft a story. Then Al, the traffic manager from the automobile company, calls me.

"Did you call my house last night?" he asks.

"No."

"A woman called. My son answered, and he didn't get her name. I thought it might have been you."

In my one conversation with Al, I had mentioned some people you wouldn't want to meet in a dark alley. When I asked if he knew them, Al said no. I've given up hope of getting information from him, so I just ask how he's feeling. He sounds terrible.

"I got a call from a couple of people you mentioned," he says. "It's kind of worried me." To my surprise, Al keeps talking.

"When you first called, I didn't feel I should risk my job or my family. It's not that big a deal. I don't see why I should risk my career and my life over those guys. You're a reporter, and it's your job. I'm glad you're doing this."

I am still feeling resentful about the PR man he set on me, but I am surprised.

"After I talked to you, people at my company phoned me," he says. "Then I got the calls from people I didn't want to hear from. Two weeks ago, I got a call from a party with an invitation. Then I got a call from another fellow who wanted to have lunch. My wife is getting a little antsy. It's nothing intimidating. They just call and say, 'How are you?' 'We haven't talked to you lately.' All the little shallow comments."

He says he has been transferred from the traffic manager's job, but "the rumor is that I'm going back into that job at a different level and with different authority. I'd view that with mixed emotions. I'd want assurances from a very high management level that I'd have considerably more – support."

I have no clue what he means, but he does not explain. He wants to tell me why he hadn't talked to me earlier.

"I was worried about you. You sound like a young person, like me. I didn't think you knew what you were getting into."

I haven't met Al in person, but I try to picture him as one of the sleek young executives I saw eating lunch that day, trying to match his voice with those faces.

The fear in Al's voice does not fit in.

We end our conversation.

Piece by piece, the story of the deals, the payoffs, and the threats is coming together. I am not sure exactly who is making certain that the Teamsters union does not object to the exploitation of the drivers. I can never get a name.

"You're leaving a trail a mile wide," DeLong, the Teamsters PR guy, tells me. "I hope you know what you're doing. I get calls about you, and someone said at a meeting the other day that if you kept going around trucking companies, one of those big truck tires was going to fall on you."

"That's lighter than a coil of steel," I say. He does not get the reference.

It is the end of March 1974, more than a year since the first telephone call about truck overloading, and I am finally ready to call Vincent Meli. To my surprise, he comes to the phone right away.

I tell him I want him to know about my story before he reads it in the paper, and I ask for an interview to hear his side. Truth is, I also want to meet him. I've been chasing shadows for a long time.

I have not yet read *The Godfather*. If I had, I would see the similarities between Meli and Michael Corleone. Meli came to the U.S. as an immigrant and graduated from college, Notre Dame. Immediately afterwards, he joined the army as an officer and went to Europe to fight in World War II, serving in army intelligence and receiving medals for bravery. Meli has no criminal record, not even a traffic ticket. His uncle, Angelo Meli, is well known in the rackets in Detroit, but Vincent is not. He moves easily, quietly, and cleanly through life, invisible in all but Mafia social circles.

When I call him, he tells me, in a voice that is quiet and polite, "I'm fifty-two years old, and I've been through this before with your newspaper. I'm Sicilian, and I know the connotations of that. The only crime I ever committed was being Sicilian. Whatever you're working on, it can't be in my interest."

"I took journalism in college. I know you're doing a job. I wouldn't want to be misunderstood, and I wouldn't want to get mad because I was misunderstood. Write your questions down, and I'll answer them."

At this point, it is a relief to drop my questions in the mail. He never answers. But a year after the publication of my stories, I will be shocked to realize that the person sitting across the dinner table from me at a gathering in Grosse Pointe is Vincent Meli himself. The host is Bill Bufalino, the lawyer representing the New Jersey Teamsters suspected in the disappearance of Jimmy Hoffa.

CHAPTER FOURTEEN:
GOODBYE HOFFA, GOODBYE DETROIT

It's July 30, 1975, and Chuckie O'Brien is pounding on my door in the middle of the night. I am living alone in Grosse Pointe, in a second-floor condominium I've recently bought. I am surprised to see him, but I let him in. He seems excited but not distraught.

He tells me Jimmy Hoffa is missing, the family is upset, and he has no clue what has happened. Earlier this day, he says, he was at Teamsters Local 299 when a gift arrived by freight from a Teamster official in Seattle, addressed to Bobby Holmes, the head of Teamster Local 337. Holmes lives in the Detroit suburb of Farmington Hills.

The gift was a large frozen salmon, packed in plastic and shipped in a box packed with ice. The ice was melting, so the frozen fish needed to be delivered as quickly as possible. O'Brien tells me he was asked to deliver it. However, he does not own or have access to a car.

O'Brien tells me he called his friend Joe Giacalone, the son of Chuckie's "Uncle Tony" Giacalone, the Mafia figure, and asked to borrow Joe's car to run the errand. Chuckie put the fish in the back seat, and it made a mess of the car.

It's a strange story, told in the middle of the night by a man who scares me more than a little, and if Hoffa really has disappeared, this is a *huge* story. I ask Chuckie if I can put him on the phone right away with Ralph Orr, my colleague at the *Free Press* who is the senior labor reporter and an expert on the Teamsters. Without a moment's hesitation, Chuckie says yes, and we make the call. O'Brien repeats this story, word for word, to Orr.

O'Brien stays a few more minutes, but I have the strong impression that the reason for his visit is to get this story out. I feel reassured that he has told Orr and me the same thing, but in the morning our editors feel it means nothing. If O'Brien, who does not have a reputation for truthfulness, has told such a weird tale —not in his interest to begin with – it must be irrelevant and worthless. The real news, as we quickly confirm, is that Jimmy Hoffa has vanished. O'Brien is a sideshow and not to be mentioned.

I disagree. We learn from Hoffa's family that he disappeared on his way to a meeting with Tony Giacalone that never occurred. According to other sources, Giacalone was visible at a Southfield health club all day long.

Hoffa had parked his car at the appointed meeting spot, the Machus Red Fox Restaurant in Bloomfield Township, fifteen miles northwest of Detroit. He waited for a long time, making several calls to complain that no one had shown up. Eventually, someone did pick him up, and he was never seen again.

Hoffa was close to Chuckie and would not have worried about getting into a car with him. During the time Hoffa vanished, Chuckie was driving a car that belonged to the son of the man who arranged the meeting. I'm seeing too many coincidences.

When my editors refuse to let me tell O'Brien's story in that day's newspaper, I feel a deep conflict between my duty as a citizen and my role as a journalist. As a rule, I do not give law enforcement officials information I cannot publish. But the Hoffa disappearance is different. Something in O'Brien's story might save Jimmy Hoffa's life.

So, I go to see the U. S. attorney, a man I do not know, and tell him in confidence exactly what O'Brien told Orr and me. At this point, local police are still running the case, but the FBI has been called in to consult, and the U.S. attorney will eventually run the Hoffa grand jury.

Chuckie's story first appears in our competitor, the *Detroit News*, citing federal sources. The *Free Press* runs it the following day. I don't like being scooped on my own story, but I feel I have done the right thing.

Joe Giacalone's car is seized and searched. Dogs indicate the presence of Jimmy Hoffa's scent in the back seat. There is blood in the car, but it belongs to the fish. Investigators do find the only physical clue they will encounter in the entire Hoffa investigation: a three-inch human hair in the back seat. Not until 2001, twenty-six years later, will DNA analysis show the hair belonged to Jimmy Hoffa. This will not suffice for a prosecution.

The working theory of the case, which has never been closed, is that Chuckie O'Brien drove Giacalone's car to pick up Hoffa on the day he disappeared. Chuckie cannot give a satisfactory account of his whereabouts between 2:30 and 4 p.m., the window of time in which Hoffa vanished.

Until I read a well-researched and sympathetic book written many years later by O'Brien's stepson[xiii], I do not realize O'Brien has misled his family and investigators about several critical things. He has told them he spent the entire night after Hoffa's disappearance at the home of his friend Marvin Adell and did not learn Hoffa was missing until the next day.

Not true. He drives or is driven by someone to Grosse Pointe, where I see him and put him on the phone to Orr. Chuckie tells us Jimmy is missing, and the Hoffa family is upset. But they have not spoken with him yet. So how does he know Hoffa has disappeared? And why, if he is not involved, does he lie afterwards about when he knew?

The story of Hoffa's disappearance balloons into a national and then an international story. Phony calls pour in with Hoffa sightings and imaginary burials as the days turn into weeks and months. The *Free Press* puts Ralph Orr and me on a team with Fred Girard, who writes quickly and well, and freelancer Dan Moldea, who later writes a book and becomes a Hoffa expert. Orr stays in touch with the Hoffa family. Other staff members put hundreds of hours of reporting time into the story.

O'Brien leaves Detroit for Florida almost immediately after Hoffa's disappearance, returning for interviews with the FBI. O'Brien will continue to live until February 2020, but I will never see or speak with him again.

In the days after the disappearance, I focus on the Federal investigation. Hoffa's son says his father's meeting was arranged by Anthony Giacalone, who offered to broker a peace deal between Hoffa and Anthony (Tony Pro) Provenzano, a New Jersey Teamsters official.

Provenzano and other Teamsters are called to Detroit to appear before a federal grand jury. The grand jury proceedings are secret, but the press corps and the Teamsters' attorney William Bufalino Sr. turn that floor of the Federal Building into quite a scene.

Members of the press corps wait in the hallway for the witnesses to come out of the elevator. In addition to Provenzano, they include two sets of brothers, Thomas and Stephen Andretta and Gabriel and Salvatore Briguglio. As they emerge and make their way down the hall to the grand jury room, we shout questions at them.

"What is this, a f — - quiz show?" snarls Gabe Briguglio. No one else says anything, no one except Bufalino, who sets up shop in a room outside the grand jury chamber.

Each time one of the Teamster witnesses is asked a question, he excuses himself and comes out to consult with Bufalino. They speak briefly. Then the witness returns, and Bufalino lectures the reporters about the American legal system and its problems. This happens dozens, hundreds of times. The New Jersey Teamsters become like characters in a Jack in the Box.

After hours and then days of sitting on the floor, at the feet of Bufalino, it is hard not to laugh at their comings and goings and the flowery speeches of Bufalino, who is accompanied by his son, William Bufalino Junior, also an attorney, even though the investigation and the situation are deadly serious.

This goes on for days and one thousand separate grand jury appearances. I'm not sure why the U.S. Marshals allow the press corps to participate in such a sideshow, but it takes place many years before anyone is particularly worried about building security.

Stephen Andretta refuses to answer any question from the grand jurors and is kept in jail, with frequent appearances before a judge in vain attempts to secure his freedom. His complaints, among other things, include his hemorrhoids. Gabe Briguglio's disposition never improves.

After many days, Provenzano returns to New Jersey, and the rest of the Teamsters are finally released to go home. Bufalino promises me an interview with them at his home in Grosse Pointe. When I arrive, they are all sitting down for dinner. That's when I realize that Vincent Meli is sitting across the table from me.

The moment I see him, I feel the hand of William Bufalino Senior on my shoulder. He invites me to leave the table for a tour of his home, including his basement, which features a miniature Sicilian village. I am even more amazed by his library. For someone who constantly complains in court and to the press that the Mafia does not exist, his library is filled with books about the Mafia.

There is no time for interviews, he tells me.

"My clients must leave for the airport immediately. If you want to ride along, you can."

I do, and when we get to the airport, Bufalino gives them permission to speak with me on the plane to New Jersey. Mentally, I call their bluff. I call my editor, pull out my American Express card, and buy a ticket. But without Bufalino to smooth the way, I fare no better on the plane than the grand jurors did in on the ground. Someone meets us at the airport and drives us to the Teamsters Hall. All I remember about the place is the garage with wall-to-wall carpeting.

My companions seem to conclude that it's a joke to bring me along, as they keep saying how much they hate Detroit and hate the press. Tony Provenzano joins us, and they invite me to go out to a second dinner with them. I don't think these guys ate well in jail.

We go to a small, isolated restaurant in what looks like a warehouse district. Just the Hoffa suspects and me. They are smoking cigars and ask if I want one. I have never even smoked a cigarette, but I take a cigar and chew on it a little.

"Ma Barker and her boys," says Tony Pro, and everyone laughs.

I don't get a word out of any of them about Hoffa. They enjoy scaring me a little. Then they drive me back to the hotel. I am glad to get away from them alive, and the next day I am thankful to fly home.

Three years later, Sal Briguglio is shot dead by two hooded gunmen in New York's Little Italy. Five years later, Tony Pro is convicted of labor racketeering and sentenced to a twenty-year term in prison, where he dies of a heart attack.

Meanwhile, in the wake of my stories about corruption in the trucking business, the agent from the Department of Labor and a federal prosecutor work with a federal grand jury in Detroit to open a labor racketeering investigation focusing on Vincent A. Meli, Jack Russo, and Roby Smith, the Teamster official who should have been protecting the drivers.

The drivers themselves testify against them when it goes to trial.

It's one of the government's first prosecutions under the Racketeer Influenced and Corrupt Organizations (RICO)Act of 1970, and the defendants are convicted of extortion and sentenced to federal prison. They delay with appeals. Meli and Russo go all the way to the U. S. Supreme Court before they lose.

Just as I reconcile myself to working at the *Free Press* for the rest of my life, two gut-wrenching events force me out. One is a death threat from the Mafia. The other is an encounter with Kurt Luedtke.

My exit begins with an invitation to lunch from the suave and handsome Neil Fink, a prominent defense attorney whose clients include senior members of organized crime. I know Fink, so I accept with extreme caution, like a rabbit invited to dine with a lion.

Anthony Giacalone is upset about his portrayal in the Hoffa stories. This I know. I have also covered his recent trial on charges of federal income tax evasion. Stories from the courtroom described him as "tight-lipped," "cold-eyed," and "mean-looking." Not mine. I did, however, quote the loan shark Rip Khoury, who called the Giacalone brothers, Tony and Vito, "animals in the shylocking business."

Fink takes me to the London Chop House and buys me an expensive meal I cannot eat. Over coffee, he tells me in a friendly way that Mr. Zerilli thinks it's time for me to take up feature writing. He does not specify which Zerilli, but he does not need to.

Joseph Zerilli, the old man, recently returned to head the Detroit crime families after his son, Anthony, was sent to federal prison. Joseph Zerilli first came to Detroit from Sicily at the age of sixteen and got his start during Prohibition running rum from Canada to Detroit. He is now one of the last surviving members of the Mafia's national commission, a man who can sit with Joseph Profaci, Vito Genovese, and Carlo Gambino.

As innocent as Zerilli's message would sound if I ever told anyone, I know it is my only warning. Usually, nothing is said. Most people remember Harvey Leach, the handsome young furniture company president who went to a business meeting the day before his wedding three years ago. He was found in the trunk of his car with his throat cut from ear to ear. Afterwards, the word went out he had mob connections. His murder will never be solved.

The quiet warning from Fink is enough to make me consider leaving town and stop writing about the Mafia. I will do both but, as fate will have it, outlive Zerilli and find myself in town to cover his funeral.

A run-in with Luedtke gives me another reason to flee, although it begins with a seeming compliment. One Friday, Kurt asks me how I would like to work in Washington, D.C. Knight-Ridder, the chain that owns the *Free Press*, has an opening in its bureau there. I've never dreamed of such a possibility. I ask to think about it over the weekend. I return on Monday and tell Kurt I'll take the job.

"Not so fast," he says. "I didn't offer you the job. I just mentioned it to you as a professional courtesy. I need you too much here." In a few days, he gives the job to another woman, a new hire. I see this as a slap in my face.

I gave up on getting an East Coast reporting job when I left Boston, but now I resolve to make another try. I'll pitch *The Washington Post* and *The New York Times,* and I'll start at once.

It's 1977. Last year, at a primary election rally in Lansing, I met David Broder, the *Washington Post* political columnist. We spent an evening talking about journalism and politics. I call him up, remind him of our chance meeting, and ask if he can arrange a job interview for me at the *Post.* He sets me up with Richard Harwood, the deputy managing editor.

I have no contacts at *The New York Times,* but I'm lucky this time. Mike Levitas has just been installed as metropolitan editor, and he agrees to see me. I send the editors at both newspapers my resume and clips, empty my bank account, and buy plane tickets.

My indignation at Luedke has faded by the time I walk into the *Post* newsroom, and I am running on nervous energy. I have time to calm down because Harwood arrives twenty minutes late.

"You have ten minutes," he says when he arrives. Then he uses up the time to describe his breakfast with Richard Reeves, a famous political journalist. I can tell he has not read my work, has no interest in me, and is seeing me only as a favor to Broder. I am desolate.

I travel to New York to see Mike Levitas. He has read my work, and we like each other, but he has a hiring freeze and no openings. I return to Detroit in a funk.

When I follow up with a letter to Harwood, I tell him I've had longer conversations in revolving doors. Perhaps my letter is passed around for laughs. I do not know, but Leonard Downie Jr., then the assistant managing editor for metropolitan news, invites me to come back at the *Post's* expense for a real interview. This time, they offer me a job on the suburban staff. The assignment, even in a great newspaper, is a step down from being a *star* at the *Free Press*. There are also reports of cutthroat competition among *Post* staff members. I am not used to this, so I am nervous. But I accept the offer and start packing to leave town.

I will also be leaving my boyfriend in Detroit, a fellow reporter on the *Free Press*. He is exceptional and very handsome, and our newsroom friends mock us as "Barbie and Ken." After meeting him, I pursued him relentlessly and eventually outran my competitors. One weekend, when he was going out of town, he said I could move my things into his apartment near Belle Isle on the Detroit River. I have been living there with him for a year.

I still do not know the difference between infatuation and love, and we both have some growing up to do. But I feel safe at his place. The apartment has a steel door, and Ken has a handgun. I never ask if it's loaded.

He comes to my farewell party and, for a while, tells people I am the only woman he has ever lost to a newspaper. Then he realizes he is in love with a friend of ours who is far more beautiful and better for him than I. They will end up happily married.

The day before I leave Detroit, someone from *The New York Times* rings me at the *Free Press*. The caller is connected instead to a printer with a similar name who has imbibed a great deal. When the call finally reaches me, the guy on the line is Nick Horrock from the Washington Bureau of the *Times*. He says the *Times* wants to talk to me about a job.

"It's too late," I say. "I'm already on my way to D.C. to work for the *Post*."

It's Friday, and I am flying out tomorrow. Nick asks me to meet a group from the *Times* tomorrow afternoon. I have nothing to lose, so I say yes.

I fly to Washington and meet in a downtown bar on Saturday with Horrock, Hedrick Smith, who is the Washington bureau chief, and Tony Marro, a reporter in the bureau who will go on to become editor of *Newsday*. Horrock tells me the *Times* is creating a national investigative team. The *Post* kicked ass during Watergate, and the *Times* never wants that to happen again.

We talk and drink for a long time, and we get along well enough that they ask me to delay reporting for duty at the *Post* for one day, long enough to fly to New York on Monday to meet Abe Rosenthal, the executive editor of the *Times*. They are describing a much better assignment than the job in the suburbs for the *Post*. I decide to take a chance and go up to New York.

Abe has a fire-breathing reputation. I have no friends at the *Times* to advise me on how to talk with him. When I get off the Eastern Airlines shuttle, I am so nervous I have my first case of butterflies in my life. Looking for a way to calm down, I go to Saks Fifth Avenue and take the elevator to the top floor. Then I ride the escalator down through all the floors, gazing at everything I can never afford to buy. By the time I walk out the door, I am numb and completely calm.

Abe is not half as scary as the Detroit mobsters. He's a good conversationalist, and I am impressed. When he offers me the job in Washington, I accept. Afterwards, I call the *Post* to thank them and say I'm sorry, but I've changed my mind and will not be coming. Then I call the movers and tell them to send the bill to the *Times*. Nothing seems real.

CHAPTER FIFTEEN:
CAPITOL BLUES

It is July 1977, and the *Times* is close to settling the lawsuit[xiv] filed by brave women I will come to know and admire over the years. Thanks to them, I now have a job beyond my dreams: working for *The New York Times* in Washington as a member of a new national investigative reporting team.

Most new hires on the reporting staff, regardless of their previous experience, begin working for the *Times* on the metropolitan staff in New York. They make an exception for the new members of the investigative team. I'm so excited about my new assignment, I don't think about the disadvantages of not getting to know anyone in New York. My editors will become familiar voices on the telephone, sending me places, asking me questions, checking to see if something is wrong. But I do not know them face to face, and it makes a difference.

The *Times* has hundreds on a staff we only half-jokingly call a paramilitary organization. I should start building myself a network within it, but I do not know this, and no one tells me. I also take for granted our common goals as journalists give us an unbreakable bond, like soldiers. This is true at best, but not always. There will be heartbreaking betrayals.

Like soldiers, we will be asked to give up many things, big and small, and many of us will risk our lives. I will count on my editors to have my back, certainly against the government and even against other editors if it comes to that. But I am not personal friends with the editors who count. They are in New York, and most of them are men.

The newsroom in the Washington bureau looks deceptively familiar. Any veteran newspaper reporter would feel at home: the same hustle, deadlines, ringing phones, and dirty coffee cups. The sign by the coffee machine says, "Your mother doesn't work here. Clean up your mess." The furnishings in the bureau are more luxurious than the vast, stark *Times* city room in New York, which has identical desks in rows. All papers must be out of sight at the end of the day, leaving only bare desktops and typewriters in view, a policy almost impossible to enforce. It does not last.

At the *Times* bureau, the difference is the human one. The *Times* is the Ivy League of newspapers. The reporters are *great*, and I am assigned to a team of stars: In addition to Horrock, my colleagues include David Burnham, Tony Marro, Wendell Rawls, and occasionally Seymour Hersh. They welcome me, collaborate with me, and share story ideas. For a while, I cannot get over their differences in technique, but it all seems to work. Burnham, Horrock, and Hersh roar over the phone at their sources, Rawls jokes with them, and Marro works his stories like a jewel thief.

One of my first incoming telephone calls is from Detroit. William Bufalino Sr. congratulates me on leaving town and moving up to *The New York Times*.

"Jo," he says cheerfully, "I see you are working from Washington now, writing about *politicians!*" He does not designate politicians as better targets than his clients, but I get his meaning and accept his wishes of good will and good luck.

As I am about to learn, Bufalino has a point. Crime by the government can be the most dangerous of all to the public good. At the end of my first month at the *Times*, I am thrown into an investigation of a such a crime, the CIA's secret post-World War II mind control research.

It was called MK-ULTRA, also *Bluebird* and *Artichoke,* and one of its goals was to create a remote-control assassin of the kind portrayed in the book and movie *The Manchurian Candidate*, someone the CIA could force to kill another person and remember nothing afterwards. The agency imagined the Russians and the Chinese already had such an assassin. As it turned out, they did not.

I hear about mind control on the last day of July 1977, several hours before deadline, when thousands of pages of formerly secret documents are released to the Washington press corps in response to a Freedom of Information Act request. To view this material, we must go to a room, sit down, and page through boxes of papers, taking notes as we go.

The original paperwork has been destroyed, including the contracts, letters, telephone records, and all details of how the agency persuaded civilian and military scientists to undertake the research. We have thousands of pages of ancillary material, such as old expense accounts and receipts. Someone has gone through these with black ink to eliminate every name and revealing detail. We see lots of orders and reports about dogs. What dogs? Where? Why?

The day after the rush of the document release, I sit down with a team from the *Times* to mine these pages word for word for any shred of information that has been overlooked, any name not blacked out, any item left on a piece of paper that may give us a clue.

I have no powerful sources. I know no one in the CIA. But I do find elliptical references to an experiment in which electrodes were implanted in the brains of people to see if their behavior could be controlled remotely.

This appears to have happened in Louisiana, and I rush to New Orleans to interview a professor whose name appears on a receipt. He's at Tulane University. I call him first, not saying why I would like to interview him, but he refuses to see me.

I go to his office anyway, and – using my best Detroit sidestep – whisk past his secretary. The professor is wearing a white coat, and he looks so much like Boris Karloff, the actor in the *Frankenstein* films, I have a horrible urge to laugh.

Dr. Robert Heath is a famous bio-psychiatrist, the founder and chairman of the Tulane department of psychiatry and neurology. He is more than surprised to see me, but he is a gentleman. Instead of throwing me out, he invites me to sit down.

We talk for a while, and he tells me of two encounters with the CIA program in the late fifties and early 1960s. In 1957 an agent from the CIA asked him to test a brainwashing drug on monkeys and later on prisoners at the Louisiana State Penitentiary in Angola. The drug was bulbocapnine. It was something Dr. Heath had already tested on cats.

"This is no secret drug," Dr. Heath recalls telling the agent. "You can find it in the literature. You can't wash any brain with bulbocapnine." Nonetheless, he tried the drug on several monkeys, and was paid $200 for his work.

"I never used it on human beings," he tells me.

During those years, as part of his private research, he performed psychosurgery and pioneered implanting "depth electrodes" in the human brain, using these to identify areas he called the brain's pleasure and pain centers. He was pursuing research on the pleasure center, seeking ways to treat patients with schizophrenia.

As I listen to him, I squirm in my chair. Just four years ago, stories in the *Free Press* by Dolores Katz and me led to the landmark legal decision *Kaimowitz v. Department of Mental Health for the State of Michigan* banning experimental psychosurgery on prisoners and mental patients. I am relieved Dr. Heath does not know this.

Dr. Heath goes on to tell me Dr. E. Mansfield Gunn, chief of the CIA's medical service division, approached him after a symposium in November 1962. Dr. Gunn wanted Dr. Heath to use his electrodes to investigate the pain centers of the human brain, arguing the Russians were doing the same. Funds for this work could come through legitimate medical research foundations.

"It was abhorrent," Dr. Heath tells me. "If I were going to be a spy, I'd be a spy. I wanted to be a doctor and practice medicine." He looks upset, even after all these years. "The offer violated the Hippocratic Oath. It promised no benefit to the patient or mankind."

MK-ULTRA never produced the desired assassin. But the experiments themselves hurt people. CIA researchers took spinal and other fluids from comatose and delirious patients hospitalized with terminal cancer, liver failure, uremia, and severe infections. Experimenting with sensory deprivation, a nurse was placed in a dark, silent room and began to think snakes were coming out from under her chair. She was later hospitalized for schizophrenia.

Unsuspecting people, including members of the military and prostitutes, were lured to parties in hotels and given drugs without their knowledge. Frank Olson, an army biochemist, drank a cocktail laced with LSD and jumped to his death from a window of the Statler hotel in New York City in 1953. Years after my reporting for the *Times,* his case will take a sinister turn when his son has his body exhumed and examined. Forensic experts will attribute his death to a blow on the head before his fall. The family, who suspects he was thrown out the window, will be unable to get the case reopened in court.

We cannot identify many of the researchers, but they came from at least forty-four colleges and universities. Not all knew the source of the money or its true purpose. The trail gets fainter with the years, as records were destroyed or vanished.

Senate hearings, which had begun in 1975, heat up after the release of the documents in 1977. Subsequent books will indicate this project seems to have been an exploration into the fine points of torture, in which mind control is everything. This possibility does not occur to me because it is unthinkable in 1977 the United States will ever engage in torture. In the new millennium, after rendition and black prisons, I will change my mind.

In August 1977, a month after I arrive in Washington and while I am working on the CIA story, a firestorm erupts in our bureau over sources and sex. Laura Foreman, a former political reporter for the *Philadelphia Inquirer* who has been hired into our office, is questioned by the FBI as a potential witness in a tax evasion case against Henry Cianfrani, a much older man considered to be one of the most powerful men in the Pennsylvania senate.

Senator Cianfranti has acknowledged giving Laura gifts that included flowers, champagne, furniture, and a fur coat. Laura is beautiful, talented, and single. As an outsider and a newcomer, I am not privy to the frantic discussions among the editors, only to the wave of fear that sweeps the few women now working in our bureau. It is an open secret another woman is sleeping with her best source, and we assume at least some of the men have slept with their sources because they do it everywhere else.

Abe Rosenthal's reaction, later published, is, "I don't care if my reporters are f----- elephants as long as they aren't covering the circus."

After a lot of drama, Laura leaves the newspaper, and no one else is put under the microscope. The affair, at least for Laura, ends well. When Senator Cianfranti gets out of prison for labor racketeering, they get married and stay that way. [xv]

It is a brutal repeat of a basic lesson: Sources are essential, but journalists must draw boundaries between us and them. We can't sleep with them, and we can't take money or favors from them — the standing rule is nothing more expensive than a drink at a bar.

Larger conflicts of interest — believing lies from our government and ignoring the truth from our enemy — do not bring down the hell meted out for love affairs.

Acts of friendship, unguarded with no ulterior motive, are so rare they are truly unforgettable. I experience such a moment just once from one of the least likely places, the FBI office in Detroit, where communication with the press ranges from silent to mute.

An agent I'll call Michael works there. If I ever manage to reach him, which is difficult, he finds the nicest conceivable way to say nothing at all. Most of the agents make their distaste for the press clear.

Shortly after I arrive in Washington, Michael calls to say he's in town. He invites me to lunch. I am so surprised, I say yes. We choose a restaurant with an outside terrace. It is a broiling hot midsummer day.

As we start to get out of the car, he says he wants to take off his suit jacket, but he does not want to eat lunch wearing a shoulder holster in plain sight.

"Would you mind carrying my gun in your purse?"

I am carrying a cotton string bag, large with plenty of room. As if this happens every day, I say yes, open my purse, and he drops in the gun. I know nothing about weapons, including the fact this gun undoubtedly has a safety. As we walk into the restaurant, I began to worry about carrying a loaded weapon.

What if it goes off by accident? What if he suddenly needs it back?

It takes at least one glass of wine before I can relax. It is an extraordinary moment. Michael never trusts me as a journalist, but, at least for lunch, he trusts me as a companion.

When I arrive in Washington, I have my first chance ever to investigate a small piece of family history. After World War II, my grandfather Willis W. Bradley, Jr., a retired Navy captain and Medal of Honor recipient, was a one-term Republican Congressman from Long Beach, California. My mother keeps scrapbooks of newspaper clippings about him and still treasures his unused Congressional stationery.

Many, many Americans have served one term in the House of Representatives, but he was my grandpa, and I adored him. My mother worshipped him. She also believes men, not women, accomplish things.

Now I'm in D.C. and working for the best newspaper in the world, I want to see my grandfather's old Congressional office. How I would love to tell him my news! I look up the room number of his office in an old Congressional directory and go to the Capitol building to find it. To my disappointment, it has become a Congressional barber shop. I do not tell my mother.

Everything has changed in Washington since I was a teenager living in Northern Virginia. I never knew anything about living in the city, and now there is nothing I can afford to rent. I look at roommate ads on bulletin boards and settle on sharing a tiny Capitol Hill townhouse with an aide to an

Arizona Congressman. As soon as we move in, my roommate adds a hyperactive Irish setter to our household.

My next lesson is also difficult. I need powerful and reliable sources, but I lack the money and space to entertain at home. Big disadvantage! It's horrible to imagine such a scenario: dignitaries invited to dine on my blue Wedgewood china, *repoussé* silver, and crystal, set out with candles and linen on our wobbling card table amid the overwhelming smell of dog. Impossible.

Instead, I invite my potential sources to lunch at the city's celebrated restaurants, dim places with mahogany walls, dark red curtains, and banquettes, not dark enough to hide the lobbyists and the famous pols and not private enough for my sources. The heavy hitters are always male. In their company, I cannot pick up the bill – as the newspaper's ethics policy requires – without creating a scene. By custom, women still are not allowed to pay, any more than we can open doors for ourselves. It is not done. I am totally stressed out in these places, smiling and treading water, knowing I'll get no information.

I fare better in the little cafes with plate glass windows and tiny wooden tables and bentwood chairs that line Connecticut Avenue. Congressional staffers are glad to join me here, and they often reciprocate by inviting me to bring a sandwich to their office. Sometimes they will share a confidential document or two, and I can use a nearby copy machine because people will assume I am someone's secretary.

My favorite staffer, a man who calls bureaucrats "cockroaches," dispenses with our lunches and just calls me now and then, demanding to leak secret documents immediately. Even after I leave Washington, I regard him as a hero. But he does not last. Twenty years from now, he will tell me, "I'm tired of wearing the cheapest suit in the room." He will sell out and go to work as a lobbyist for offshore corporations.

In June 1979, I meet two former marines who helped clean up the rubble after the bombing of Nagasaki in World War II. One of them, James J. McDaniel, tells a press conference he was just twenty-four years old when he helped the marines clean up in Japan. He drove a dump truck, and "no one even mentioned radiation."

"I helped pick up metal," he recalls. "It was cold – there were puddles and frost on the ground – but the metal felt warm in my hands."

The other marine, Harry A. Coppola, also assigned to cleanup duty, was sent home from Nagasaki with constant nausea and vomiting. "You could take bricks, and they'd turn to powder," he says. "I used to kick it around, that stuff. You'd kick it, and it'd turn to dust."

Both men have bone marrow cancer they believe was caused by their exposure to residual radiation near the site. McDaniel's claim for compensation with the VA has been rejected on the grounds he cannot show his disability is service connected.

"I don't feel I want to take anything from the government," he says, "but I'm too young to retire, I can't draw Social Security, I'm getting weaker, and I'm going to need help."

Coppola says he has not been able to work for five years. His claim with the VA has also been rejected. "If I break a bone," he tells us, "I'm really in trouble."

After writing my story, I make some calls and learn the Centers for Disease Control is trying to track down others who were exposed to atomic radiation during their military service, including the 3,212 participants in Shot Smoky, a nuclear weapons test in the atmosphere in Nevada in August 1957.

The Defense Nuclear Agency, the successor to the Manhattan Project and the Armed Forces Special Weapons Project, which conducted the tests, is trying to reconstruct radiation exposure records for the troops who participated in this test and many others. Information about them has been kept secret from the American public that was also exposed to their dangers.

The truth about radiation damage to humans during the tests began to emerge when President Jimmy Carter ordered the operational records of the Atomic Energy Commission be made public a year after I arrive in Washington. Many journalists begin looking at the paper trail as documents are declassified.

The idea of an "atomic battlefield" arose from a wishful fantasy that armies could use atomic weapons in conventional warfare. In pursuit of this notion, hundreds of soldiers were marched into the Nevada desert in the 1950s to view atomic bombs detonated above ground. They wore only their uniforms and sunglasses for protection. Sailors were also ordered to watch the bombs go off on Bikini and other atolls in the Pacific. The radiation badges of most of the military participants, to the extent anyone had them, have disappeared.

At the Nevada Test Site alone, 126 atomic bombs were detonated in the atmosphere over twelve years. Each of those 126 blasts released radiation comparable to the explosion of the Soviet nuclear reactor at Chernobyl. Everyone lied about the danger. No one knows the extent of the damage.

Slowly, strange details emerge. The unexplained deaths among 14,000 sheep and other animals were caused by radiation. A cloud of radiation enveloped a Greyhound bus on its way from one unknown place to another, its passengers never identified or warned. Many local ranchers and their families became ill, as Carole Gallagher will chronicle in 1993 in *American Ground Zero; The Secret Nuclear War,* [xvi], her moving and terrifying collection of photographs and first-person accounts. But in 1978 and 1979, we are just starting to learn the truth.

Many soldiers and sailors who participated in the atomic test maneuvers are dead or terminally ill with cancer without knowing how much radiation they received or whether it made them ill. I want to hear from them or their families.

I travel to Scottsdale, Arizona to speak with Dorothy Benne, the widow of Lieutenant Colonel Louis C. Benne. He waited until the night before he died in 1978 to tell his wife he had been exposed to unexpected excessive radiation years earlier.

Colonel Benne was a World War II fighter ace, shot down in Hungary after fifty-two missions. The hospital where he was taken after the crash was bombed, and he survived. He lived through eight months in a German prison camp before escaping on a motorcycle. He was a brave, tough man. After the war, his light plane crashed with a B-25 bomber, and he was the only survivor.

At the age of fifty-six, one month after passing a rigorous flight physical, he began to bleed from cancer in his bone cells. The night before he died, he asked his wife Dorothy to bring a tape recorder to his bedside. Then, for the first time, he told her a story of being exposed to radiation while in the Pacific in 1951 for the atomic tests. A wind shift exposed him to radiation.

"When we arrived at Eniwetok, or even before we left Hawaii," he told her, "we got a briefing that said a lot of people were concerned about the roentgens that we would be exposed to on these atomic shots." At the time, the Atomic Energy Commission's permissible level was 1.3 rems a month. A rem is a unit that measures the effect on the body of one roentgen, a measure of radiation.

"The army said there was nothing to worry about because there was no doubt in their minds that five roentgens a month is nothing," Colonel Benne told his wife. "And so, they said they would make it ten. Then they said, 'Let's make it twenty – and twenty is nothing.' So, they said that 'Anyone who had twenty roentgens' exposure goes home on first boat. But we aren't going to do that. We are going to show you how few you are going to be subjected to. We are going to set it at five.'

"Well, funny thing is, blowing off, the wind shifted, and everyone got about ten to fifteen, so they had to up the roentgens to twenty on the first shot and, of course, we still had about six shots to go. So anyway, Dorothy, it was a big joke."

Hours later, Lieutenant Colonel Louis Benne died.

Dorothy Benne's claim for compensation from the Veterans Administration was rejected on the ground that her husband's radiation exposure cannot be associated with "disabilities occurring at a remote date." Hers was one of 291 radiation claims filed between 1968 and 1978. Of those, 214 were denied, half of them from cancer patients or their survivors.

The veterans are caught in a cruel numbers game. Out of any 250,000 Americans their same age, sixteen percent, or 40,000, will die of cancer. The veterans' challenge is proving excessive radiation caused their cancers. Most individual exposure records are lost, and many army personnel records were destroyed in a 1973 fire. The veterans are trying to calculate their exposure from memory, reports of troop movements, and radiation measurements that, in many cases, are still classified.

Back in Washington, I team up with a new reporter, Arthur Sulzberger, Jr., who will eventually become my publisher. We to go out to the Defense Nuclear Agency to interview the director, Vice Admiral Robert R. Monroe.

The walls of the admiral's office are lined with huge photographs, the size of those in movie theaters, showing mushroom clouds of every color and size. The admiral is proud of his work.

We are living in the era of Mutual Assured Destruction – MAD – an apt acronym for the line of reasoning that two superpowers like the United States and the Soviet Union will not be insane enough to blow each other off the face of the earth. But the admiral makes it clear to us this strategy relies on having the best and latest means of destruction. At the same time, he assures us, the armed services have taken diligent care of their soldiers, sailors, and marines and always will.

The common idea that vast numbers of veterans are dropping like flies is simply wrong, he says. "There was immense concern to avoid excessive radiation exposure. The Atomic Energy Commission had almost complete authority in these matters and set permissible levels. Troops, observers, monitors, and participants got only a tiny fraction of that."

His face is a study in indignation. "The public has the perception that people were sloppy. The facts show the opposite. There was an occasional accident. We hope to identify every one of them. A second idea is that there were massive overexposures. That's wrong. Wrong as hell. The average exposure was less than half a rem."

Notwithstanding, no one knows what individual radiation exposures were, especially in the military, where an entire platoon might have gotten one radiation badge. No one knows the names of all 100,000 participants. Too many records have disappeared.

The admiral invites us to sit down with him and watch old movies of the atomic tests, black and white films in which sailors, waving and smiling, come up on deck in suntans and short sleeves to watch the detonation of an atomic bomb. In other films, soldiers march blithely off into the desert.

The experience is shocking. It is years too late, but I still want to yell out "Stop!" to warn them before the camera pans to the searing blast emerging from the ocean or rising from the sand and expanding into a gigantic cloud like an evil genie, like the end of the world.

But everything has already happened to the veterans, and they cannot prove a thing. I am not sure what our stories can do for them.

After we see the films, we examine the troop movements plotted on the radiation maps. Where did they go afterwards? Where are they now? When I write the story, I describe the posters of mushroom clouds. I cannot bear to describe the cheerful grins on the faces of the men, nor the panic and sadness I feel on seeing them.

My story runs on the front page, previewing a hearing by the Senate Committee on Veterans Affairs that day, where the Veterans Administration promises to take another look at the several hundred claims they have rejected. They also promise to issue new guidelines to improve the handling of radiation-related claims. From now on they will take the word of a claimant that he was present at a nuclear test unless military records show otherwise.

Unlike Detroit, I have not excelled as an investigative reporter in Washington. This work is speculative, takes a huge amount of time, and can cost massive amounts of money. Often it fails. Always, it needs support from the top.

It is easier to report investigations. This is what New York keeps asking me to do. But as a newcomer, I am not well positioned to do this.

Many top journalists are competing for the same sources. If you are not known, even if you are someone from the *Times,* sources will hesitate to risk their jobs for you if they can leak to a trusted friend at the *Washington Post.* My bosses in New York can see this. After two years, I am still an outsider, both in the city and in the Washington bureau. My journalism career is on life support.

As he will tell me later, David R. Jones, the national editor in New York, decides to try to save my job by sending me out on a few writing assignments, but time is running out in Washington for me. When the Miami-Caribbean bureau becomes available, I made my pitch for it on the grounds that I speak Spanish. To my delight, Jones tells me I can try out the job for a few months, working from Washington until the Miami bureau chief is reassigned.

CHAPTER SIXTEEN:
SUGAR AND OIL

There's an elbow in my ribs, someone is pushing me from behind, and my blouse is soaked with sweat. I'm in Port-of-Spain, Trinidad, fighting my way to the ticket counter to get a seat on a commuter plane operated by Trinidad & Tobago Airways. There's no air conditioning, no line, just a mob of potential passengers. This is the kind of third world travel you can't see from the Duty Free, and I must get a ticket.

On board, I join a planeload of reporters, locals, and very few tourists. No one seems to care about seat belts, but alcohol is much in demand. During the flight, a bottle of rum makes its way up and down the aisle from hand to hand. Every time the plane takes a plunge, which is often, the locals cheer. The more they drink, the louder they yell.

It's July 1979, and I'm on my way to cover a shipwreck. Four nights ago, in heavy rain and thick fog, two of the largest ships in the world crashed, exploded, and caught fire. *The SS Atlantic Empress* was sailing from Saudi Arabia to Texas. The *Aegean Captain* was heading from Aruba to Singapore. Together, they were carrying 3.6 million barrels of oil when they collided just eighteen miles from the white beaches of Tobago, an island that lives or dies on tourism.

Rescue and recovery operations are headquartered in Tobago. There's a press office and a hotel for reporters, but the desk clerk gives me an apology when I check in. "We have a slight water problem." Shen hands me a bucket for flushing the toilet and a small box of coils resembling Fourth of July fireworks "for the mosquitoes."

Just as I wonder whether I am going to smoke or blast the mosquitoes away, I see fellow journalists stampeding past my door, shouting we're returning to the airport. The press headquarters has moved to the Hilton in Port of Spain.

At the Hilton, small groups of blackened and exhausted sailors are draped on sofas and chairs around the lobby. The last of the ships' crews, still wearing clothes from the day of the accident, are waiting for official clearance to leave the country. Most appear to be Africans, and they shrink from us. Before they are rushed out of the room, someone assures us the sailors do not speak English. In hindsight, I have my doubts. It would be worth hearing the story straight from them.

The supertankers were only six hundred yards apart in the darkness, fog and rain when they first saw each other. They were so close together and so big, they could not change course. When the bow of the *Aegean Captain* struck the side of the *SS Atlantic Empress*, it set off a giant explosion.

The captains of both vessels ordered their crews to abandon ship. Aboard the *Aegean Captain*, all but one escaped, but the crew of the *Atlantic Empress* panicked. Twenty-six jumped into the burning seas or died in the flames. The radio operator and the captain of the *Atlantic Empress* were the last to leave. The captain walked through the fire to escape, but he inhaled the flames. He was severely burned and was flown to Galveston, Texas, for treatment before I arrived.

The light crude oil carried by the *Atlantic Empress* is now on fire, billowing into the sky in giant black clouds. It is also spilling from the ship's ruined hull into the sea. We cannot see a thing from land.

The oil belongs to Mobil, so Captain Phillip Neal, a Mobil firefighter who has flown over the ship, is brought in to brief us. After a day, another huge explosion rips the *Atlantic Empress*, and UPI reports her sunk. To the consternation of my editors, I cannot confirm this, and I am relieved when UPI refloats her.

Tugs are pulling the *Atlantic Empress,* still burning, out to the open sea, while the *Aegean Captain* is towed toward Curaçao for offloading. As we await developments, government and oil company officials assure us the oil spill is dispersing into a thin sheen on the top of the water.

I will be called home before the fate of the supertankers is known. The *Aegean Captain*, travelling partly under her own steam, will head west and travel more than five hundred miles to safety in Curaçao. But the *SS Atlantic Empress* is doomed. Two weeks after the collision, amid more fires and explosions, the tugboats will finally release her. She will sink with her cargo of oil and come to rest in 14,000 feet of water, 260 miles east of Barbados and 350 miles east-northeast of Trinidad. She will be the largest ship ever to sink, as Captain Neal will report. The human cost has been enormous, but an environmental catastrophe has been postponed. No one knows if it will ever take place.

While I am waiting for the drama to play out at sea, I can see a huge transformation going on around me in Trinidad, where the oil was discovered four years ago. Sugar has long ruled the Caribbean – the Dominican poet Pedro Mir once described these islands as an "unlikely archipelago of sugar and of alcohol" – but you can now add oil.

Sugar was king for centuries. The natives of the islands died quickly on plantations. To replace them, thousands of people were kidnapped from Africa and enslaved to work and die in the fields.

Slavery is gone, but the plantations remain. Sugar is still the main cash crop on most islands, and many have quit growing enough local food to eat. The descendants of the slaves are free, but most are desperately poor. They own little land, except on three islands: Cuba, where the state holds the land in their name; Haiti, so populous the land is worthless; and Puerto Rico, where agriculture has vanished.

Now, the region is in a crisis. The price of oil is up, and the price of sugar is down. Most Caribbean nations cannot buy enough oil to produce their sugar crops, keep the lights on, and buy food.

Only three places are getting by. Cuba has a $3 billion annual subsidy from the Russians. Puerto Rico is living on U. S. Food Stamps. And Trinidad and Tobago, situated near Venezuela, has found oil. It's drowning in oil money, a bonanza and a migraine.

I'm not talking about the oil now threatening the beaches and the tourist trade – that is a catastrophe in itself – but the new social problems wealth creates. Trinidad cannot accommodate everything its newly wealthy society suddenly demands. Roads. Water pipes. Telephone service.

Overnight, there are five times as many cars, even though most people do not own a car. Drivers compete in traffic with carts pulled by water buffalo. Automobile accidents have skyrocketed.

Even the rich do not have running water at home yet. I watch a Mercedes pull up to a public standpipe in search of drinking water. They fill up a carload of plastic jugs.

The telephone service has collapsed. In these days before the advent of cellphones, almost no one has a home phone that works. The spokesman for the telephone company tells me his phone is out of order, and the Prime Minister tells the newspapers he feels like throwing his phone into the sea.

I have a telephone on the table next to the bed in my room at the Hilton, so I try to call my office in New York. When I fail, the hotel operator advises me to book my international calls at the telephone office downtown. When I go there, I sign in, and the clerk tells me to take a chair. I will need to wait my turn in a private booth.

Sometimes the wait is minutes; sometimes, hours. Calling in a story on deadline is impossible. Talking to editors is difficult. As a newcomer to foreign reporting, I am unaware that telex, not the telephone, is the way to communicate. This failing on my part brings me luck.

One morning, waiting in the telephone office, I pick up a local newspaper and read that the Welsh Arts Council has just awarded its National Writer's Prize for international achievement in literature to a poet from Trinidad. I buy one of his books on my way back to the hotel.

His name is Derek Walcott. His poetry is stunning in its beauty and so acute that it puts me in the exact center of the tropical contradiction that is Trinidad. I ask around and find that he lives at a nearby hotel. I call him from my hotel room and, miraculously, get him on the line.

"When you called," he says in greeting me, "I thought it was a joke."

Walcott is forty-nine years old, moving past middle age and looking thin and worn.

He is working on a song for a musical, and his office is two chairs outside his room in a dismal hotel where he's living while getting a second divorce.

"I start writing at five in the morning," he tells me. It's too early for the hotel restaurant, so he mixes instant coffee with hot water from the sink. At mid-morning, he is working on a bad case of nerves, so we adjourn to my room at the Hilton and sit on the balcony overlooking a green savannah.

We sit, and Walcott lights a cigarette. I open my notebook as he starts talking about his work and his life: the difficulty of being a Caribbean poet who can't earn a living here, who is not appreciated by the people who are the heart of his work. Money is plentiful, but patrons are scarce.

"While the wealth of this country grows, the coarseness and the vulgarity of the people who have the wealth also increases, like any boom town," he says.

CHAPTER SEVENTEEN:
THE HEART OF THE STORM

I meet the Dominican historian Frank Moya Pons shortly after my stop in Trinidad and Tobago. He says he can sum up his country's history in two words, "poverty" and "violence." It started with Columbus, who encountered 400,000 Indigenous people when he landed on Hispaniola, the island that includes the Dominican Republic and Haiti. After thirty years, all the native people were dead.

The early Spanish settlers were so poor they celebrated mass at 3 a.m. so no one could see their rags in daylight. After centuries of colonial and neocolonial rule by dictators who used murder, torture, and terror – and once the help of 15,000 U.S. Marines--to stay in office – it is 1979. Poverty persists. Three-fourths of all Dominican children are malnourished.

The whole country is living off one cash crop: sugar. An American corporation, Gulf and Western, owns one fifth of the country's land. A few Dominican families and the government own the rest.

The good news is that the Dominicans have elected a president who has managed to stay in office for a year. The sad news is the collapse of the world price of sugar and the soaring price of oil.

"We could just sit down and start crying," the governor of the Central Bank tells me, "but we are a country with a lot of potential." What he doesn't know – and neither do I, as I file a story and leave Santo Domingo – is that things are about to get worse.

Jeff Gerth, my colleague at the Washington Bureau of *The New York Times*, calls me at my hotel in Miami and asks me to return to Santo Domingo to pick up documents for an investigation he's doing. Earlier, Jeff and I wrote about a lawsuit the Securities and Exchange Commission was preparing against Gulf and Western in connection with the Dominican Republic.

I agree to go get the documents. There is no Weather Channel, no ubiquitous 24-hour weather news, so I do not know two hurricanes are also on the way. I arrive hours ahead of Hurricane David and check into the Hotel Santo Domingo, overlooking the ocean and downtown. By the time I learn the storm is coming, the airport is closed.

As a child, I lived through a hurricane in Puerto Rico – we just shut the louvers that served for windows and hunkered down – and no one at the hotel seems very worried. I don't see anyone boarding up windows. I pick up the documents for Jeff Gerth. Then I buy a flashlight and new batteries for the small portable radio I take everywhere. I go back to my room, run water in the bathtub, draw the curtains, and prepare to wait things out.

The hurricane strikes at night. After the power goes off, I curl up in bed and listen to my little radio as the wind howls around the building. I'm on a high floor. I start to worry when the large windows begin bulging in and out. Then someone knocks on my door. It's a hotel employee with a flashlight, beckoning me to come with him.

"*En seguida, por favor*. Right away, please."

He leads me down dark flights of stairs that have become water slides until we reach the lobby, now standing wide open to the outdoors. I follow him through heavy plate glass doors into a restaurant that faces the registration desk in the lobby.

The restaurant is a room with no outside windows. Other hotel guests, including a Japanese movie crew, have crawled under the tables. I get on my hands and knees and join them. For hours, we look out through the glass doors as palm trees, bushes, and other debris fly through the lobby like props from the *Wizard of Oz*.

By dawn, the storm is over, and we creep out of the restaurant and over the junk in the lobby toward the front desk, covered with debris. From underneath, a phone rings. Just once. Someone digs it out. It's the *Times*, calling for me from New York. Before I can get on the line, the phone dies, and all the telephones are dead after that. To communicate with the States, I can try telex, the others tell me. The Western Union office may have emergency power.

No journalists are arriving – the airport is closed – and the only American journalist I encounter is from the tabloid *National Enquirer*. He tells me his sole assignment is to learn if a famous Siamese twin, separated from her sister at birth in a rare operation in Philadelphia six years ago, is still alive. Her sister died in an accident at the age of three, and the family's home in the Dominican Republic was right in the path of this hurricane. The *Enquirer* reporter leaves to find the twin, who is later reported alive. I go out to see about the rest of the Dominicans, many of whom are not as lucky.

Every block is a spiderweb of downed electrical wires. The power was turned off before the storm struck, and it will stay off for days. The hurricane has smashed windows and buildings, shredded signs and awnings, and pulled up stately trees like turnips. Great rocks and pieces of cement hurled by wind and sea litter streets and lawns.

I've got no car. How am I going to find the Western Union office?

By luck, I see a man in an empty taxi, flag him down, and beg him to take me to Western Union, explaining that I am an American journalist, and my story about the hurricane may bring aid to his country, Luckily, I also have a lot of cash, and that persuades him. We make our way through a maze of streets running with water, changing course with every blockade of downed trees and power lines. Miraculously, Western Union has emergency power, and I send my story to New York by telex for the first time.

The radio is reporting major rivers are flooding, and bridges are torn apart in the countryside. Helicopters begin picking people off rooftops. I want to see, but so many roads are closed, it would be impossible to travel by car, even if I could find one.

Then I hear the American military will be taking medical aid and supplies to stranded areas by helicopter from a local airport, and I find a seat on a *público* that is going there. A *público* is a cross between a taxi and a bus on which people and animals sit in crowded conditions – imagine a clown car with chickens at a circus. With a little extra persuasion, it gets me there.

At the airport, I find the officer in charge of the supplies going out on Navy Sea Stallion helicopters. Their huge size is reassuring because the weather is still rainy and terrible. The officer tells me there's a waiting list. I can get my name on it and hope for a seat. He writes my name down, and I wait.

Load after load goes out until the day ends, and I sit and wait. The next day, when I return, more reporters have arrived from the States and are trying to get on the list. My name is at the top. The officer tells them they have no chance of making the trip. I am the only likely passenger.

After several hours, when I am finally seated on board, the other reporters give up and leave. Just before takeoff, however, a senior officer arrives, sees me, and orders me off the helicopter.

No! I've waited too long for this! It's not fair! I won't get off!

"I work for *The New York Times*," I tell him, "and I have been waiting here for two days."

"I don't care who the hell you work for," he snaps. "You're not coming. Get out of here."

Slowly, I get off.

My friend from *TIME* magazine, Bernard Diedrich, has stuck around, hoping to get on with me at the last minute. After I am ejected, he suggests driving his car – Bernie always manages to produce a car – and trying to drive into the flooded areas.

We spend hours trying to get a look at the drowned parts of the country but, as we have been warned, they are inaccessible. After dark, we return to our hotel and walk into the bar. The reporters there meet us with shocked faces.

"You're alive!" they say to me.

"Yes. So?"

The helicopter I boarded crashed and burned while returning to its base at the airport. Three people were killed, and three others were critically injured. My colleagues assumed I was among them, as I had not returned. U.S. Embassy officials, confused about the number of people on board, has not released names. Luckily for my family, no one has reported my death. [xvii]

I spend the night in a stupor, unable to comprehend the chain of events that both infuriated me and saved my life.

It is part of the great unknown in which we all live.

I now believe the angel who rescued me as a baby toddling through a moving train intervened again for reasons unknown to me. Whatever those reasons, I am thankful.

Still, I hesitate the next day when a Dominican journalist, a friend of mine who has heard of my narrow escape, offers me a seat in a helicopter owned by his newspaper They are flying out to talk to people and survey the damage. Then I say yes because I am there to cover the story, and this is what journalists do.

His private helicopter is a small, flimsy looking craft, compared to the Sea Stallion, but it putters steadily through the rain toward the interior of the island. The death toll has risen to one thousand, and more than 100,000 are homeless. The storm brought wind, rain, floods, and landslides. Thousands of Dominicans have only broken trees to shelter them from the relentless rain.

Dark flood waters cover the land, and drinking water has disappeared. Dominican mothers, like others in the third world, have been enticed to give their infants powdered formula instead of nursing them. With no clean water for mixing formula, the babies are screaming with hunger, and their frantic mothers have dried up. The authorities suggest making the contaminated water safe by boiling it, but no one has electricity to heat water or any fuel to burn.

As families run out of food, armed police guard truckloads of plantains, trying to make sure they are distributed, not grabbed up for resale. A few days ago, a group of hungry people with leprosy attacked a truck carrying food and mattresses, not knowing it was destined for their colony at Nigua, south of the capital.

In the mountains west and north of San Cristobal, one of the cities hardest hit by Hurricane David, I see hundreds of people living in caves. They have even installed a small chapel in one of them. With life in danger, it is important to safeguard the life of the spirit and the appearance of normalcy.

When I walk up to a woman in San Cristobal, she fishes into a mountain of shattered furniture, pulls out a chair, and insists I sit down and be comfortable. I come upon another woman ironing a pair of slacks with a cold iron plugged into a socket with no electricity. "It doesn't work," she concedes, "but it makes me feel better about things this way."

The pair of sandals I took for my overnight stay in Santo Domingo have been dissolving in the rain. The mud pulls the straps to pieces I tie back together. The stores are closed, and the power is still out in our hotel. I have not been able to change clothes or bathe for days. The first drops of the next hurricane, Frederic, are beginning to fall.

Back at the hotel, I find my *New York Times* colleague and friend Rich Meislin. He arrived when the airport reopened. Rich gets a bottle of Irish whiskey from his suitcase, pours me a drink, and insists I take the plane home to Miami before Frederic closes the airport again.

I thank him profusely and check out. As my flight takes off, I feel overwhelmed I have survived Hurricane David and death by helicopter. At the same time, I feel guilty because I am leaving thousands of people to face another hurricane with no safe place to go.

My relief ebbs away, but the sense of guilt lingers. Over the years, the suffering of others will cast a shadow over my soul. The only forgiveness I can offer myself is my belief that someone must be a witness and tell the truth. This is my life's work.

CHAPTER EIGHTEEN:
CHASING THE SHAH

In January 1979, the Shah of Iran was deposed from the Peacock Throne. It happened far away from me, and I paid no attention.

The Shah's enemies expected him to head straight for his friends and allies in the United States. Instead, he began a long odyssey of rejection around the world, starting in Egypt, where he was not wanted. He then sojourned in Morocco, made a stopover in the Bahamas, and then lingered in Mexico, growing increasingly ill.

At the urging of some of the Shah's powerful friends, American doctors came to examine him and recommended he be allowed to enter the United States on humanitarian grounds for medical care. On October 22, 1979, the Shah was quietly admitted to the New York Hospital-Cornell Medical Center. Iranian leaders were astonished and enraged.

The Iranian Prime Minister Mehdi Barzargan did not believe the illness explanation, and his government eventually fell because of the Shah's entry into the United States. On November 1, Ayatollah Ruhollah Khomeini made a radio appeal to students to "expand with all their might their attacks against the United States and Israel, so they may force the United States to return the despised and cruel Shah."

On November 4, mobs responded by storming the American embassy in Tehran. They took fifty American diplomats and citizens hostage and held them captive. In total, they will be detained for 444 days.

Before the Shah left Iran, his oldest son, Crown Prince Reza Pahlavi, came to live in Lubbock, a town in west Texas. He arrived in the summer of 1978, when he was eighteen years old, to train as a jet pilot with the U.S. Air Force. His sisters and a brother joined him in January 1979, when their father left Iran.

Bill Stevens, the *Times* correspondent based in Houston, went to the house several times, doing his best to interview the family. Stevens is an artful and dogged *Times* veteran. He was the reporter with the beard and the tee shirt that I saw outside the Mack Avenue stamping plant during the auto talks in Detroit. He was the *Times* bureau chief there.

The Shah's arrival in the United States and the subsequent hostage taking enraged many Americans. On Dec. 2, the Shah left the spotlight in New York, flying to Texas for treatment at Wilford Hall, the major Air Force medical facility near San Antonio. Again, Bill Stevens was on top of the story for the *Times*.

Until he was not. The Shah has left for Panama, and Stevens has no passport.

I'm in a Miami hotel when the phone rings in the middle of the night. It's the foreign desk. The Shah has left the country, Stevens can't follow, and I am the closest reporter with a passport. I get on the plane for Panama City. Once I arrive, I have no idea where to find the Shah.

The Panama City airport is a sweaty mass of busy people, milling around. I grab a taxi and ask to go to the American Embassy, hoping to get a lead on the Shah. The driver looks at me.

"*¿Periodista?*" Are you a reporter?

"*Sí.*"

"*¿Ud. no quiere ir con los otros?* You don't want to go with the others?"

"*¿Dónde?*" I ask, "Where?" I am frantic to know where other members of the press are. They are surely tailing the Shah.

"Contadora."

¿Dónde está? Where is it?

"*Isla.*" An island.

Bad news. You must fly there.

"*Aeropuerto!*" I yell, whirling my arms backwards like a windmill. Let's go back! We reverse course through the hot traffic.

A ticket. Oh, where do I get a ticket?

Flights to the island go on a small commuter airline, and the agent tells me I am in luck.

"This is the last flight. They're closing the island. The President and the General are there. So are all the reporters. *El Shah. Conferencia de prensa hoy.*"

A press conference today! I'm late! I'm too late! Now I feel like the White Rabbit in *Alice in Wonderland.*

I am the only journalist on the little plane. When it lands, I bolt from the terminal, hop in a taxi, and beg the driver to take me to the press conference as fast as he can. He knows the place, a seaside villa, the home of an industrialist, a former ambassador to the United States.

On the lawn, I can see journalists crowded together, cameras and recording equipment bobbing in a forest of heads and shoulders. Around them is a cordon of heavily armed Panamanian National Guardsmen. I run to them and twist my way in, slipping through the bodies and arms of the journalists. I am stopped by a human wall of enormous bodyguards planted shoulder to shoulder around the speakers. I cannot see through them, and I am too short to see over them. I hop up and down, but it is useless. I have come so far, and I can't see the Shah.

The press conference has just begun. The Shah is introduced, along with his wife, Empress Farah, and the President of Panama, Aristides Royo. Fortunately, I can hear them.

The Panamanian President says he knows it's risky to host the Shah, but he hopes that taking him in will be seen as an effort to foster peace between Iran and the United States. He does not explain why Panama, which has helped national liberation movements in places like Nicaragua, would help a dictator like the Shah. "Panama is not an enemy of the people of Iran," he says. It is helping the Shah as a "person who has certain problems."

The Shah speaks for just three minutes. He thanks Panama for its hospitality and says he hopes his departure from the United States will encourage Iran to release the American hostages.

In a flash, the press conference is over. The great herd of reporters, photographers, and camera crews disperses, rushing to file our stories at a nearby resort hotel. We arrive to find all communications from the island cut off: telex as well as telephone. Then we learn that the airport is closed until further notice. We cannot leave the island to file our stories or photographs.

Hotel security tells us their hands are tied: government orders. It is one of those fiascos where the official in charge of public relations is not talking to the official in charge of security. Frustrated, most of us go back outdoors, trying to figure out what to do next. There are no taxis in sight.

I decide to walk back to the airport. A few yards from the hotel, a private car comes along the road, and I wave it over and get in. The driver, a local man, knows the way to the airport, but he is very drunk. When the airport comes into view, I ask him to stop, and I get out. This is a wise move because my companion drives into a ditch shortly afterwards.

The airport is empty except for a few security guards inside and some peacocks on the runway. As I approach the guards, I decide on something I've seen my male colleagues do successfully, but never tried myself. I pitch a temper tantrum.

I tell them I work for *The New York Times* and have an extremely important story for the entire world! The stupidity of someone in security means that the wisdom of their President and generosity of their government will not be understood outside the tiny island of Contadora because no one can tell that story!

"I need to get to Panama City now to send my story to New York so the world can read it. If I can't, your government will be extremely upset! Someone needs to help me right away!"

The angrier I pretend to be, the angrier I get, and then I flounce over to an empty bench and sit down. There isn't much more I can do.

After about twenty minutes, a soldier walks in and beckons me.

"The general says your plane is ready."

He must be joking, but I follow him out to the runway, and a small National Guard plane is waiting for me. It flies me back to Panama City, where I go to a hotel, check in, and file the only story that gets out of Contadora Island for hours.

After reading it, a copy editor calls me.

"How did the Shah look?"

Everyone wants to know whether the Shah is ill or faked his illness to gain admission to the United States. Journalists have not seen him since he entered the United States.

"I couldn't see him," I admit. "I was too short."

Before publication of the final edition, the Associated Press manages to send a photograph of the Shah seated at the press conference. He's smiling, looking happy but frail. He is wearing a blue open-necked shirt and a pair of dark slacks.

The photo appears at the top of our front page, next to another reporter's story in which the Iranian Foreign Minister Sadegh Ghotbzadeh hails the Shah's flight from the U.S. as a victory for Iran.

I never knew which general sent the plane for me. General Omar Torrijos, head of Panama's National Guard, who met privately with the Shah before the press conference, or General Manuel Noriega, the strongman who later took over Panama. He was in command of security on Contadora.

The colleagues I left behind on the island started to worry after the drunk driver and his car were found in a ditch, and I was missing. For a time, they had the Panamanian National Guard out looking for me. When they learn the truth, that I took a plane back to Panama City and filed a story before they could, they are not happy.

I stay in Panama the next day to cover loud street protests that General Torrijos is "a man of the Pentagon" and to wait for Alan Riding, the *Times's* Latin American correspondent, who arrives shortly and takes time to walk me through the jungle to see the Panama Canal.

That morning or the next, one of the local newspapers features a large photograph of the biggest boa constrictor I have ever seen, captured in what I hope was some other place in the jungle. The snake is so heavy and long it takes a line of five or six men to hold it up in the air. It is big news.

I leave Panama with a huge sense of relief, as I know nothing about the place and do not care for snakes.

CHAPTER NINETEEN:
HELLO, HAVANA

I look at Miami differently this time as my flight approaches. It will be home, not just a place to change planes. Its downtown has low white buildings facing a blue harbor with cruise ships, marinas, and islands. Still to come are the glass towers that will dominate the skyline, some of them condominiums that will serve as safety deposit boxes for the drug trade, now in its infancy here. A few will be ghostly, with no residents, the only noise coming from the packed discos on the ground floor.

When I first arrive, the airport resembles a giant mall. Passengers head for ticket counters with appliances they hope to check as luggage, not cargo. Most are television sets or smaller, but here or there I see a stove or washing machine. I am astounded to hear as much Spanish as English. Hello, Miami. I have come to Latin America to live.

Eleanor Sherman, the *Times* office manager, is waiting with my new company car, a disappointing dark green sedan that looks like a standard issue vehicle for the police or FBI. I am consoled by our drive out to my new apartment in Key Biscayne. We soar over the blue water on the Rickenbacker Causeway, which includes a drawbridge, often open to sailboats. Who, other than a journalist, would fret about delays?

Aunt Mary, who is Eleanor's great aunt and my benefactor, has located a condominium to rent in her building, furnished down to the potholders. All I need is my toothbrush. The place has two bedrooms and plenty of space for my few pieces of furniture and all my books. The low building has a fountain. The sound of splashing water follows us up the stairway to the second floor.

It's winter, the weather is fine, and the air conditioning is turned off. As I open the apartment door, an ocean breeze from a screened-in porch ruffles my hair. The living room is dark, with peach wall to wall carpeting and white French provincial furniture. Not my style, but who cares? The salt air welcomes me. I am going to live one block from the beach and the Atlantic Ocean. Paradise.

"Just drop your things," says Eleanor, a woman passing through middle age at a rapid clip and a veteran journalist herself. She and her husband Fred, a journalist with the *Miami Herald*, bought a house on the Key years ago, before prices skyrocketed during the Nixon Administration. "You'll love the *Times* office."

It's on a high floor of the tallest building downtown, overlooking a marina filled with boats and birds. Now and then, a pelican will make a spectacular dive past one of our office windows. I could spend hours looking at the view, but I don't get even a few minutes. Before I can say more than hello to the other people in the office, the foreign desk is calling from New York, telling me I need to get to Cuba. I have a visa for a press conference with Fidel Castro in Havana. There are no direct flights from Miami. I don't see how I can get there on time.

Eleanor picks up the phone and calls the television networks. NBC has a charter going from Fort Lauderdale. I drive north on Interstate 95 and make it to the private terminal before the press plane takes off. The network has leased an old DC-3 once owned by a Prince of Denmark, something out of an old Alfred Hitchcock movie. A crew from CBS and several other print reporters are already on board, and I am thankful to join them.

"Fidel's Follies," cracks Bernard Diedrich. He's the journalist from TIME magazine I met after the hurricane in the Dominican Republic. Our visas are good for twenty-four hours. We'll have to leave as soon as the press conference is over – no time to talk to anyone or look around. The Cold War is still underway, but relations between the United States and Cuba have thawed under President Jimmy Carter enough to crack the door open to journalists. The opening, however, is not very wide.

As soon as we disembark and walk into a shaded arrivals area, trays of frozen lime daiquiris arrive, loaded with Havana Club, Cuban rum. They are delicious. It's raining, but the heat is suffocating, and the drinks are oh so cold and welcome.

The TV crews take large cases full of equipment off the airplane. The Cubans ask them to unpack each one. There are mountains of stuff. We wait as the Cubans inspect and list every item, down to the last lens and gizmo. As we wait, we drink more daiquiris. By the time a bus arrives to take us to the press conference, I am so mellow I have forgiven the delay.

But as I am getting off the bus, I slip on the step and catch myself against the muddy side of the bus. It's my nerves, perhaps giddiness from the daiquiris. A large brown stain appears on the front of my white dress. It's raw silk. I have no way to clean it off.

When Fidel Castro appears, I've seen so many photographs of him that he seems familiar in person. The same dark beard, same army uniform. Although the press conference is for Americans, Castro speaks in Spanish, and I am surprised he believes we will all understand him. He uses the press conference to accuse President Carter of being unduly suspicious of him.

As part of the Cold War, American surveillance photographs recently revealed the presence of a Russian military brigade in Cuba. It has a rocket battalion, a tank battalion, and two infantry battalions – totaling 2,300 to 3,000 men.

"What does the United States have to do with those personnel moving about?" asks Castro, ignoring years of enmity. "They are subordinate to our armed forces. What you call a brigade, we call a training center. We do not constitute the slightest threat to the United States."

When I return to Havana on my own, in April 1980, people recognize me on the street, even though months have passed. The video of Castro's press conference has been replayed repeatedly on Cuban television, and there I am, muddy dress and all.

The Cuban government books me into the Hotel Capri, a high rise reserved for journalists and official guests. It is a

1950s building, a former casino kept ice cold with air conditioning. The bathroom toilet has no seat. Except for embassies, I never see a toilet seat in Cuba. They are considered an unnecessary luxury.

I think my hotel room must be bugged because it is searched regularly. After it has been cleaned, I return to find small items moved, not in any frightening way but just enough to keep me on my toes. I worry about hidden cameras. I do not invite anyone to my room. Later, I learn such an invitation is illegal. Cuba was once the brothel of the Caribbean. The ban on visitors has not stopped prostitution, but it does keep me from inviting sources, friends, or lovers to my room. As time passes, I will meet them elsewhere.

Every foreign journalist is assigned a minder, a government official who says he or she is with Cuban Foreign Affairs but works instead for the Ministry of the Interior, or Cuban Intelligence. My minder is Rosa Maria Abierno, a bottle blonde like me. She wears red lipstick, a status symbol in a country where most women can't buy cosmetics. Her haircut is short and jazzy.

"Yo," she says when we are introduced. In Spanish, the letter "J" is silent, and "Ho," the Spanish pronunciation, doesn't work for her or any other Cuban I meet.

"Yo! You don't wear makeup!" She scolds me when she gets to know me. "And your *clothes!*"

I don't bother with lipstick, and I've brought cotton shirts and trousers and a couple of lightweight cotton dresses that make me stand out on the street. Cuban women make do with hot, ugly synthetic fabrics in terrible colors from Eastern bloc countries. The women look beautiful anyway because they are naturally gorgeous and dress as scantily as possible. For work or school, they wear uniforms.

Rosa is my own personal government spy watchdog. I try to hide my resentment that I cannot move around freely – we have a driver – and I try to make use of what she offers by asking her to arrange official interviews. Some people speak with me. Others refuse. Rosa always sits nearby, and no one speaks candidly. After a couple of days, I ask for a break. She is relieved.

I want to speak with ordinary Cubans about daily life here, but every block has a Committee for the Defense of the Revolution, gossips on steroids! They spy on every detail of their neighbors' lives and report anything suspicious to the police – church attendance, a possible gay dalliance, something odd in a shopping bag. I do not want to get people in trouble.

I walk around Vedado, a decrepit but still lovely downtown neighborhood where pre-revolutionary mansions have been cut into offices and apartments. Mildew and grime blanket the walls because paint is almost impossible to find. Tropical greenery breaks up the sidewalks and reaches over the lawns. People grow flowers in old tin cans on steps, balconies, and porches.

At the end of one block, I can see women standing in line, and I join them. We make small talk, but I look too foreign, too different to start a conversation. As we turn the corner, I realize we are waiting for our turn in a beauty salon. Too soon, I am holding an empty notebook and sitting in a chair in a room where the main smells are burning hair and harsh chemicals. I've just had my own hair done in Miami.

"*Sí?*" the hairdresser asks.

"Uh. Uh…" My mind goes blank. "*Champu.*" She gives my hair a good scrubbing. Afterwards, she combs my hair into rollers and puts me under an old-fashioned hair dryer. That hasn't happened in years.

Strolling out of the shop, I meet a young couple and strike up a conversation because, luckily, they are from Mexico, not Cuba. He's a veterinarian, and his family owned a farm in Mexico where Fidel visited before the Cuban revolution.

After a while, they invite me home with them, and we pile into their ancient VW Beetle for a trip downtown to their apartment and coffee. For a few hours, it almost feels like a normal afternoon.

CHAPTER TWENTY:
THE PERUVIAN EMBASSY

The next day is Good Friday, April 4, and I hear something is happening at the Peruvian embassy. It's a long way from my hotel. In Havana, taxis are called *los incapturables* for good reason. You cannot get one. I have no car, no chance of renting one. I do not want to call Rosa.

In my purse, I have a telephone number for the veterinarian and his wife. I call them and ask if he can give me a ride out to the Peruvian embassy. To my surprise, he says yes. We drive to Miramar, a fancy neighborhood, past the construction site of a huge new Soviet embassy. The Peruvian embassy faces Avenida Quinta, a main traffic thoroughfare. The treetops in the median are clipped into geometric shapes: cylinders, hemispheres, and cones.

A fence with locked gates surrounds the Peruvian embassy, but there are no guards, and I can see people climbing over the fence. On the other side, men are milling around on the embassy lawn, and more people are standing in the gardens. I get out of the car, walk to the fence, and climb over.

The people inside are excited, but after I introduce myself, many are afraid to talk with me. A few say they have come alone to seek asylum with only the clothes they are wearing. Several adults have children with them. Eventually, I locate the Peruvian chargé d'affaires. He is reticent. "The situation is under consideration at the highest levels in Lima," he says. Nothing more.

As it turns out, six Cubans seeking asylum crashed a city bus through the embassy's gates three days ago, on Tuesday, April 1. One of the Cuban guards fired a bullet that ricocheted and killed another guard. It was the second attempt in five days to crash a bus into the embassy. The first try failed. After the second, the Cuban government placed guards with machine guns at the embassy gates and rolled giant boulders onto the driveway.

Latin American nations have a generous tradition of granting asylum, so the Peruvians already have twenty-five asylum seekers living in their embassy. The Venezuelan embassy has fifteen, and the Argentine embassy has one.

The Peruvian and Venezuelan embassies have been targets for break-ins with large vehicles because they are the only Latin American embassies on Avenida Quinta, a major street where a truck or bus can get up enough speed to crash through a gate. Cuba refuses to give safe conduct to anyone who enters an embassy by force. The Peruvian ambassador has been reprimanded and recalled to Lima for agreeing with the Cubans on this point.

Today the Cuban government has withdrawn its armed guards and removed the boulders, announcing on the front page of the official communist party newspaper *Granma*: "We cannot protect embassies that do not cooperate in their own protection."

When I arrive in the late afternoon, forty-three Cuban adults and three children have made their way into the gardens of the Peruvian embassy. In the next twenty-four hours, two thousand more people will turn up. There is no food, water, medicine, or sanitation.

Fidel Castro drives by the embassy twice this first night. Some of the asylum seekers are still fond of him. "I wish he could come inside," I hear one woman say. "He could see how happy we are."

Castro seems to be everywhere. When I leave my room at the Capri Hotel at six the next morning, I am surprised to find the dark and silent lobby filled with shadows who turn out to be soldiers and police. Cups of coffee are set out on the front desk, and members of the hotel staff stand at the door. A large black limousine idles in the driveway. Someone asks me to wait to leave the building.

The elevator doors open, and Castro walks out, accompanied by other men. Offstage, he is still dressed in his signature fatigues and cap, a tall, powerful figure who dwarfs his companions. I am surprised to hear a hotel employee fretting about him afterwards.

"Fidel has been working night and day. I'm worried about him. He's losing weight."

It is hard to find a ride to the Peruvian embassy today. I end up joining a group of Latin American reporters who persuade Pepe, a driver assigned to chauffeur a group of Russians around Havana, to drive us to the embassy after dropping off his charges.

Pepe spends the long trip to Miramar ridiculing and criticizing the Cubans seeking asylum. He says the Cuban government has confirmed they are parasites and scum. When our group finishes our interviews and looks for Pepe, he and the car are gone. Later, I find Pepe among the asylum seekers. Joining them seemed like a clever idea, he tells me.

The police let anyone enter the embassy grounds, but early in the afternoon, Cuban officials begin urging people to leave. In view of the overcrowding, they offer safe conduct passes for anyone who wants to go home and return to the embassy. Also, anyone who has not entered the embassy by force is free to leave Cuba if another country will give them a visa. Shouts of *"Libertad! Libertad!"* greet these announcements, but the people on the lawn say they are afraid to leave.

I'm standing outside the fence, where it's mass confusion. Some people around me are shouting for their relatives. Others are just shouting abuse at those inside. *"Parásitos!"* and *"Escoria!"* "Scum!"

A baby is crying. I look down and see a tiny girl crawling on the ground, alone among the shuffling feet. I retrieve her, a toddler, wet with tears and sweat. She clings to my neck as I edge closer to the fence, trying to shield her and looking for anyone who may have lost her.

Amid the yelling, her frantic parents call louder than anyone else. They arrive in a matter of minutes. When they see her, they begin laughing and crying at the same time. I'm not strong enough to lift her over the top of the fence, so I grab at the sleeves of some of the men who have been hurling insults.

"I have found a lost child!" I say in Spanish. "Her parents are right here! Please help me give her back to her mother!"

I don't know why I expect them to help people they hate, but they do. Gently, we raise the child up and over, headfirst, to her parents. The people around us send up a cheer. I can still see those little feet going over the top.

The Cuban government seals off the embassy after the third day, when the crowd reaches ten thousand people. Some of them accept safe conduct passes to go home, and the government agrees to help the rest, who include three thousand children. The grounds have become a sea of excrement and mud, and they need food, water, medicine, and sanitary facilities.

Some of those bringing help to the asylum seekers – the drivers of an ambulance, a water truck – decide to stay and join them. They elect their own leaders, including a surgeon, a law student, and a car thief. Among those I meet inside are political prisoners – no surprise – several performers from the Tropicana night club, and a composer.

As the police tighten their cordon, a man in a stolen taxi crashes through the police barricade, drawing a burst of gunfire that injures a seven-year-old child and two adults inside the compound. That same day, April 9, I decide to investigate rumors that many Cubans coming from far away to seek asylum have been arrested and others have been beaten by mobs. I go searching for them.

In the lobby of a small hotel in old Havana, I meet a woman in her thirties who tells me her plans to enter the Peruvian embassy failed. She agrees to speak with me privately, but she is frightened as she leads me up a dark and filthy flight of marble stairs to her airy, spotless hotel room.

Huddled together on the bed are her children and another family, a mother and three children who also made the twenty-two-hour journey by train from Oriente Province in the hope of getting asylum in the Peruvian embassy and likewise failed.

The first woman brought her children, nine and ten years old, to Havana for reasons of faith and ambition. "I am a Roman Catholic," she explains. "I want my children to believe." She had an office job as a comptroller, "but I can't show I believe in God. It is considered counterrevolutionary." I decided to come to Havana to seek asylum so I could do the work for which I am qualified."

On the way to the embassy, she says, the police detained her and the children at 84th Street and took them to a police station. A mob was waiting out front, armed with electrical cables. "They beat me on the head. They beat the children, too. The police did nothing."

The beatings aren't the worst of it. "The police let me go, but they took my identification card. They will show this at my job. I will lose my job. I have no hope."

The other woman in the room has just lost her husband. He was twice a political prisoner, and they lived with anxiety and poverty. They arrived in Havana with their three children at ten o'clock in the morning the day before.

"We borrowed a car to see what chances there were at the embassy. Several blocks away, they stopped us, put us in two police cars and took us to the station. My husband was taken prisoner. I went today to ask about him, and the officer said he couldn't say. He said there were four thousand being taken to the Combinado del Este prison by train.

"People are shouting in the street for their husbands and their sons. They are saying that there is a Peruvian pavilion at the prison."

The women's grief is terrible. I have the sensation of being back on that bus in Cincinnati fourteen years ago with Mary, the woman who can't see, has no glasses, and will lose her job sorting mail. I don't know how to comfort or help these women either, but I leave the hotel determined to tell their stories and to find out what is happening to others like them.

As I walk through the city, I can see slogans posted on the windows of homes and buses and painted on banners strung across the way. "Let the Scum Go!" "Get the Parasites Out!" "Let the Delinquents Leave!"

A scraggly man recognizes me and asks me to stop. "*¿Es usted periodista Norteamericana?*" "Are you an American journalist?" His cultured accent is a surprise, as is his use of the formal form of "you," rather than the familiar *tu* in universal use, regardless of rank, in Cuba.

When I say yes, he introduces himself as a former university professor. He has lost his job after ten years of teaching and works as a manual laborer to avoid being convicted of *peligrosidad* or dangerousness. Then he inquires, hesitantly, if I have been to the Peruvian Embassy and if those inside are truly scum.

"My daughter is with them," he says before I can answer. "She is fourteen."

I do my best to reassure him.

This afternoon I can still slip through the police barricade and into the embassy compound to check on the fast-deteriorating situation there. Just after I climb back out over the fence, a man on the sidewalk catches my arm. I am startled but reassured when I see he is an ordinary guy.

"*Gracias a Dios*, I thought you were the police."

"I am the police," he says. "Get out of here." He lets go, and I run a few blocks until the embassy is out of view. My path takes me past the Triton, a beautiful new hotel by the sea, where a party is underway on the terrace. A tropical buffet is set out next to tables covered with white tablecloths fluttering in the breeze. A loudspeaker blares "Get up and boogie," in English, but only a few people are dancing. Curious, I walk over to take a closer look. The faces of the people gathered in little groups are stricken, and the party has a funereal air.

The hotel and the party are for members of the "community," Cuban exiles allowed to return to Cuba to visit family members. They bring in $10 million a year in foreign exchange. They were once denounced as *gusanos,* worms, but now "the worms have become butterflies," as more than one Cuban has pointed out to me. This is the night their visit ends, and they have to say goodbye to their relatives. They are just a few blocks from the Peruvian embassy, a hungry place so crowded you cannot sit down, with foul air full of anxiety and anticipation. A police cordon separates the two worlds, those trying to leave and those who left so long ago they can return.

Later that night, Rosa comes to tell me I am leaving for Miami in the morning with the *gusanos.* Other news organizations are complaining to the Cubans about favoritism to *The New York Times* because I am the only American journalist in Havana. My visa is still good, but the Cubans are done with me.

Rosa drops me off in the International Departures area at José Martí Airport to leave with the exiled tourists. But my ticket does not guarantee me a seat. I have no reservation, and the group leaves me behind. There are no other flights to the United States, and I have no way to contact Rosa.

I sit for hours as flights to other countries arrive and leave. I have no visa to re-enter Cuba. Finally, as they are closing the airport and turning out the lights, a guard tells me I must leave. When I say I can't come back to Havana because I don't have a visa, they say they'll have to arrest me. At this point, I start to cry. Someone calls the Ministry of the Interior, and Rosa shows up to retrieve me.

The next morning, I am booked on another flight. Rosa stays to make sure I get on. But the plane breaks down on the runway before anyone boards, and the mechanics say it has no hope of taking off. Rosa takes me back to the Capri, and I have another day of reporting.

I call my new acquaintance, the veterinarian, to help me out. Rosa has been no help, but I still need to speak directly with someone in the government who has information about what's going on. He drives me out to Vedado, and I am reminded that *Vedado* in English means "forbidden." It comes from the days the area was a closed military zone, cut out of an ancient forest by the Spanish *conquistadores*. The sugar barons came here later to build their extravagant mansions. My friend stops in front of one of them.

"This could be the right place," he says. He doesn't explain, and the look on his face tells me not to ask.

The building looks like a private home, a large white villa surrounded by lush greenery. No fence. No official markings. When I see an armed man in uniform at the front door, I am tempted to stay in the car.

Instead, I walk up and identify myself as a reporter for *The New York Times.* The guard writes down my name and says, "Someone will help you with your case." Then he points to a large waiting room lined with plastic chairs. As time passes, it occurs to me that the lovely wrought iron scrolls covering the open windows are not just for decoration. It's hot and humid here, and there's no breeze. Only insects. The room has no fans or air conditioning. I'm sweating as I watch flies dance across the floor.

The other people in the waiting room, all adults, seem upset. You might expect this in a police station. What's odd is the silence. No one is saying anything. Not one word. Many are smoking. Here and there, I see piles of cigarette butts on the floor, signs of nervous people who waited a long time. A woman in an orange dress has fallen asleep. Another woman, wide awake, is trying to hide her tears. Now and then, someone arrives to escort a person to an inner room.

I'm not wearing makeup, and one of my sandals is broken and tied together. I'm blonde but that's not rare in a city where hairdressers are handy with bleach. In this room, it's my cotton dress that brands me a foreigner. My dress stands out like a scream.

After what seems like forever, a woman sitting near me whispers, *"¿Quién eres?"* – "Who are you?

"I'm a reporter from the United States," I tell her in Spanish. "From the newspaper *The New York Times.* I'm here for an interview."

"An *interview*?" She seems incredulous. "You *want* to be here? No one *wants* to be here."

"Why?" I ask her. "What is this place?"

"You don't *know*?" She gets up and moves to another seat. The others in the room regard me with suspicion. No one says anything.

I wait another half hour. The woman who spoke to me is taken out of the room. So are some of the others. At last, I give up and walk over to the front door.

"Since it doesn't look like I'm going to get an interview," I tell the guard, "I'm going to leave. I have a deadline. Thanks anyway."

I turn to step out, and he stops me.

"No one leaves," he says. "Go sit down. They will take up your case in a little while."

"I don't have a case," I say. "I'm a journalist."

"Go sit down," the guard says and means it.

It dawns on me I'm in trouble, but I don't know how much. I go back to my chair and wait.

Rosa is going to be mad.

Sitting here, I'm hoping a man I barely know is still waiting for me out in the car or will tell someone if I disappear. The terror of the asylum seekers is starting to feel real.

Before coming to Cuba, I interviewed former political prisoners, including Huber Matos, who spent more than a year imprisoned in a small concrete box, never seeing the light of day.

I do not want to fall into the wrong hands here.

More time passes.

At last, a woman walks up to me and says, "The general will see you now."

She leads me into an office that looks like it belongs to a police chief and introduces me to General Fabián Escalante. He is dressed in civilian clothes, a knit shirt, and trousers. He looks to be about my age, in his thirties, and he is tall, trim, and handsome. He takes a seat at his desk and invites me to take a chair in front. Then he asks who I am and what I'm doing.

I don't know that General Escalante has an excellent command of English, so I introduce myself in Spanish and explain I have been waiting for an interview with someone in charge. He nods his head and says nothing more, so I ask my first question, "Are the people seeking asylum in the Peruvian embassy being detained?"

He does not reply, just writes down my question, in much the same way FBI agents have done during my interviews with them, as if wanting to make sure he has the question straight. So, I keep going.

"Are the police having problems with violence in the area around the embassy?"

Again, no answer. More writing.

This is going nowhere.

"Are busloads of people trying to get to the Peruvian embassy in Havana?"

He is treating this like a case against me, not as an interview.

I push this doubt aside and keep going.

"Have you set up a Peruvian pavilion at the Combinado del Este prison?"

In silence, he keeps writing. When I am done, he puts down his paper and pen and looks up at me. "We have no problems," he says in Spanish. "They are all criminals."

It's clear our interview is over when another man enters the room. He's also in civilian clothes, a suit this time. He says he is from the Ministry of the Interior, and he is courteous. He also speaks with me in Spanish.

"Miss Thomas, you clearly do not understand our system. We *never* give interviews to reporters. *Never.* If there are any government statements, you will have to read them in the party newspaper *Granma*."

Then General Escalante stands up, indicating my visit is over. While the man from the Ministry of the Interior remains behind, the general opens the door to his office and personally escorts me to the entry hall and front door of the building.

On the other side of the waiting room, the woman in the orange dress still sleeps. The general motions to the guard that I may leave. The guard looks doubtful but steps aside. Heart pounding, I walk out of the building.

The VW beetle is still in the same parking spot. The driver is dozing off. I knock on the car window, wake him up, give him a big smile, and thank him. Then I get in and close the passenger door. After he has pulled away, I begin to scream.

"Where in the *hell* did you take me?"

"The headquarters of the secret police," he says, "the Department of State Security. They know everything."

"Yes!" I shriek, "But they don't tell!"

"Well, it was worth a try, wasn't it?"

I am breathless with anger and fear. When I collect myself, I realize I still have time to make today's deadline, so I go to my hotel and try to summarize what I've seen. The old Western Union office still operates here, under Cuban control. When I take my story there to be typed into the telex machine and sent to New York, the reaction of one of the operators, normally cool and professional, gives me a glimpse of the subterranean tensions here.

She hesitates when she reaches my paragraphs describing the scene at secret police headquarters. Then she cries out, "*¡Estamos perdidas!*" – "We are lost!" – but resumes typing and sends the story.

To my surprise, when Rosa appears the next day, she mentions no pushback from her bosses at the Ministry of the Interior. She drives me to the airport, and the Cubans finally get me out of the country. In less than a week, they give me a visa to return.

Afterwards, I learn that my visit to the secret police caused an uproar behind the scenes.

"They were running around like crazy!" a high-ranking member of Cuba's intelligence community will tell me many months later, laughing. "They didn't know how a reporter from *The New York Times* got into their office, and they didn't know what to do with you."

I do not know what a feat it is to puzzle General Escalante, even unintentionally. At the time I meet him, he has a large spy network inside the United States and knows a great deal about us. When he retires years later to teach and write, he will report on saving Castro's life during 634 assassination attempts.

The person who tells me about the shock I created by showing up at the general's headquarters is a Cuban who worked closely with Che Guevara for many years. He never tells me this about himself. When I meet Ulises Estrada in Jamaica, he says he is a diplomat and nothing more.

CHAPTER TWENTY-ONE:
MARIEL

The chaos in Havana has upended Miami, home to half a million Cuban exiles. Marches in support of the asylum seekers in the Peruvian embassy appear and dissolve in streets all over the city. In Hialeah, where car honking is routine, blaring horns show support for the asylum seekers. In just eight hours, the police log three hundred horn-honking complaints.

In Miami's Little Havana, several dozen people are entering their second week of a hunger strike. Among them is Armando Ruiz, sitting on a mattress in his makeshift tent. He tells me he and his family stole a city bus a year ago in Havana and rammed it through the gate of the Venezuelan embassy on Avenida Quinta. After 109 days, they left for Caracas.

Tons of food and medicine intended for the asylum seekers sit in warehouses in Miami in the hope it can be forwarded to Havana, but its fate is uncertain. The asylum seekers are in the same situation. Just as I return to Florida, several hundred are sent to Costa Rica on an "air bridge" provided by the Costa Rican airline, which makes a daily trip to from San Jose to Havana. I board a plane for Costa Rica to catch up with them.

I find them in the old presidential residence, surrounded by gardens with clouds of pink and red blooms, brilliant sunshine, and cool mountain air. They are lying on hastily installed mattresses, oblivious to the beauty of their surroundings. They are chain-smoking, pining for broken families, and trying to figure out what to do next.

I ask them how they managed to live outdoors at the Peruvian embassy for so many days without food. And what happened to those who gave up and went home on safe conduct passes?

"We ate a cat," Mario Leyva recalls. "Someone found two dogs. We ate the black one, but the white one hid. We ate a papaya tree from the leaves to the trunk, and then we pulled the roots out of the ground."

Frank Gallardo accepted a safe conduct pass and went home with his four-year-old son Henry, now seated on his shoulders. "Our neighbors threw rocks at our house. Our neighbors. We lived for twenty years in the same house. Our neighbors did it out of fear."

At this moment, a Peruvian official shows up to gather names for the first flight to Lima. Most of the Cubans want to go to Miami, not Peru.

"You can choose where you want to go eventually,' he tells them, "But not yet."

"Oh, no!" and there are more groans and cries.

"If we don't get the names in an hour, the airplane won't leave today," he tells them. Then he sits down on the only available seat – a trash basket – and begins taking names.

By late afternoon, the stranded Cubans are still trying to contact relatives in the United States, but most have no money and no telephone for a call. Costa Rican officials whisk them swiftly back out to the airport, trying hard to ease their traumatic path toward an unknown destination. I can't imagine fleeing to a place you don't want to go, unable to reach those you love, with nothing in your hands but hope.

I return to Miami for a change of clothes and a new visa, then fly to Havana and join a large group of American print and broadcast journalists to watch more than a million Cubans march for thirteen hours past the Peruvian embassy in a show of support for Fidel. The demonstrations fall on April 19, 1980, the 19th anniversary of the Cuban victory over the Americans at the invasion of the Bay of Pigs, known in Cuba as *Playa Girón.*

The parade is staged by local Committees for the Defense of the Revolution, playing on the theme *gusanos.* Posters show worms of every description: worms carrying suitcases, worms being flushed down toilets, gangster worms, worms wearing too much makeup. Another popular motif is Jimmy Carter protecting a worm or President Carter simply being kicked in the seat of the pants by Cuba.

The government of Costa Rica tells Cuba it will give permanent asylum to all ten thousand Cubans who came to the Peruvian embassy, but Cuba stops the flights to Costa Rica, demanding refugees go directly to the countries where they will be resettled. Spain starts to fly refugees to Madrid, but crowds gather at the airport to throw eggs at departing passengers, delaying the flights by hours.

Three days after the million-Cuban march, Rosa appears at my hotel with an offer to drive me out to Mariel, a small harbor west of Havana. The Cubans have started giving permission to small boats from the United States to enter the harbor, and ten small boats flying American flags are gliding like minnows through the Soviet and Cuban freighters at anchor.

"We're sending out calls over radio stations in Miami to anyone with a boat," says Hildo Romero, one of the first Cuban American boatmen to arrive. "A lot of people want to help." His boat is tied up at the landing, and he's buying fuel and food. He tells me Cuban officials have even checked the weather reports for him.

As I watch from the dock, a large shrimp boat boards groups of Cubans ready to leave, women and children first, old people next, then couples holding hands. By the time they are all on board, they are crowded shoulder to shoulder on the deck. A Cuban official keeping count tells me there are 217 passengers in all, and the boat's crew is hoping the weather will not deteriorate on the way home. They can make the journey of ninety miles to Key West by sea in fair weather.

I ask Rosa, who is still standing with me, if I can join the refugees on one of the other boats leaving today and travel with them to Florida.

"No. *Punto final.*"

"But I'm the only one here, except for the boat crews, who has a passport to get *into* the United States."

"*No es nuestro problema.* If you want to come *here*, you can't go there."

I am both disappointed and relieved. I am so prone to seasickness I could get seasick in a bathtub. Even thinking about a boat ride to Key West makes me nauseated. It would be a great first-person story, but it isn't worth losing my Cuban visa and everything in my stomach.

As I turn away from the dock, I see three elderly women dressed in black, each carrying a small suitcase. They've been left behind in the dust. I walk over to talk with them. All are widows.

"My sister called yesterday," Armelia Ortiz explains. She is wearing a cameo, her dress is trimmed with lace, and she is holding a straw purse in a trembling hand. She and her friends traveled fourteen hours by bus from Oriente Province to Havana, then came by car to Mariel, where port officials stopped them. To leave, they need exit documents.

The women have been waiting five hours in the hope of finding a bus back to Havana. Señora Ortiz is sunburned, footsore, and surrounded by a large group from the local Committee for the Defense of the Revolution, a mouse encircled by cats.

With an eye on them, she insists she is a good revolutionary, not someone who went to the Peruvian embassy. She just wants to go to Miami to live with her sister. "I'm alone," she says. "I'm a widow. I'm old."

Her companion Carolina Torres wants to visit her daughter in Florida. She'll only stay three months and then return. Honestly. She is the custodian of bus drivers' uniforms in her town. "I have my job," she says. "I have four sons, and one is a captain in the army."

An ancient yellow Buick approaches, and the crowd flags it down. The three women get in for a return trip to Havana. First, they plan to look for a hotel, then the paperwork they need.

The downtown office issuing this paperwork is surrounded by barricades and besieged by crowds seeking exit papers. Anyone from the Peruvian embassy can get them, and so can anyone with a relative and a boat from the U. S.

The telephone office downtown is also jammed. People without home telephones can place calls here, but its capacity is two hundred calls a day to the United States. All calls go through undersea cables that have not been repaired or replaced since the Cuban revolution. The total capacity is about 650 calls a day. If you have a home phone, you need to book a call with an operator before seven in the morning if you want to get through that day. Thousands of people are trying to call their relatives.

Overnight, the harbor at Mariel becomes a floating city, with more than thirteen hundred American boats and Cuban boats selling groceries, tee shirts, souvenirs, cigars, and liquor. "The blockade is broken," *Granma* rejoices. "There is a great demand for Havana Club rum."

Cuba's ten million people have the best access to health care and education in the Caribbean, and it is a place where social mobility is possible. On a future trip, when I can wander unattended, I will come upon an ancient cane cutter who learned to read after the revolution. His grandson is a neurosurgeon. A doctor's clinic is within walking distance of every home, and the Cubans have beautiful teeth. The Russians, who are footing the bill, arrive with mouths full of metal.

The Russian trade assistance, oil for sugar on favorable terms, keeps the Cuban economy going. The problem resides in the nature of the exchange, which is one of barter, so the

Cubans end up with no dollars to spend. Instead of buying, they trade for consumer products from the Soviet bloc. Unfortunately, Soviet suppliers often lack what Cuban consumers want. TV sets are available, but soap, linens, and mattresses are not. "Wouldn't it be better to get more towels and fewer TV sets?" Castro asks.

To get a few dollars to spend on the international market, the Cubans export everything they can. They grow citrus, but it's hard to find an orange or a lime in Havana. They're sent overseas for sale. A cotton blouse, if you can find one, may cost a month's salary. The Cubans at Mariel want out.

Disagreements break open among Cuban families and neighbors. Four nights after the boatlift begins, I am overpowered by the stench of rotten eggs as I walk through downtown Havana. I follow the smell down a side street and hear chanting and someone beating on a pan. I turn a corner to see a house dripping with eggs, surrounded by a mob chanting *"¡Escoria!* Scum! *¡Gusanos!"* Banners wrap the hedges. *¡Traidores!*

Six people are trapped inside: the captain of a fishing vessel from Florida and five leading members of the Committee for the Defense of the Revolution. The house, the largest in the neighborhood, once hosted the committee's social events. The committee members, including a doctor and a schoolteacher, were the most revolutionary of the revolutionaries – until the Sunday before, when the captain showed up to get them.

A large man, also a member of the committee, mops his sweaty forehead and tells me, "They were the most militant party members. They deceived everyone. They were opportunists."

"If these were ordinary people, they could just go," says another committee member. She offers me a seat on her porch, and I sit down beside her. "Three others have left this neighborhood – good riddance. No problem. But these people got everything from the revolution. They're traitors."

Her next-door neighbor walks over and joins the conversation. "Their house is a palace. Two cars, two televisions."

"Come into *my* house," the woman sitting next to me orders. She is going to show me how miserable it is, compared to her neighbors,' and she is so strident, I am reluctant. But I get up to follow. She opens her door and reaches back to take my hand. Even in the stifling heat of that night, her hand is cold.

She's afraid.

"You have to understand," she says in a whisper, once we stand her front room, "some of us are living with double personalities." She points back outside toward another man standing slightly apart from the crowd. "He was behind Batista," she says, referring to the dictator overthrown by the Cuban revolution. "Now he's behind Fidel. He goes wherever there's power."

"I have a picture of Che on the wall and a picture of our Savior behind the furniture," she says. "I am a member of the committee, but I do not approve of this" – she motions out toward the crowd besieging the house in the dark.

Is she crying?

I am back on her porch before I know it, then out in the street.

Did I dream that conversation?

I walk away.

Returning to my hotel on foot, I encounter another shattered home, a first-floor apartment in a building daubed with crude red letters, *"Escoria 5 ½"* or "Scum 5 ½." The front windows have been shattered and boarded up from the inside. The only person in sight is a member of a committee sitting on the front steps of the building. I walk past him up the stairs and knock on the door.

I can hear someone undoing a series of locks. The man who opens the door motions me to come in. The room is stifling hot, and four other adults are sitting there in the darkness — the electricity has been turned off — while a toddler sleeps on a cot nearby.

The man does not seem surprised when I introduce myself as a reporter from *The New York Times*, just numb, incapable of reacting. He introduces himself, his wife, his parents, and his sister. The sleeping toddler is his son. The other adults are very frightened, and the man explains their predicament in a jumbled rush.

They have wanted to leave the country for a long time. In January, they finally asked the government for permission to leave, not expecting much. Then on Sunday, "my aunt called to say there were people with boats in Mariel. We thought it could be a joke, so I spoke with my uncle in Miami, and he said three boats had left to go to Mariel."

In their excitement, one of them confided this wonderful news to a friend or a neighbor – in hindsight, no one is too sure just who. But "at midnight on Monday, someone came to ask if it was true that we wanted to leave."

By seven the next morning, their apartment was under attack by neighbors, their windows smashed, and hateful red letters scrawled across the front of the building. To be sure I understand what they mean, the man translates them for me:

"They say 'Let the scum go, five and a half.' My son is the half-scum" –

The loud pounding on the front door stops him in mid-sentence. Slowly, he walks to the door and opens it. It's the police.

"Who are *you*?" they ask, looking at me.

"A reporter from *The New York Times*."

"A *reporter*?" They look as if they have discovered a giant cockroach.

"Come with us."

I have not counted on this. The neighbors, yes. The police, no. They paid no attention to the violence that took place at this apartment. But I go with them. Once outside, they put me in the back seat of their car and drive me to a police station.

As we walk in, I see a telephone on the wall. "Can I make my phone call?" I ask. In my panic, I forget the rules are different here.

"Phone call? *What* phone call?" they reply. "Sit down and wait."

After an hour, Rosa appears.

"Yo! What have you been doing?" It is well past midnight, so this is a rhetorical question. Politely, the police release me to her custody, and I take a trip back to my hotel.

"Why can't you just stay at the hotel bar and drink like everyone else?" she asks.

I *have* been going for drinks – just not at the hotel bar – with as many diplomats as I can. Most are from Latin American countries sympathetic to the Cubans. I need information, and Cuban officials are always under surveillance and not allowed to speak on background.

The beautiful and popular wife of one Caribbean diplomat, who ends up becoming a good friend of mine, invites me to the first of many dinner parties that always includes dancing and chances to wander out into her garden for a conversation.

If you are laughing and dancing the merengue, a conversation can begin. In a garden too dark for cameras, lit with tiny lights, sometimes you can talk. Sometimes you can't. You always worry about electronic bugs.

I also go for drinks with other reporters from all over the world. Spanish is our common language. Most are real journalists in the sense they are looking for the truth, even if they cannot publish it. There are exceptions, such as the reporter from East Germany who insists on taking me for drinks at *El Gato Tuerto*, The One-Eyed Cat, for a drunken lecture about the greatness of his country and how inefficient the Cubans are.

"*If only* they were more like the Germans!" he keeps repeating.

Thank God they're not, I think as I plot my escape from him.

A few days later, on May 2, some of the Cubans staying home launch an organized attack against those who want to leave. Men armed with chains, pipes, and clubs arrive by bus and viciously beat people in a crowd of several hundred standing in line outside the offices of the United States Interests Section. The building is a tall slice of glass facing the Malecon, the broad seafront esplanade that wraps around downtown Havana. Those in line, including women, children, and former political prisoners, are waiting to ask about immigrating to the U.S.

Other American reporters who are there to interview the political prisoners say later they could hear the attackers coming, banging their pipes on the sides of the bus so loudly it sounded like gunfire. Some victims are seriously injured as four hundred others flee into the building.

By nightfall, the victims are still inside, and the screaming crowd out front has swollen in size and rage. The glass in the front of the building is broken, but Cuban police are keeping them back. The screamers are in a nasty mood. As I walk toward them, I see quite a few American and other foreign journalists watching from a safe distance. The empty, lighted space around the entrance to the building reminds me of a bull ring, dangerous and loud.

Marlise Simons of the *Washington Post* joins me in looking for the man in charge of the situation, who turns out to be a Cuban general, José Abrantes. When we find him, we ask if he will let us pass through the police line to go inside.

"It's our embassy," we say, "and we would like to speak with our *jefe* Wayne Smith."

General Abrantes looks at us, and he looks at the angry crowd and shakes his head. "No."

But we want to go. "Smith is our guy," we say. "We are journalists. We need to talk to him."

After a few minutes' hesitation, he decides to dare us.

"If you want to walk over there," he says, nodding toward the ugly crowd and the shattered front of the darkened building, "go ahead." He smiles. He is very handsome, and his friendly smile is a mistake on his part, because it makes us trust that he will not let us get hurt. We decide to risk it.

We walk close together across the empty space, past the mob, up to the door of the Interests Section and ask the Marines to let us in. They do. The power is off in the building, and it is stifling hot inside. We interview Smith, who refuses to let us speak with any of the Cubans in the building. When we leave, no one lays a hand on us.

Ten years later, General Abrantes, who in 1984 will rise to become Cuba's powerful Minister of the Interior, will be charged with being part of a huge conspiracy to import cocaine into Cuba and sentenced to twenty years in prison. He will endure just three years before dying of a heart attack.

Rosa Maria, who will rise to the rank of Captain in the Ministry of the Interior, will be charged and convicted in the same conspiracy. She will serve five years in prison and be released to die of cancer in three months.

I still cannot believe their lives ended this way, in such tragedy.

∽ᘐᘖᕲ

The floodgates open on May 6, 1980, when President Carter declares an open arms policy for those who want to leave Cuba. He also declares a state of emergency in Florida. More than 86,000 Cubans leave in the month of May alone, while the Cubans who are still stuck in the Interests Section are subject to an eight-hour parade past the building in which hundreds of thousands shout, "Worms go home."

I trot alongside the marchers, notebook in my hand. When I identify myself as a *New York Times* reporter from Miami, people give me a smile. Some insist on giving me the name, even the address, of a relative in Florida. The marchers, unlike the men on the bus, are in a festive mood. This is an anti-American parade against American policies but not against Americans. I never feel afraid.

The boatlift gets less orderly as it gets bigger. Boat captains complain they are threatened with large fines for leaving without passengers and turned back if they try to leave empty. The Cuban government denies this, but ordinary prisoners are mixed in with the political prisoners, and the world "Marielito" will come to have a bad meaning in Miami when some former prisoners commit crimes or join the drug trade.

CHAPTER TWENTY-TWO:
LIBERTY CITY

I am in Miami on May 17, 1980, when a racial disturbance erupts in the Black neighborhood of Liberty City. It is a spontaneous explosion of community outrage. Scholars will later call it "unprecedented in this century" because its sole purpose is to beat or kill white people. It lasts three days and leaves eighteen people dead.

The spark that lights the fuse is the decision in Tampa by an all-white jury to acquit four white Miami-Dade County police officers charged with killing Arthur McDuffie, a Black insurance executive after he fled from them on his motorcycle. They handcuffed him and beat him to death with their flashlights.

Although "probably as many Blacks saved whites from harm as did the harming," a Ford Foundation study will conclude, the crucial factor that marks the disturbances in Liberty City is "the general air of approval that pervaded the scenes of violence."

A car driven by a white man is hit by a stone, goes out of control, and strikes a Black child. A mob beats and stabs the driver and his brother to death while hundreds of others watch. The victims are nineteen and twenty-two years old. A taxi driver saves a white woman passenger.

It's night, and Liberty City is on fire by the time I get to the first set of police barricades and talk two patrolmen into escorting me toward the police command center, where I hope to get information about what is going on. We do not make it that far.

I get out of my car and take cover in a telephone booth, and the police officers leave. I can't see a thing. When I call the national desk in New York, they keep telling me to speak louder. They can't hear me over the noise.

"What's that banging?" they keep asking.

"Gunfire!"

"Get the hell out of there!"

I can't see anything but confusion, and I don't contribute much to the story that runs the next morning under another reporter's byline. My presence gives them the Miami dateline. It's possible that I am the person identified in the story as the "white stranger" who "asks a Black youth the reason for the violence."

"People like you all, killing us," he says.

When I go back the next day, the violence is still going on. I find a group of Black kids with a van and ask if they will take me into Liberty City to talk with their families. They don't want to do it but finally agree if I lie down on the floor in the back of the van so no one can see me. I do, and off we go.

Every few blocks, people on the street stop the van. They question the driver and the passengers, but no one ever opens the doors or looks inside. When we finally get to the home of one of the kids, he persuades his aunt to come outside. When she opens a door and sees me on the floor of the van, she begins to shout.

"Get out of here! As far as you're concerned, this is Vietnam! It's dangerous for you to be here! And it's dangerous for us to be with you!" She tells her nephew to get back in the van and leave. They take me back to Biscayne Boulevard and drop me off.

I call New York and tell them to send a Black reporter. Unlike Cincinnati, my white skin is too big a liability in Miami. Nathaniel Sheppard, Jr., a Black colleague and friend, is already on the way. It is a dangerous assignment for him because of the police, but his chances are better than mine.

As in other places, righteous anger has been a long time coming in Miami's Black communities. A long history of racism, discrimination, and police brutality – put in a pressure cooker with tens of thousands of new Cuban refugee arrivals – has made the explosive mix that blew up with the McDuffie acquittal.

I have been so involved in the Caribbean I have no sources or connections whatever in Liberty City. I know from my experiences in Ohio that this can be, and should be, an all-consuming story. I want the *Times* to cover it. This time, I want someone else to cover it because I am the wrong color, and I can't get up to speed fast enough to do the story justice.

CHAPTER TWENTY-THREE:
BACK COUNTRY HAITI

While I am in Cuba, the United States changes the rules for refugees from Haiti. Before now, they have not been allowed stay like the Cubans, even though they have been fleeing one of the region's most oppressive regimes, under the Haitian President Jean-Claude Duvalier, and even though they have been desperate enough to travel six hundred miles in the open sea to reach Florida.

Every now and then, they appear on the local television news, staggering onto the beach among startled sunbathers or being rescued by the Coast Guard, but mostly the Haitians are invisible, and sent home almost immediately.

In April 1980, however, a federal court decides the Haitians and Cubans must be treated the same, and the number of Haitians explodes. By the end of the year, 30,000 Haitians are living in Miami, a Little Haiti appears, and a big political debate is underway.

Our government does not want the Haitians, nor does it want to offend the Haitian government. American factories assemble clothing and electronics in Haiti and manufacture most American baseballs there. The Carter Administration urges the Duvalier regime to give democracy a chance.

Jean-Claude Duvalier, who is known as "Baby Doc," was only nineteen when he became the world's youngest president. His father, "Papa Doc," François Duvalier, passed along the title President-for-Life shortly before he died in 1971.

Papa Doc, a former medical doctor and intellectual, was elected President in 1957 but became a totalitarian despot. He depended on a network of killers and spies, the Tonton Macoute. The name was Haitian for "Uncle Knapsack," the Haitian bogeyman who came to get naughty children and take them away in a knapsack (*macoute*). Papa Doc transformed his brand of voodoo, a religion Haitians practiced in tandem with Roman Catholicism, into something evil, full of threats of zombies, torture, and death. Over the years, thousands of people were arrested, tortured, killed, or disappeared.

When Papa Doc died, his son did not particularly want his job. He preferred a career as a playboy and let his mother run the government. But that changed in 1973, when he took over, announcing a policy of "liberalization." He gave the Tonton Macoute a new name: Volunteers for National Security, and everyone has been waiting to see if he will do more.

In the summer of 1979, my first summer in the Miami Bureau of *The New York Times,* two political parties appear in Haiti, the first in twenty-two years. They announce on the same day, July 5, and – not knowing of the other's plans – choose the same name, the Haitian Christian Democratic Party. I go to Haiti to interview the party leaders.

I find one of them, Grégoire Eugène, fifty-four years old, a professor of civil and constitutional law. His sold-out book, published earlier in the year, observes that Haiti's Constitution permits political parties. Most Haitians do not know this. Eugène tells me he wants a "moderate, centrist party like Christian Democratic parties elsewhere in the world."

Unknown to Eugène, a pastor named Sylvio Claude, who was beaten, tortured, deported, and jailed when he returned to Haiti, has been released from jail. He announces his own new political party on the same day with the same name as Eugène's. Things do not go well.

Three days after my story about the "freer political climate" in Haiti appears in the *Times*, the police raid Claude's party headquarters. Claude jumps out a window to escape. The police shoot at Claude, striking him in one finger. He runs to a radio station to report his plight on the air, but he is arrested anyway. The police arrest the radio station operator too.

This is when I first meet Georges Salomon, Haiti's Ambassador to the United States and later its Minister of Foreign Affairs. He is a dignified, educated, well-spoken man, and he tries to put a civilized face on the Duvalier regime. I do not know if he believes what he says.

He gives me a wild story, which I repeat in print, that Claude will be charged with plotting to set fire to gasoline stations on the day Hurricane David was expected to arrive. The government discovered this so-called plot after arresting Claude, Salomon says.

Claude will be in and out of prison for the next four years. After the exit of the younger Duvalier, he will criticize the new regime of President Jean-Bertrand Aristide, and it will cost his life. A lynch mob will come for him on September 30,

1991. Claude will run for protection to a police station, but they will not help. The mob will take him, set him on fire, and burn him to death.

Eugène's political party fares a little better. It holds its first rally on November 8, 1979, and shuts down immediately. A group of sixty thugs shouting "Jean-Claude Duvalier!" charges into a gathering of about three thousand people as soon as the president of the Haitian Human Rights League, begins to speak. They break furniture, and they beat the speaker and his wife.

The next day, Eugène tells me, "We're waiting for conditions to improve. Everyone is waiting to see what will happen, but no one can say." Within the year, Eugène will flee the country. He will die in exile in Miami.

Although Haiti is a nation of poverty and fear, there are places you cannot see the beggars and the dirt. Looking down from the hills of Pétionville in November 1979 when the rain stops, all I can see are clouds of red poinsettia and lavender bougainvillea. The Hotel Oloffson, a white confection of wooden porches and Victorian architecture, is situated in this suburb, and I love walking into its airy bar.

Aubelin Jolicoeur, a tiny old man as narrow as a shadow, is always there, and he welcomes me with *"Bonsoir, cherie,"* as soon as I come into view. He coils around me, asking for news. Jolicoeur always wears a three-piece white suit and carries a cane with a gold handle. He writes a column for a local newspaper and wants information and gossip. But he is not a true journalist. As a childhood friend of Papa Doc and lifelong friend of the Duvaliers, he was the inspiration for the police informer and journalist Petit Pierre in Graham Greene's novel *The Comedians.* [xviii]

Jolicoeur is something of a celebrity, and his legend includes once playing piano with Bobby Short when the musician was a guest at the Oloffson, but I do not want to join his circle of friends. He seems harmless, but I take him seriously enough to fear him. After a few stays at the Oloffson, I switch to a family run hotel to avoid him.

It is clear to me that democracy is dead in Haiti. But what about the Haitians who were not active in politics, who reached the United States and were then deported? By sending them home, we took a hand in their fate. What has happened to them? I want to find out.

In the early fall of 1980, I obtain several lists of names of people deported from the United States to Haiti: eighteen men sent to the port city of Gonaives, and twenty-three men to Bombardopolis, a small town in the mountains. Both are in Northwest Haiti, the poorest region of the country.

Northwest Haiti sends most of the boat people. It has 300,000 inhabitants, three doctors, and four kinds of malaria. Gonaives is a port town and large, but Bombardopolis is small enough for gossip. People there will know what has happened to neighbors who went to the States and got deported. Were they arrested when they returned? Were they tortured, killed, or disappeared? Did they ever come home?

Sitting in Miami and looking at a map of Haiti, I thought a trip to find these people would not be difficult. As the crow flies, it would be a journey of less than a hundred miles. In Port-au-Prince, however, things look different. Most of the Northwest is mountainous or desert, and there are no paved roads. No tourists go there, and there are no maps. I will need a four-wheel-drive vehicle and someone to show me the way, including where to cross creeks and other obstacles, like gulleys.

The bigger problem is language. I don't speak creole.

To find the people on my lists and then persuade them to talk with me, I need a translator. I can't just hire a translator, because I don't want to put anyone in danger by asking them to help with a *New York Times* story the government may hate. I have no way to protect them.

There are also logistical problems. The trip may take two weeks, and the Northwest has no potable water, little food, and no gas stations. I'll have to take my own supplies. I'll need to camp overnight, as there are no hotels or guest houses. My little camera will not do the place justice, and I really want company, but I'll have to make the trip without a photographer.

I am second-guessing myself. Am I going or not?

I can't ask any of my journalist acquaintances in Haiti for advice or help. They have enough worries and troubles, and I don't want word of my project to leak to the government.

I finally decide to go ahead with the trip.

I'll speak Spanish.

Many Haitian peasants go back and forth to the Dominican Republic every year to work in the cane fields. Someone on the scene may need to translate my Spanish into creole, but communication no longer seems like an insuperable obstacle.

I hire a jeep and persuade a teenager I'll call Andre at the jeep rental place to travel north with me from Port-au-Prince to Gonaives, where I plan to spend a few days looking for my first group of deportees. I'm hoping he can help me search and then help me find someone to replace him as a translator and guide to travel farther north.

Andre is a skinny, cheerful kid, dressed in a castoff New York Yankees tee shirt and rags. He's strong, and he helps me load huge jugs of drinking water, big metal cans of gasoline, food, camping gear, and extra tires. Then we hit the road,

I am an anxious, careful driver, and this is the first time I have ever driven a jeep. It's huge but basic, wide open to the elements. I whisper thanks to my dad, who insisted from the first I learn to drive a car with a manual transmission. The streets of Port-au-Prince are chaotic, full of cars, trucks, pedestrians, carts drawn by animals, and circus-colored buses called tap taps.

You're kidding me! No one has brake lights! After several near-rear end collisions, I consider giving up. But as soon as I hit the national highway north, the roadway grows less crowded.

Beautiful trees line the highway. Later I will learn they are a rapidly growing species planted as part of an American project to reforest Haiti's bald landscapes, where the trees have been chopped down for charcoal. Most trees in the new project have met the same fate. The survivors line the highway and vanish after I pass Duvalier's seaside home at Carries.

What I will most remember about our first night is the bullwhip. After our late start, I learn that an American doctor has a clinic along our route. I hope that Andre and I can stay with him for the night. I hate camping and would much prefer company, conversation, and information.

I find the doctor in a cluster of buildings with patients as thin as scarecrows, one to a cot. Their families care for them, do their laundry and bring their meals. Otherwise, the clinic looks like a large farm, with a great flock of chickens in the yard.

The doctor turns out to be a dentist who is practicing medicine because there is no one else to help his seriously ill neighbors. Many have tuberculosis, and some have blood on their clothes. The windows are open; the heat is terrible. Flies buzz in squadrons around the room, and a large bullwhip hangs on the wall.

The dentist is a genial and hospitable fellow. He has no room for guests, but he has a small wooden storage building where one person can spend the night in a sleeping bag.

"If you close the windows, you can keep the bugs out," he tells me. "Andre can sleep on the porch, which is better than the ground." We share with our host some of the food we've brought for dinner.

As we eat, he explains his project. His patients are very frail, so it is essential for them to eat their meals. Their families come every day to attend to them, and he keeps the bullwhip on the wall, ready to use whenever he needs it.

"Do you whip the patients to make them eat?" I ask.

"The patients? Of course not! I use it for the chickens!"

"The chickens?"

"They belong to my neighbor, and he won't build a fence. They come over here and steal food from my patients, who are too weak to fight them off. That's when I use the whip."

During the night, the heat in the little storage room is insufferable and the mosquitos are insatiable, even after I cover myself with netting from head to toe. Slapping, itching, sweating, and wide awake, I hear drums beating and lie there listening for hours. Voodoo has been invisible to me, but it is everywhere, and the drums are the heartbeat of the night.

I can't interview most of the eighteen men I'm seeking in Gonaives: Half gave U.S. officials false addresses or no address at all. Three went back to Miami, and three have moved away. Three are still here, and two of them speak with me.

"I spent two days in jail when I came back," one tells me. "Now my main problems are too many children, no money, and no work."

The other man at first denies ever going to the United States. "I was not deported," he says. Then he relents and admits making the trip and being sent back.

"What happened to you? Did you go to jail?"

"Not saying anything about it."

Just as I am about to thank him and leave, he asks, "If I make another try, will you keep me? Will your government let me stay if I try again?"

"I have no idea." This is getting difficult, speaking through a teenager who himself is becoming anxious. "Do you think you will try again?"

He will not say.

Andre does not know the Northwest countryside, but he asks around in Gonaives and finds another teen, Marc, who speaks Spanish and agrees to take me further north, all the way up the coast past Anse-Rouge to Môle-Saint-Nicolas and Jean-Rabel if I want to go.

I tell him I want to go to Bombardopolis. Anse-Rouge is on the way, so that's fine, and I might as well see the other places. "They sent many boat people."

"And Boeing people," Marc says.

The Boeing people are those who scrape together enough money to go by airplane to Canada.

At Anse-Rouge, a seaside town, a strange building sits among the mud huts. It is a modern guesthouse with plumbing and electric lights that do not work because they are not connected to anything. Anse-Rouge has no public utilities.

The guesthouse was built with money from the U. S. Agency for International Development (AID)for the Haitian Community Help Organization. It was intended to house visiting health and agricultural experts. After finishing construction, AID stopped funding the community group, thinking the Haitian government would support it, but it did not. Staff members joined the boat people and went to Miami. [xix]

It reminds me of other foreign aid projects I have seen in Haiti: technology not suited for the place and not supported for the long haul. In Port-au-Prince I once watched a crew of about eight men filling the bucket of a large front-end loader by hand, using shovels, treating it like a wheelbarrow instead of the powerful and expensive machine it was.

In Anse-Rouge, an aid project much smaller than the guesthouse has transformed the town. A well for clean water was completed last year. Although the town is still a collection of shacks with dirt yards, a new banana tree grows next to every home.

Not every water project has succeeded. Near Bombardopolis, an isolated settlement in the mountains where I hope to find news of twenty-three deportees, a nonprofit group capped a spring with concrete to supply clean drinking water to a public fountain. But the residents believed that capping the spring angered the god who lived inside. They called voodoo priests to preside as they chopped off the concrete and made the fountain into an altar.

The Northwest is the part of Haiti where slaves fled their French masters after the 1804 revolution and set up family farms. Over generations, the ownership of these farms stayed in the same families, but they were divided into smaller and smaller pieces. Now they average three acres each, too small to be sustainable. Disaster is coming. Swine fever is making its way west from the Dominican Republic. In a year, the government will order the slaughter of all the pigs in Haiti. For thousands of families, a pig is their only wealth.

The roads in the Northwest are made of dirt by hand. On our way to Bombardopolis, sometimes we can find the roads, and sometimes we cannot. Here and there, Marc must walk up and down the banks of a creek to find a place to cross. I feel as if we are actors in a Disney nature movie, but not a family movie, a scary one. I kept thinking our jeep will tip over, and no one will know. As I have come to learn, the countryside is so crowded, even though it does not appear to be, I do not have to worry about not being seen.

To reach some of the deportees, young Marc and I must hike up steep dirt paths. I am in my late thirties and fit, but I do a lot of huffing and puffing. One day a farmer sees my red face and walks over to ask where I am going. He then brings over a sturdy brown horse, with a bridle but no saddle, and invites me to get on. I can return the horse on my way back, he says. I'm surprised and touched by his trust and generosity, and I hope he will not change his mind as I ride away. The horse makes the climb possible.

Of the twenty-three deportees I'm seeking, sixteen turned around and made it safely back to the United States. Another tried to return and drowned. His brother witnessed his death, the family tells me. Of the remaining six, three are not known in the town, and the rest still live in Haiti but had to leave home to find work. To buy passage, they sold their land and all their belongings. They had nothing to come home to.

One woman there has become a local celebrity because she has tried to leave four times and failed each time. She is not young. She gives me a brilliant smile when I tell her I am from Miami. "I am going!" she says. [xx]

The generosity and hospitality of the poor continue to surprise me. At one mud hut where I stop to talk for a long time, I tell the wife I need to use the bathroom, using the Spanish idiom which is bath, and she tells me to wait a moment.

I just need to find a spot to pee, but the wait seems to stretch on and on. Finally, I realize the family has gone to draw water so I can take a bath, a huge effort for them in a place that is a desert. I am ashamed of my mistake.

Several times, while driving over the rough terrain, I drive over sharp thorns that pierce the jeep's tires and make them go flat. I have spares, but they are huge and very heavy. Peasants always appear within minutes to lend a hand. On the road back to Port-au-Prince, the jeep's engine dies. It is not overheated. It just stops. Marc opens the hood, and we look at it, helpless. We have plenty of gas, but we are in the middle of nowhere.

Again, a group of Haitian peasants appears, as if out of the ground, to help us. They examine the engine like surgeons. Then one of them goes away and returns with a little piece of wire, not much more than a paper clip. He fiddles with it for a while, sticks it into the engine, and motions for me to turn the key and hit the gas. The engine starts. I am overjoyed, and so are they. They ask for nothing. I don't have much food or money left, but I give them everything I have and head down the road.

Writing for the *Times*, I say the United States is not having much success deporting refugees to Haiti. Although they don't seem to be harmed by the government when they return to Haiti, they are so poor they cannot stay there. If possible, they come back to the United States.

Georges Salomon, the Haitian Foreign Minister, calls me to say how much he likes the story. He is trying to portray the Duvalier regime in a kinder light. His call makes me uncomfortable.

On a Friday two months later, I stand on a dock in Port-au-Prince in a big crowd of reporters, police officers, and plainclothesmen carrying walkie-talkies and guns. We are waiting for the *Lady Moore*, a Bahamian government vessel. She is bringing a load of Haitians who have been stranded for six weeks on Cayo Lobos, a desert island off the coast of Cuba.

The shipwrecked Haitians resisted when police from the Bahamas finally came to rescue them. The Haitians said they preferred death on a desert island to life in Haiti, but Haiti was their only choice. They were not welcome in the Bahamas, where some thirty thousand Haitians are already being deported.

In Port-au-Prince, the forced return of more than a hundred marooned and unwilling Haitians on the *Lady Moore* has drawn a crowd of international reporters, but the vessel runs into a storm and does not arrive that Friday.

In the evening, to put the best face on things, the Haitian government hosts a cocktail party for international journalists. The director of the Haitian Red Cross promises us every effort will be made to help the homecoming men and women, and the head of immigration assures us the government "had not taken any action against those who have returned." This is not true for everyone.

Two weeks earlier, unknown to me, Evans Paul, a journalist with the independent station Radio Cacique, was arrested at the airport in Port-au-Prince when he got off a flight from New York, where he had interviewed Paul Magloire, a former Haitian President nicknamed *"Bon Papa."*

After his arrest at the airport, Paul was taken to the Casernes Dessalines and held incommunicado for ten days. He later told Amnesty International his captors tied him into a ball and beat him with sticks until the skin on his buttocks was torn away, and "you could say that the sight of my blood excited them even more. When I was on the point of dying, they untied me and dragged me to a dark cell."

Paul was released without charges, but a judge called his broadcasts subversive. The government clamped down hard on broadcast journalists because most Haitians were illiterate and got their news from the radio. Paul had an audience of thousands.

The day after the government cocktail party, Saturday, I wait for the *Lady Moore* all day. She does not arrive.

"Engine trouble," they say.

I go back to my hotel. As I walk into the lobby, I am surprised to find Jean-Robert Hérard, a journalist with the weekly publication *Le Petit Samedi Soir,* waiting for me. His publication has been a thorn in the side of the Duvaliers. He wants to talk out on the front porch, which is empty. We stand looking out over a wide flight of stairs down to the drive.

"Can you get me asylum in your embassy?" he asks.

"No, I don't think so," I say, my heart in my mouth. "We don't do that in friendly countries. You must walk in and apply to immigrate." I want to help him, and I know I cannot.

"I'm afraid," he says. "The police are after me. I've been to other embassies today. No luck at all." He is frightened. "I don't know what to do. Can you hide me?"

"In my room? I'm in a Haitian hotel. Where would I hide you? Where would I take you? I want to help you, but I don't know how."

He is sweating, and he has a wad of small photographs in his hand.

Just then, a gold Porsche convertible pulls up in front of the building, and a Haitian man I've never seen before gets out and calls my name.

"Miss Thomas! Miss Thomas! I saw you at the cocktail party last night. I want you to see Port-au-Prince with me tonight."

He is older than me, from the look of him, and wearing a white silk shirt, open at the neck, with a lot of gold jewelry. He starts up the stairs.

Jean-Robert knows him. "Take these," he says, jamming the photos into my open purse. "I can't be found with them." Then he turns and calmly walks back into the hotel lobby.

"Sorry to interrupt," the man says. "One of your sources...?"

"Just an old friend," I say, turning so the top of my purse closes over its contents. "And you are?"

"Pierre Duvalier," he says. "Jean-Claude's uncle, and it would be my pleasure to escort you tonight to see the sights and sounds of the real Port-au-Prince. There are so many beautiful places I am sure you have not seen." He gives me an engaging smile. I have the feeling the invitation is a command.

"You have a convertible," I say. "I'll just run and get a scarf."

I can hide the photos in my hotel room and get rid of them.

"No need," he says, motioning down the stairs. "I always have a scarf for the ladies."

And we walk down the steps and get into his car.

I do not like performance automobiles, and Pierre Duvalier – or whoever he is – has me gripping my seat in his Porsche. We rocket along narrow, winding roads, up and down hills in the growing darkness. He takes me to candlelit clubs where partygoers dance and drink while I float in a fog of fear.

Many men wear handguns on their hips. The holsters bounce as they dance. Afraid Pierre will ask to see the photos in my purse, I fasten it shut and make sure it is underneath my chair every time I get up. When I can, I pull a chair leg over the strap.

I can't call for help. I am already dancing with members of the police. I pray they do not also belong to the dreadful VSN, and I wonder if I will ever return to my hotel or simply be dropped off dead.

None of the women talk to me or even seem to look my way. I am the only foreigner, as far as I can tell, and certainly the only journalist. I am afraid to drink anything. Pierre offers me Scotch – that's what he drinks – when I turn down the Haitian rum.

"No, it's Irish whiskey or nothing."

Fortunately, they don't have it, and I get away with drinking soda out of the bottle.

I do have to dance with him. For hours. I shift my chair and my purse every time I stand up. I'm sweating, trying to focus on the great Haitian music. My fake smile would make a stripper proud.

As the time drags on, voodoo appears. My memory is hazy, perhaps because I am poised to run for my life. It's dark, too, and crowded, hard for me to get a good look. I recall flames, smoke, drums, and costumes. Finally, I tell Pierre I am exhausted and need to leave. We drive more slowly back to my hotel, where he lets me out in front. I use my last strength to walk slowly – not run – up the stairs.

When I reach my room, I worry someone may have hidden a camera while I was out. I do not want to be caught with Jean-Robert's photos. Leaving the lights off, I pull the stack from my purse and fumble around in my suitcase for my fingernail scissors. Then I cut the photos into pieces and flush them down the toilet, a few at a time. I do not look at them. They are not my secret.

The next day, the *Lady Moore* finally arrives. The Cayo Lobos passengers, both men and women, are gaunt and hollow-eyed, still dressed in rags. Some stagger. Others faint and must be carried in stretchers. The Haitian captain of the boat shipwrecked on the island is one of them. Along with other journalists, I walk up and try to speak with him, but we are shouldered aside. He is taken away and put on a stretcher before he can say anything.

Arguments break out later over discrepancies in the head count. Twenty-nine passengers are missing, but I am kicked out before anyone realizes this.

While the refugees are still disembarking, a short, stout Haitian woman I don't know approaches and orders me to leave the dock. She is well dressed, but she is angry and full of menace. To my surprise, she gives me a shove. She does not say what authority she has, nor does she tell me her name.

"I'm not going," I say. "I have permission from the government to be here, and there are lots of other reporters." Journalists and police officers are surging around the line of refugees unwinding from the boat.

"You leave!" she shouts.

Again, I refuse, and I am still saying no when several uniformed police officers appear and escort me off the dock and into the street, where they make sure I remain while the rest of the arrivals come off the boat and are taken away.[xxi]

A Haitian friend who watched the affair speaks to me afterwards.

"Do you know who you were arguing with?"

"No. Some horrible woman. She didn't give me her name."

"You should be more careful. She was Madame Max Adolphe."

I am not well briefed in Haitian politics, so I look her up when I return to Miami. She is the mayor of Port-au-Prince. She is also one of the most feared people in Haiti. Formerly, as a leader of the Tonton Macoute, she was Papa Doc's iron fist. He made her warden of Fort Dimanche prison, where there were reports she invented and conducted gruesome and often sexual tortures on hundreds of prisoners, including children and the elderly.[xxii] Jean-Claude replaced her at the prison when he took over, but she remains a terrifying presence.

I wonder why she was so angry with me. I doubt she cared about my reporting: other journalists had permission to stay on the dock. Perhaps she heard I was out dancing with some of her men and took offense. Although I will return to Haiti, I never see her again. In 1986, when she is sixty years old and the Duvaliers flee the country, she will disappear without a trace.

After the Cayo Lobos refugees return, publicity about them and their complaints infuriates the government, which is

desperately seeking a bailout from the International Monetary
Fund and struggling to woo foreign investors, who are starting
to balk.

Factory wages in Haiti are still low because there are so
few jobs – urban unemployment is 75 percent, and a bribe is
necessary to get a job – but labor peace is no longer a sure
thing. Haitians went on strike at four factories in the fall of
1980. Encouraged by workers' movements elsewhere, 36,000
workers signed up to join a union.

In late November 1980, two weeks after the arrival of
the *Lady Moore*, the police begin arresting dozens of labor
organizers, politicians, teachers, medical students, and print
and broadcast journalists, including my friend Jean-Robert and
his brother. I go back to Haiti, determined to ask Duvalier if
he has ordered these arrests himself and what was going on.

The foreign minister, Georges Salomon, has been
promising other nations his president-for-life is sincere about
"liberalization." The American embassy shares this hope. The
United States does not want to support an international pariah.
Salomon liked my stories, and I plan to ask for his help in
getting an interview with Duvalier.

When I arrive, I learn the foreign minister has just
suffered a heart attack. Given the collapse of his promises and
hopes, I am not surprised. I decide to try to speak with him
and find him in the hospital during visiting hours. He is in bed
but not hooked up to life support. I am relieved to see him
alone.

"Miss Thomas! What a surprise!" He seems glad to see
me.

"I was sorry to hear. How are you feeling?"

"Better. But the atmosphere has not been helpful."

Salomon assures Jean-Claude is a reasonable man and will surely have a good explanation for the arrests, one more in line with what he, Georges Salomon has been telling investors and the international human rights community.

"That may be, but no one can get to him," I say, as politely as I can, looking around to make sure no one else is walking toward the hospital room. "Do you think you can arrange for me to speak with the president?" I refer to Duvalier in the third person, thinking it sounds more respectful.

After a pause, Salomon says, "Yes, I believe so. If I can, I'll send word to your hotel."

Six days pass, and world events overtake the Haitian arrests in the news. On December 2, three Catholic nuns and a lay worker, all Maryknoll missionaries from the United States, are raped and murdered by five members of the El Salvador National Guard.

Currently, Central America and the Caribbean are a joint assignment for most news organizations, and my colleagues race to El Salvador. The *Times,* with more reporters and focus on the region, has correspondents assigned to both the Caribbean and Central America. I can stay in Port-au-Prince and wait.

After two more days, the government trucks in tens of thousands of Haitians to stand on the brown lawn of the great white presidential palace near the Champs de Mars to support Duvalier. Dozens of electric lights blink out "Jean-Claude Duvalier: President for Life." Plainclothes security men with machine guns thread through the crowd. Without a trace of irony, the peasants shout "Long live democracy!" Some participants hold signs they themselves cannot read. "Down with anarchy!" the signs say, and "We say no to communism!"

I see one child who embodies the whole charade. She is covered with running sores, but someone has dressed her up a white pinafore, washed and freshly ironed.

Duvalier appears and addresses the crowd in creole. He rails against international communism and assures his listeners they are well off, adding, "Haiti does not need charity!"

This is a reference to the annual meeting of donors of foreign aid, the lifeblood of Haiti, set to take place in just four days. He must know the top United States and Canadian officials will not show up.

On the day of that annual meeting, I get an invitation to the palace to interview the president. We will speak in French, and an interpreter is waiting for me on the second floor of the palace at the door of Duvalier's office.

It is a high-ceilinged room, dark and as cold as a cave. The air conditioning is running at full blast. There is no daylight. The only light comes from a lamp on Duvalier's desk. He is sitting down, wearing an expensive European suit, dark with a white shirt and an excellent silk tie. He is a large man, wide and as dark as the room. He has a small Christmas bouquet at his fingertips, and he does not smile. He is just twenty-nine years old – I am thirty-six – but my age advantage gives me no comfort.

After the introductions, which the translator handles in a straightforward manner, I begin our interview by saying, "I would like to ask you about the events of the last few weeks, especially about the arrests of journalists, teachers, and trade union organizers."

Even with just two years of college French, I know that what the translator tells him bears no resemblance to what I have just said. Duvalier looks puzzled and says nothing. I turn to look at the translator and see him tremble.

I try again, speaking in English.

"*Monsieur Le President*, you have described yourself as an advocate of liberalization, but recently many journalists and other professionals have been arrested. Is this something you ordered, or is this an initiative of the army, the VSN, or the police you are simply going along with?"

This time, the translator says nothing.

I try to smile. Then I say, in my best college French, "Can we excuse the translator and continue this discussion in French? I will do my best to ask my questions correctly. My readers and people in government in the United States are interested in knowing what you are thinking at this moment."

My grammar is atrocious, and my accent is worse.

Duvalier answers me in English. He excuses the translator, who flees from the room. Then he turns to me. "*Mademoiselle*, Politics is not a matter for children."

He assures me he might not like everything he's doing, but he had to act fast because he's certain the journalists are subversives. The human rights advocates protesting the arrests are communist sympathizers who are trying to destabilize the government by undermining support from the international community.

"Are you worried so many arrests will make aid donors think twice about helping Haiti?" I ask, remembering his remark that Haiti does not need charity. I have in mind the no-shows at this morning's meeting.

He gives me a smile, the only one of our encounter. It is not a nice smile.

The Haitian government "is not at all disposed to accept dictates from those countries, nor interference in the internal affairs of our country," he replies.

"So, just to be clear, all these orders for arrests are coming from you? And you are not being pressured by the army or the VSN?"

You are getting the explanation from "the head of the government, not from the chief of police," he says, and he rises from his chair, dismissing me. [xxiii]

When I open the door to leave, the members of Duvalier's cabinet, unable to get in to see him, are waiting outside in the hall. So is a man who introduces himself to me as the American ambassador.

"What did he say?" the ambassador asks me.

"He said he ordered the arrests himself, and if the United States doesn't like it, we can lump it," I tell him.

"If he said that, he didn't mean it," the ambassador replies. The Cold War is underway, Cuba is nearby, and the United States needs an anti-communist regime in Haiti. I can't get a simple road map of Northwest Haiti, but the U. S. Army --working with the Haitian Army-- and the CIA have been mapping Haiti since at least 1962. [xxiv] When the Duvaliers eventually flee the country, it will be on a United States Air Force plane.

I return to my hotel and write two stories, one reporting my interview with Duvalier and another describing the situation in Haiti. I ask my editors not to publish them until I get out of the country. I leave on an Air France flight the next morning.

After my articles appear, the newspapers controlled by the government run front page stories criticizing my interview with Duvalier. One calls me "a little too impertinent." Another declares me "an enemy of the Haitian people." I am not eager to return to Haiti.

Jean-Robert and the other Haitian reporters and editors are released and go into exile, but Haiti remains a deadly place, especially for broadcast journalists. One of them, Jean Dominique, who will cycle between exile and return, will be shot to death at his radio station.

When I leave Haiti in December 1980, I do not know I have contracted an illness that is rare elsewhere in the Caribbean. It almost causes my death by assassination when I arrive in Jamaica shortly after.

CHAPTER TWENTY-FOUR:
THE HOT ZONE

Kingston has been a hot zone in the Cold War between the United States and the Soviet Union since the 1972 election of Jamaican Prime Minister Michael Manley, a democratic socialist and friend of Fidel Castro. Manley begins conducting sweeping reforms in a country where wealthy professionals and men of commerce live like landed gentry while many workers live like livestock.

Manley's government nationalizes some industries and opens free public schools for all. New labor laws institute equal pay for women and a national minimum wage. Health centers go up, and Jamaica's infant mortality rate drops in half. Poor families get forty thousand new homes. After four years, Manley is re-elected in a landslide.

But Manley and his Progressive National Party are undone by economic trends beyond their control. Jamaica, like the other Caribbean nations, has no oil, and the price has increased one thousand percent in the last decade. The island's industry, natural resources, and tourism cannot make up for the difference.

To stay afloat, Manley borrows from the International Monetary Fund, but its requirements crush the poor. Private foreign investment dries up, and Jamaica's foreign debt rises to a billion dollars. As the economy falters, members of the middle class worry that Jamaica will become "another Cuba" and start leaving the country, taking their money and their skills.

In February 1980, saying "No country can overcome a crisis without a clear path," Manley calls for elections in the fall. The United States favors his opposition, the Jamaica Labor Party led by Edward P.G. Seaga.

Violence, long a deadly undercurrent in Jamaican politics, breaks out as soon Manley announces elections, The news is full of shootings, stonings, and stabbings. Among those wounded is Prime Minister Manley himself, shot on a visit to his own district.

When I arrive in May, I go to see the aftermath of the Gold Street Massacre, as the newspapers call it. Men in black with semi-automatic weapons appeared at a Seaga fund-raising dance on Kingston's South side and sprayed a house and its dancers with bullets. The shooters vanished before the police arrived. Four people died, and ten are wounded.

One of the victims, Yvonne Morgan, was hit by five bullets. She lives in a little house on Maiden Lane, a poor, muddy street. I step over a pig on my way to her door. At twenty years old, she is already the mother of three children. I find her twisting uncomfortably in her chair, trying to relieve the pressure of a bullet still in her belly.

"I heard a shot," she tells me. "The furtherest place I could run was inside, but the bullets still coming in. I ran back up Gold Street. I heard someone say, 'Kill her! Kill her!' I have bullets in my legs, my hips. I'm running fast, not looking back. I come in my yard and fall."

As bad as it is, physical violence is only one torment in Jamaica. People fear running out of food. The imports are almost gone, and locally produced food is in jeopardy. Small stores have closed. Housewives have been attacking supermarkets, accusing the owners of hoarding. On the street, they can still get rice from a vendor if they pay an outrageous price for a non-food item, such as a $3 pen.

There are other frightening signs: A poultry farm, unable to get corn, is compelled to feed its chickens with wheat intended for flour, then slaughter the chicks before adulthood. A factory that makes cans for Jamaican food runs out of metal before the pineapple and carrot crops are harvested.

Pineapples and carrots make poor leading characters in a high stakes political drama. *The Daily Gleaner*, Jamaica's leading newspaper, singles out a flamboyant villain, the Cuban Ambassador Ulises Estrada. The Jamaican government has cordial relations with Havana, but the opposition leader Seaga, a favorite of *The Gleaner*, has already accused Cuba of sending communist agents to make trouble in Jamaica, and when Estrada arrives, the newspaper gives uncritical space to Seaga's claims.

Prime Minister Manley's critics ignore his pledges of an undying commitment to democracy and insist he intends to turn the country communist. "KGB OUT" and "DGI Out" graffiti covers the walls of Kingston. DGI is a reference to the Cuban intelligence service.

Although it is not known in Jamaica at the time, and not known to me, Estrada has a long history as a communist revolutionary. He went to Bolivia and to Africa with Che Guevara. As he will later write, Estrada was the lover of "Tania," the *nom de guerre* of the East German revolutionary Tamara Bunke. Tania was killed fighting alongside Guevara in Bolivia in 1967. Before Jamaica, Estrada was Cuba's ambassador to Yemen.

After being attacked in *The Gleaner*, Estrada responds by holding a press conference and accuses the newspaper of not playing fair. As a diplomat, he cannot answer the newspaper's allegations without being accused of meddling in Jamaica's internal affairs. *The Gleaner* then accuses Estrada of threatening both the newspaper and Jamaica. Seaga demands Estrada be declared *persona non grata*. Prime Minister Manley refuses.

Subsequently, a deadly international game of tit for tat begins.

In July, the name and home address of a man described as the chief of station of the Central Intelligence Agency in Jamaica, along with the names and addresses of other embassy officials, are given out at a news conference in Washington, D. C., by a co-editor of *Covert Action Information Newsletter*, a Washington, D.C. publication. The editor accuses the United States of trying to subvert the Manley government.

Within forty-eight hours, the home of this alleged CIA chief of station is machine-gunned in Jamaica. No one is hurt, and Manley deplores the attack. But before he knows about it, he is asked about the allegations in the *Covert Action* newsletter. He says: "Anybody who has lived through Jamaica in the last year knows that there is a calculated and deliberate destabilization program at work."

I decide I must meet Ulises Estrada. What Michael Corleone said in *The Godfather* is good advice for journalists: "Keep your friends close but your enemies closer." If Estrada is pulling the strings in Jamaica, I want to make his acquaintance.

He agrees to an interview at his home in Kingston. He answers the door in his swimming trunks. No one else is there. He has a pool in the back yard, and he tells me his wife and family are in Cuba. I admire photographs of a blonde woman and children and take a seat in a folding chair next to the pool while Estrada finishes taking a few laps. He is an Afro-Cuban, very dark and fit, and his head is shaved bald.

Although his English is fine, he seems relieved to converse in Spanish, and he knows I have been working as a journalist for the *Times* in Cuba. I ask him about his quarrel with *The Gleaner*, his experiences in Africa, and his activities in Jamaica.

Earlier in the year, Jamaican authorities seized a shipment of 200,000 shotgun shells sent from Miami to a firm managed by a Cuban in Jamaica. Documents showed the ammunition was heading for Jamaica, but Jamaica's minister of national security investigated the matter and concluded the shipment was in transit to Cuba. It was illegal, then and now, to send ammunition directly from the United States to Cuba, but each leg of the shipment was legal.

Estrada's critics say the ammunition was intended for the political gangster gangs attacking Seaga's supporters in Kingston. Estrada denies this. As far as Cuba is concerned,

Jamaica is a friendly country, he says. Cuba does not want to hurt Manley's chances in the election or see Kingston in flames. Cuba wants Jamaica to succeed.

Estrada says he is a diplomat, not a spy. At the same time, he is proud of being a communist and a revolutionary. To me, communists outside Latin America suggest the Russians, the hydrogen bomb, and *Darkness at Noon*. Estrada's communists are guerillas fighting the generals who run Argentina and Chile and murder the poor in Central America. During this talk and others, he never mentions his past friendship with Che Guevara. Looking back, I am amazed.

Still, after being stonewalled in Havana, I cannot believe I can sit down for a long afternoon with a Cuban official, not to mention this one, a half-dressed ambassador in a bathing suit. Confidence is not something Ulises Estrada lacks.

He is also a flirt. After several hours, he is telling me, in English, "You make me feel like a Sunday morning." Coming from an atheist, I wondered if this has a double meaning, but it is impossible not to laugh when he says it.

While I am working in the Caribbean, Abe Rosenthal, executive editor of the *Times*, tells me, half-joking, he will never assign me to Central or South America "because you are a romantic. You would run off with the guerillas."

I will not know, until a brief obituary appears after Estrada has died as an old man, that he was the liaison with all the guerillas in Latin America, the second in command of the Americas Department of the Communist Party in Havana. When I meet him, he is so charismatic it would be tempting to run off with him myself, were he not married and made me an offer, which he does not.

After we talk for a few hours, he walks me into a little office and shows me a stack of papers, his cables to Havana.

"Do you want to look at my spying?" he asks. "Here."

He picks up the papers and hands them to me, many pages of them.

They are authentic diplomatic cables, harmless, with information any smart person could glean from the newspapers or with available materials.

"Take them with you. I've sent them. You can have them. You work for the Empire, *The New York Times*."

I try to hand them back.

"Take them!'

I do. I fold them up, put them in my purse, and eventually take them back to Miami with me. Now and then, over the years, I will look at them and remember that moment, that afternoon with the sun glinting off the pool and that combination of defiance and trust in his eyes. The documents are harmless. Eventually they will disappear during one of my many moves around the world.

This is a good place to say I do not try to interview the putative CIA station chief in Kingston or anyone else in the agency. I do not want their information. I will also refuse the few requests I receive from the CIA to brief them after I return from Cuba.

One of the biggest dangers to journalists in the field is the suspicion we are spies. Journalists are arrested, jailed, and sometimes killed for this. It's true we are seeking information many governments do not want us to have, but it is for the public, not for our government. And we are seeking the truth, not trying to harm someone in our country or anywhere else.

The only defense for U.S. journalists — and it may not be enough — is to have no contact at all with the CIA. I made that choice at the outset. I'll leave those "sources" to journalists who can stay safe at their desks in Washington, D. C. My choice of defense, however, has not always been sufficient.

In late September 1980, when I return to Kingston on a flight from Miami, I find myself running a high fever I can't shake. All the bones in my body ache so badly I can't move. The palms of my hands turn red, and I have a bad rash. I go to a Jamaican doctor who says he has not seen this combination of symptoms before and cannot diagnose my illness.

When I return to my hotel, I call Estrada, remembering that he's worked in Africa and must know something about tropical diseases. I'm guessing I have picked up a mosquito-borne illness during my recent trip to Haiti, where I was bitten from head to toe despite the mosquito netting.

I ask Estrada if there is a Cuban doctor in Kingston who has worked in Africa or has experience with tropical illnesses. I need someone who can come to my hotel and look at me. I am too sick to get out of bed again. He sends a doctor who examines me and tells me I have dengue fever, which is not found in Jamaica. He writes a prescription, and I send it out to get it filled. After a few days, I feel much better.

I call Estrada to thank him.

"Glad he could help," Estrada says. "He was an army doctor in Africa."

"What kind of doctor?" I ask.

Estrada laughs. "A psychiatrist."

I have no idea that I came within minutes of dying – by gunshot, not by fever – while I was lying in bed at my hotel. A team of killers was stopped on their way to assassinate me.

The Jamaican Prime Minister, Edward Seaga, who has defeated Michael Manley in the election, tells me about it later, when we are alone.

I go to interview him and fly with him and a pilot in a small plane to a place where he plans to make a speech. Once we are airborne, sitting side by side, he says, "You were almost killed."

"What?"

"We were told an assassin was coming from Miami to kill Bruce Golding, a leading member of our party. We had the name of the airline and the flight number. Then we were told the assassin was a woman."

"No!"

"Some of our people went out to kill this assassin, and fortunately they checked with me first. They told me they had the name of the person, and what's more, she was a friend of the Cuban ambassador."

I am starting to get the picture.

"I asked them the name," Seaga tells me, "And they said, 'Jo Thomas.' I told them, NO, YOU FOOLS! She's the correspondent for *The New York Times*!'"

"Jo, you came this close."

I haven't been mistaken for a spy. I've been mistaken for an assassin.

All the while, I have been worrying our little airplane will have trouble landing in a field of sugar cane, which it does handily. After this, nothing else in Jamaica worries me.

CHAPTER TWENTY-FIVE:
A DEADLY MEAL

Sometimes when you go looking for one thing, you find something else, much more important, death for sale, ready to eat at the kitchen table. This happens to me in Puerto Rico.

The *Times* has been tipped off about a giant agricultural boondoggle here. A multi-million-dollar government-sponsored project to grow rice has resulted in just two hundred acres under cultivation. A rice mill has been built for the project and needs to process 12,000 acres of rice a year to break even. What went wrong? I hope to find out.

I've learned that Puerto Ricans eat as much rice as any population in the world, a hundred pounds a year for every man, woman, and child. When the idea for growing rice arose, the island didn't grow a single grain. Instead, it was importing 380 million pounds a year. Puerto Rico has good soil, two growing seasons, and 50,000 acres of humid coastal valleys with plenty of water for irrigation.

A small pilot effort had failed at a cost of slightly more than half a million dollars. Salt water got into the fields, herbicides and pesticides were poorly used, and a small mill could not handle even the little crop that was produced. The project was abandoned.

A second try became snagged in an argument over the shaping of the fields. Should they be contoured, as in Southern rice-growing states, or leveled, as in California? They decided to level the land using outside experts, high tech instruments, and local workers, but they got the slope wrong. The water ran out of the first field they planted. A record 126 inches of rain bogged down their heavy equipment. Two hurricanes struck the island and destroyed the first seed farm. Meanwhile, the estimates for the cost of the rice mill kept rising.

As I piece together this tale of woe, several people tell me it's been a crazy idea from the beginning because no one will purchase locally grown rice anyway. It will be too plain. Puerto Rican housewives will only buy "pretty" rice.

What are they talking about?

I make a trip to the grocery store. On the shelves, I find boxes of rice and buy several brands. Back in my hotel room, I open them up and pour some rice from each box into a little pile on my desk. The rice is shiny, coated with a mixture of talc and glucose. Labels on the boxes instruct consumers to wash off the coating before they cook the rice.

This is strange. Why do they do this? Can they really wash it all off?

This odd practice, coating rice with talc, was introduced back in 1960, when new rice packaging plants opened in Puerto Rico and wanted to qualify for tax exemptions as "manufacturers," not just packagers. Since then, shiny rice has dominated the market. Talc coated rice is also being sold to Puerto Ricans in New York.

I wonder if eating talc has any effect on their health?

I make a trip to the Central Cancer Registry in Puerto Rico. I also look at data from the Census Bureau and the National Center for Health Statistics. The per capita cancer rate in Puerto Rico is lower than any state except Alaska with one huge exception: stomach cancer. The per capita stomach cancer rate is the highest in the nation.

This red flag sends me to the Puerto Rico Cancer Institute, where I meet Dr. Angel Roman-Franco. In our interview, he tells me he has done a two-year laboratory study of the possible effects of ingesting talc. His findings indicate that eating talc can cause cancer. He went to the Puerto Rican Secretary of Health and recommended banning the use of talc on rice. Dr. Roman-Franco has been ignored and silenced, and he says he is afraid of losing his job.

"Stomach cancer takes a long time to develop, about twenty years," he tells me. "Puerto Rico is only now beginning to see cancers that started in 1960. We will be seeing the results of 1980 in the year 2000."

Dr. Roman-Franco's lab studies have been conducted with cells from the stomach linings of mice. Japanese studies have shown these kinds of cells, in humans, ingest talc. Dr. Roman-Franco's early findings indicate that talc acts as a co-carcinogen with commonly eaten contaminants in food.

Although little talc is absorbed by the stomach, once it is there, it accumulates over time, the doctor tells me. "It is an indestructible material." In addition, he says, "Japanese investigations have shown nine washings do not remove all the talc."

When I ask the Puerto Rican Secretary of Health about it, he tells me Dr. Roman-Franco's study shocked him. He did not disclose the findings or act on them because he wanted more tests.

But Dr. Roman-Franco has told me he repeated his experiments at the health secretary's request and obtained the same results.

Then I call the vice president of the Rice Growers Association of California, which controls slightly more than half the rice market in Puerto Rico. He says he is unaware of Dr. Roman-Franco's study but insists, "the representations made to us by the Food and Drug Administration and the producers of talc have been that talc is absolutely safe."

Consumers have been worried for some time about contamination of talc by asbestos. For this reason, an article in *Consumer Reports* warned people not to buy coated rice. Puerto Rico's Department of Health once published its intention to ban talc but withdrew this after the supplier certified his talc had less than one percent asbestos contamination.

During the asbestos controversy, a nutritionist with the Food and Drug Administration sent a widely-publicized letter to a chain of cooperative food stores chastising the "unfortunate succession of unsubstantiated, misleading, and inaccurate messages concerning talc-coating rice that has been foisted upon the Puerto Rican population in recent years – first by the lay press and regrettably more recently by uninformed government and state agencies."

He wrote that "no evidence, to my knowledge, has been produced to prove that ingestion of talc used in this manner is carcinogenic or harmful in any way." California rice industry representatives have cited his letter as proof that talc is not harmful on rice.

After my article appears in the *Times*, Puerto Rico's Secretary of Consumer Affairs bans the use of talc on rice imported into Puerto Rico or processed or sold there. On March 3, 1981, he gives rice processors forty-five days to sell or dispose of their inventory. In his news conference, he says, "adding talc to rice represents only a cosmetic benefit for the rice dealers and not a nutritional benefit for the consumer."

Professor Carmin Bueso is president of a nutrition committee that has been trying to get talc off rice for eight years. When I call her, she is delighted about the decision: "Now we'll be eating rice the way it should be eaten."

As for the rice-growing project: the worst error came at the beginning: the decision to depend on the advice of experts from rice growing states like California and Texas, where the land is flat and the weather is different, instead of consulting with one of the world's largest rice producers, the Philippines, islands like Puerto Rico.

Locally grown rice will not reach grocery shelves in Puerto Rico for thirty years. It will arrive in 2016. A year later, Hurricane Maria will come along to destroy the rice crop and everything else.

If there is a bright spot, the stomach cancer rate in Puerto Rico will fall over the years to be on a par with states where people eat their rice with everything but talc.

CHAPTER TWENTY-SIX:
AND BABY MAKES TWO

As my career with the *Times* takes off, my romantic life is crashing. I discourage a brilliant, handsome, and ambitious younger man who may want marriage. I have hurt and divorced one good man. I don't want another commitment.

I turn instead to men who simply want to talk, drink, dance, flirt, and have sex – sometimes in the opposite order. Each is different, and all are exciting at first, but the aftermath tends to be dreary and disappointing. I'm in an apartment or hotel room by myself, wearing a towel or nothing at all, gazing into the mirror at a face that's difficult to recognize as mine. I wonder how that face will look in a few years.

I avoid sex with men I could love for fear of losing their friendship. Sometimes they dump me anyway. I refuse to sleep with sources. I turn down most men for all the usual reasons. Still, I have a hollow place in my soul and a sense time is slipping away. To fight the feeling, I focus more on work. It is easy to do. I have a twenty-four-hour workday.

Birth control pills have levelled the playing field for women when it comes to sexual freedom, but we are still at a disadvantage because we can get pregnant. This reality is underscored to me in my thirties when I start having violent headaches every day and must stop taking the pills. My doctor says they are putting me at risk of blood clots and a stroke. Casual sex is not worth dying for, so I am left with the usual alternatives to the pill. For years, I make do.

My work is more interesting than the men I meet. Although I spend the first months of 1981 traveling from one island to another, I am also spending a lot of time in Miami. South Florida has become the nation's port of entry for cocaine, and the drug trade is a huge story. The flow of drugs is bringing an ocean of cash and a blood tide of homicides. Ads for semi-automatic weapons appear on the benches of bus stops, and one particularly memorable shootout takes place at the mall in the linen department of a popular department store.

In the office of the homicide squad, the red line on the chart of the year's murders climbs off the paper and runs up the wall. The atmosphere there is one of palpable despair. No one can trust anyone else. Corruption, the police tell me, is everywhere.

"I can't go out on a date," one of the unmarried homicide detectives confides, "without having a woman offer me cocaine."

In late June, I go to Atlanta, where thirty children have been the victims of a serial killer. A suspect has been arrested for questioning, and I am sent to seek interviews with the parents of some of the victims. I am not familiar with the city or the cases, but I do know how to talk with grieving families. I drive around Atlanta and ring their doorbells. Sometimes they invite me in. Other times, I stand on the doorstep, one hand on the screen door, listening as they weep, trying to remember their exact words long enough to write them down as soon as I return to my car.

The sorrow of others is contagious, and the pain twists around inside me, worse than usual today. I'm feeling so nauseated by early evening that I beg off when other reporters invite me to join them for drinks and dinner.

I still feel sick the next day when I get home to Miami, as if I'm getting the flu. I make an appointment to see my internist, who runs some tests and asks me to wait. After a while, he returns and looks at me for a moment. He is going to say I have some new tropical bug. Or I'm working too hard, run down and anemic.

"You're pregnant. When do you want to schedule an abortion?"

What? You give me this news, and then you just say this?

"Why?"

"You're single, aren't you? What about your career?"

Go home. Just go home.

I do not reply. I stand up, get dressed, and walk out.

I find a woman ob-gyn in the telephone book and ring her office to ask for an appointment.

"I'm not married," I explain, "and I think I'm pregnant." Then I go to bed, even though it's the middle of the afternoon. I tell no one.

In a few days, when the second doctor gives me my results, she says, "Congratulations."

It cracks my heart. I weep at her kindness. I cry in shame.

No one in my family has ever had a child outside of marriage.

As soon as I got the news the first time, I knew I did not want an abortion. I will not legislate for any other woman in my situation, nor will I judge her.

As for me, there is no question of marrying – or even telling – the child's accidental father. Somehow, I will tell my family, my friends, and my colleagues I am pregnant. Then I am going to hold up my head and have this baby. My baby.

To my surprise, my conservative parents, who have given up on ever having a grandchild from me, are supportive, and my friends all think I quit trying to find a husband and got pregnant on purpose. They cheer for me and prop me up, start to finish.

My preparations are not realistic. I go out and buy a small house in South Miami, move in, and decorate a nursery. In my haste, I fail to consider that babies are not like suitcases, to be carried from one island to another. I will have to find a new assignment, and we will not be able to stay in our new house.

Like a sleepwalker, I keep working day and night as if nothing has changed, and my editors are content to keep me busy. We are all in denial. But as I became more visibly pregnant, the airlines are less willing to take me as a passenger. My efforts to conceal my belly at the ticket counter fool no one.

⁓ා౬⁓

As it gets more difficult to travel out of the country, a local story makes me think I may be killed, or at least forced to give birth, in a swamp.

Back in March 1981, I had discovered a group of Nicaraguans, former members of the Nicaraguan National Guard, together with a group of Cuban exiles, training openly in the Everglades for guerilla attacks on the Sandinistas in Nicaragua. About sixty men and a few women dressed in camouflage were based in a camp they called "Cuba," outside Miami and just beyond some new housing developments and a trash dump. One of the leaders, Jorge Gonzalez, who called himself *Bombillo*, or light bulb, told me there were three such camps in Florida.

Another man, who said I could call him "Frank" or "Ronald," but wouldn't give me his last name, said six hundred Nicaraguans in all were training in the United States. More were training in Central America.

"We'll fight the Communists with the same means they use – weapons. They don't use roses," he told me.

I asked him if he thought they were violating the Federal Neutrality Act, which forbids conspiracies to injure or destroy the property of the government of a nation with which the United States is not at war.

He said they would leave the country when they thought they were breaking the law.

When my question was asked at a Senate hearing after my story appeared, a representative from the FBI testified the Nicaraguans would not be breaking the law if they were training on private property and not using automatic weapons.

I had been so shocked to see the Nicaraguans training openly on American soil to overthrow a government not at war with the United States, I hadn't thought to ask who owned the land they were using or whether their weapons were fully automatic.

In December 1981, I learn the group is still training out in the Everglades with a new name, the Inter-American Defense Force, and I drive out to see them. This time I look at their weapons, AR-15s, the civilian semi-automatic version of the military M-16 rifle, and Ruger Mini 14's, carbines that use M-16 cartridges. United States army rangers and Vietnam veterans are among the instructors.

A man named Hector Fabián, a Cuban, is running the place, and he is not happy to see me. Fabián spent eight years directing the New York operations of Orlando Bosch, a militant Cuban exile leader who was accused of masterminding the 1976 bombing of a Cuban airliner in which seventy-three people were killed. Bosch was acquitted for lack of evidence. Years from now, the FBI will release a damning report from an informant in Caracas Venezuela, quoting one of the men who planted the bomb on the airliner and sent Bosch a message afterwards. It said: "A bus with seventy-three dogs went off a cliff and all got killed." [xxv]

When I ask Fabián if his group is breaking the law, he tells me it's simply a problem of interpretation. "Under the Carter and Nixon administrations, what we were doing was a crime. With the Reagan administration, no one has bothered us for ten months."

He offers me a ride around the camp in his jeep. I am just days away from my baby's due date, but I climb up on the seat with him, and he takes off at a good clip. The tour around the swamp is so bumpy I wonder if he is driving through the worst spots on purpose. I do not want to disappear into the swamp with him, and I am being bounced so hard I think I may go into labor on the spot.

"Thanks," I tell him. "I've seen enough."

I return to my car, parked on the pavement, and go to my office in Miami to report that paramilitaries are still training to invade Nicaragua and subsequently intend to attack Cuba and Panama. My story runs on the front page of the *Times*, and my daughter Susan is born at South Miami Hospital two days later. The soldiers in the swamp, who are sponsored by the C.I.A., leave Florida for Central America and become known as the Contras.

Many decades later, while taking in the delightful and fantastic television series *The Americans*, I will see a fictional version of two undercover Russian spies discovering this very same camp for the first time, an effort that requires disguises, a hijacked vehicle, a chase, and a gun battle. I was alone when I found them, and I was nine months pregnant.

The birth of a child changes your life completely and forever, but you do not realize this right away. After her birth, my new daughter is brought to me in a big red stocking because it is Christmas Eve. Susan Elizabeth has dark curls and my face in miniature. Since we're in Miami, every newborn girl in the nursery is getting pierced ears and gold studs for Christmas. I ask the staff to skip piercing my daughter's ears. I'll wait until she can decide for herself. This will happen in a suburban mall when she's ten years old, and I am not along.

My mother arrives from Texas to help me with the baby. On her way to the hospital, she stops by my house to pick up clothes. In my refrigerator, she finds only a plate of freshly baked Christmas cookies and a bottle of gin. I assure her I have been saving, not drinking, the gin.

Eleanor Sherman, who has become a close friend, borrows her Aunt Mary's Cadillac. It's black, the size of a yacht, and we drive home from the hospital in style. At my house, we dump the gin, get out the plate of cookies, and make coffee. We need it. Like every baby in my family, Susan will develop colic and cry without ceasing for three months. We walk the floor for hours, take her for rides in the car, and sit in the shade at the beach. She cries, and I listen to Floridian delights – reports of northern snowstorms – on my transistor radio. As Susan calms down and I come to my senses, I realize I must change my plans.

I call my mentor, Dave Jones, the *Times* national editor, for help. He arranges an assignment for me in the Washington bureau covering the Department of Justice. On the surface it makes sense, but it does not work out. I still have no sources in Washington, and the *Times* is going head-to-head with the *Washington Post* on stories out of the Department of Justice.

When I get calls from New York at night to match a story in the *Post*, I have no way to leave my baby and go looking for information. After a few weeks, I call Jones again. He offers me a day job in New York as an assistant national editor. My mother comes back from Texas, helps me pack up again, and we head for Manhattan.

Jones has been national editor for ten years, and he lives with his family in a beautiful house in Montclair, an upscale New Jersey suburb. He thinks I should look for a place to buy there, so my mom and I rent a room at an inn in Montclair, a place with few restaurants, and we live on the raspberry coffee cakes my mother keeps in one of the dresser drawers.

I end up buying a shambling, charming wooden house in Verona, New Jersey, even farther from the city than Montclair, but a real bargain. I wonder about the cheap price. Later, the neighbors will tell me the former owner killed himself there.

As we wait to close on my new house, I sublet an apartment for the summer in Stuyvesant Town in lower Manhattan. The place is furnished and looks clean, but it has so many roaches I will not let Susan learn to crawl on the floor. Instead, she learns on the king-sized bed, the first I have ever seen.

The apartment has no air conditioning. To escape the heat, Susan spends her days outdoors under the trees with a babysitter from the Caribbean we call "Miss D," available because her employers are away on vacation. Everyone in the neighborhood knows my baby, as I discover when I take her in her stroller to a nearby D'Agostino's for groceries.

"Hi, Susan," people call and smile, and Susan smiles and waves back at them. Stuyvesant Town is our introduction to city life. A kiss and a goodbye to Susan and Miss D in the morning and coffee from the cart on 43rd Street at Seventh avenue, half a block from the *Times* front door. On the second morning, the proprietor remembers I want mine with cream and sugar. A few days later, he remembers my name. "Okay, Jo." The city does not seem so big, even at Times Square.

This summer is also my introduction to life as an editor, working with my former colleagues on the national staff. I find the transition difficult. I am uncomfortable suggesting changes in their stories. I do not like pressuring them to go places they do not want to go.

My reluctance is countered by my superiors. Why haven't I fixed a story they wanted changed? Why didn't I tell someone to move faster and get on a plane?

It is the reporters or me. I learn to swallow my discomfort. Every day, no matter what, I need their stories in my hands before the deadline.

Another part of my job is overseeing "stringers." These are journalists who work for other news organizations but will cover the occasional spot story or feature story for the *Times*. We have a list of about seven hundred stringers, but many telephone numbers on the list have changed or been disconnected. Of those I can reach, many are not available when called, no matter how much I wheedle. Then there are exceptions, superstar stringers who end up joining the *Times* staff.

One day I get an invitation from Bob Reinhold, the Houston bureau chief. He's in town for a visit and wants to go for drinks at Elaine's, the go-to bar for literary celebrities. Reinhold is not your typical rumpled journalist. He favors Armani suits and Gucci loafers, and he is slim, handsome, and gay. He tells me to bring Susan.

He has a seat for me at the bar when we arrive. Elaine's is a place you expect to see eccentrics of all kinds, but not babies. Bob and I talk while Susan bangs her fists on the bar as if infants were regulars. After ten seconds, I stop feeling anxious. Reinhold is serene, as if he owns the place. When I think about it later, stuck out in the suburbs at night, our evening at Elaine's seems like a dream.

My days and nights have a fixed routine, faster or slower with the traffic in the Lincoln Tunnel. I take an early morning bus from my house in New Jersey into the city, work nine hours at the *Times,* then dash back to the Port Authority Bus Terminal for the DeCamp bus home. Now and then, someone invites me for a drink at Sardi's, a long-ago favorite of mine, but I always say no. I am gutted with guilt for spending too much time away from Susan.

My old wooden house with six bedrooms has plenty of space for a live-in babysitter, but a good babysitter is hard to find. The first babysitter, the highly recommended daughter of a policeman, turns out to be a heroin addict. Her long sleeves hide the tracks on her arms, but my mother, who has returned until I can replace Miss D, catches her going out the front door with my silver spoons in her purse.

Several other women try out for the job but quit after a few days. Then Maria, a Honduran refugee, answers my ad and comes to stay. I promise to help her through the legal maze of immigration. Then I find her a lawyer and keep my promise.

My mother stays for a few more days, and this saves us because she knows everything about babies, having raised six. Susan, who is eight months old, has stomach flu and is crying a lot. Mom helps Maria walk the floor with her. Then she calls me at the office.

"You'd better come home," she says. "I've seen a lot of sick babies, but I don't think I've seen one as sick as Susan."

When I reach the house, I pick up Susan, who is still crying, and call her pediatrician. "She has a fever and diarrhea," I tell him, "And she's looking kind of hollow around the eyes."

"Bring her to the emergency room now," he says. "Don't wait. Come as fast as you can. I'll meet you at the door."

On the way, my mother sits with Susan in the back seat.

"Hurry!" she says. "She's turning blue."

The doctor meets us at the door to the ER, takes Susan, and runs inside to put her on an IV. She is near death. Although I saw babies suffering from dehydration during the hurricane in the Dominican Republic, I did not recognize dehydration in my own daughter.

They want to keep her in the hospital overnight. She will be tied down so she cannot pull out the IV.

"We'll take good care of her," they tell me. "We're sorry, but there is no room for you to stay."

I refuse to go. I can imagine Susan waking up, frightened, and tied down, alone in a strange place.

"She will not remember it," they say.

"I don't care. I can't leave her. I'll sleep on the floor."

And that is what I do, curled at the bottom of her crib.

They have assured me a nurse will come if a baby cries, so there is no need to worry, but many babies wake up and wail long and loud, and no one comes. I do not dare call the nurses on duty for fear of being thrown out myself. When Susan wakes up during the night, I pat her. My voice and my presence soothe her. She quickly goes back to sleep. She does not remember that night, but I do.

Maria, our babysitter, lives with us until we leave New Jersey. She is learning English, but mostly she speaks Spanish with Susan and me. She takes loving care of Susan and cooks wonderful meals, but life is lonely for all of us.

Maria cannot see her own children, who are back in Honduras. I see Susan early in the morning, at night, and on weekends. Every time I leave for work, she cries. We meet our nearest neighbors, who are elderly, and one couple at church with a baby Susan's age. Susan's closest friends are the characters on Sesame Street. We have a cat, and that is our world.

Working as an editor on the national staff, I have not been paying much attention to the growing animosity in Washington to the government of Grenada, an island in the Caribbean, my old home ground. A former British colony, Grenada is still a member of the British Commonwealth, and many Americans attend medical school there. But the Cold War is underway, and in 1979, a Marxist-Leninist party, the New Jewel Movement, came to power in a coup under Prime Minister Maurice Bishop.

President Reagan is worried about the airport there. It was built when Grenada was a British colony. The Canadians designed it, the British financed it, and a London firm oversaw the construction. It has a ten-thousand-foot runway. The President thinks long-range Soviet aircraft could use it as a base to attack the United States. The government of Grenada says the airport is intended only for the intercontinental tourist trade.

On October 20, 1983, Grenada's prime minister is overthrown and then executed, and his deputy takes over. Five days later, the United States invades Grenada. Early reports are that government forces are putting up little resistance, but the Cubans on the island are fighting back.

It's a Tuesday night, and the foreign desk calls me at home in New Jersey to ask me to go immediately to Havana. American reporters have been unable to get onto Grenada and are covering the fighting from Barbados, more than 160 miles away. The main armed resistance against the American invaders is coming from the Cubans, but no one knows how many are there, or what the situation is. Little information is coming from either the U.S. or Cuba.

Earlier in the day, the *Times* asked to send a reporter to Havana, but the Cuban government refused. Given the hostile relations between the two countries, the Cubans did not want to give visas to any U. S. reporters. When the editors countered by suggesting me, the Cubans agreed. I don't know why. Perhaps because they knew me from before.

I tell the editors I can't go. Maria will not stay alone in the house with Susan overnight. She does not want to be responsible. When my editors insist, I think of Amy and Doug Halsey, good friends of mine who live in Miami. Their son Mark is five months younger than Susan. Amy replaced Eleanor as manager of the *Times* bureau in Miami before Mark was born, then quit to become a full-time mom. Doug is an attorney.

I call Amy to ask if she would take care of Susan if I brought her to Miami.

"You know New York," I tell her. "Everything is an emergency with them. I'll only be gone for a day or two until they can send someone else, but right now, I'm the only one who can get a visa to Havana, and the Cubans are the main players in Grenada."

Amy laughs because it's an outrageous request. But she knows me, she knows the newspaper, and she's my friend. So, she says yes. The *Times* books tickets for the next morning, and the Cubans say they will have a visa waiting for me.

Susan is not two years old when I drop her off with a family she does not remember. She has always been at home, never even to day care. She is a quiet child, late talking. She understands English and Spanish, but she speaks only a few words. I know Amy will take loving care of her, and the Halsey's house is set up for toddlers. It's even decorated for Halloween.

I glance at the screened-in swimming pool. "I wish I could stay. She can't swim, so please don't let her near the water!" Amy is shushing me during the handoff, giving Susan a hug and me a tiny push toward the waiting taxi, assuring me all will be well. Still, I worry all the way to the airport and on the flight to Havana.

The fighting in Grenada is still being covered from Barbados when I arrive in Havana. The Associated Press is reporting that six hundred Cuban soldiers and two hundred Cuban civilians have been captured. Some were photographed near the airstrip by photographers who were among the dozen journalists whisked over to the island for a brief tour while hundreds of paratroopers were arriving and the fighting continued.

President Reagan, who gets the banner headline in the *Times* today, says the U.S. troops arrived just in time to keep Grenada from becoming a full-fledged Soviet-Cuban colony dedicated to exporting terrorism and undermining democracy.

Others disagree, including the UN General Assembly. Within a week, by a vote of 108 to nine, they will condemn the invasion as a "flagrant violation of international law."

Two days before the invasion, a huge truck bomb killed 241 U. S. Marines in their barracks at the airport in Beirut, Lebanon, where they had been sent as peacekeepers. As pundits will say in years to come, it's possible Reagan "kicked the cat" in Grenada to divert attention from those dead Marines. [xxvi]

I am wondering if this invasion is something of an overreaction. It's true that the Prime Minister, Maurice Bishop, was friendly with the Cubans and the Jamaicans, but he also belonged to the Non-Aligned Movement, a group of developing nations not aligned with any major power bloc. I met his deputy prime minister, Bernard Coard, the man now in power, during a recent visit to Grenada. He reminded me of a sociology professor, with nothing particularly sinister or anti-American about him.

Here in Havana, the Cuban government says it has little concrete information. Its embassy has lost contact with Cubans in defensive positions, and Cuban forces are under heavy attack. The government publicizes a note from the U. S. State Department. It says, in part, "there would have been no problem in the first place between us if the Cubans in Grenada had not fired first against our forces."

The Cubans want to get their people out of Grenada. They have agreed to let Colombia and Spain serve as mediators. As the hours pass, the government in Havana says six hundred Cubans, including one hundred wounded, are now prisoners. Another one hundred are missing. The number of dead is believed to be small.

Looking for better numbers, I decide to speak with members of the diplomatic corps, starting with the British ambassador, who I have not met before. Although Grenada gained independence from Britain in 1974, Britian still has a governor general in residence there. Perhaps the British ambassador in Havana has news he will share. He turns out to be a delightful man with a big house and a large staff. He is happy to meet me but has no information to share. He says to check back with him.

I then try my old friends from the Caribbean diplomatic corps, hoping someone from the socialist countries will introduce me to the Grenadian ambassador, but he is back in Grenada. I leave word for the chargé d'affaires, who sends word he will speak with me.

Early the next afternoon, I interview Ricardo Alarcón, Cuba's deputy foreign minister. I have known him for several years. He calls President Reagan's assertion that the Cubans are exporting terrorism from Grenada "a lie," one of "several big lies."

Alarcón tells me that the Cuban ambassador in Grenada has still not been able to establish contact with the United States military commander there. He does give me the total number of Cubans on the island, including diplomats and children, 790. He also tells me Cuban construction workers have only "light weapons for their defense given them by the Bishop government in case of an attack." He has no accurate figures on the number of Cuban dead or injured.

That same day, I get an anguished call from Miami. Amy Halsey is on the line.

"Susan hasn't stopped crying since you left!" she says. "I just don't know how to comfort her! When are you coming home? I thought you were only going for a little while!"

My heart shrinks into a knot. This story is not going to stop any time soon, and there are no other American reporters in Havana.

"If I can get permission to bring her here, do you think you can get her on a plane?" I ask.

"You're kidding me!"

"I don't know what to do, Amy. I'll call you back."

The timing of her call is terrible. I have just missed a chance to make a personal appeal to Alarcón for a visa for Susan. But I call my minder from the Ministry of the Interior and beg for one.

"Why should we give a visa to a baby?"

"She's stuck in Miami. I have never left her before, and she won't stop crying."

"This is not what we do. I don't think it will be possible."

"Please think about it. If she can't come, I do not think I can stay here and keep working."

The machinery of bureaucracy grinds slowly and rarely kindly. My minder says she will call me back. I am not optimistic. I am a reporter looking for a favor from a country that is shooting at mine.

Before I file my story, I stop by to see the British ambassador again, just in case he has inside information he can share from London or the governor general in Grenada.

Again, no. Or if he has, he is not saying. Then, seeing the dejected look on my face, he asks what's wrong. When I tell him about Susan, he says I should certainly bring her to Havana – no problem. He has plenty of room for guests. We could both stay at his residence. He can arrange a nanny for her while I work.

When I return to my hotel, there is good news. The Cubans have agreed to a visa for Susan, and I have an interview lined up for tomorrow with the first secretary of the Grenadian Embassy, who had been left in charge here. I want to ask him about the invasion and the killing of Maurice Bishop, the Prime Minister.

First, I call Amy Halsey and tell her about Susan's visa. Amy has Susan's passport. Together, we arrange to buy a ticket for her on a flight bringing relatives to visit Havana the day after tomorrow, and Amy agrees to find a woman passenger willing to carry Susan on her lap for the trip.

In these days, airline travel is much more informal than it will be in the future, and this includes travel in and out of Miami International Airport, even travel to Cuba. In hindsight, I should be more worried about the possible traumatic effects on Susan of such a trip, but I have seen Cuban women with their children, and I am certain that any woman who agrees to bring her on the plane will be kind. I am desperate to comfort my daughter.

I tell the British ambassador Susan is on the way and send a cable to New York to explain Susan will be joining me, with a place to stay and childcare all set. Then I file a long, detailed account of the overthrow and death of the Prime Minister of Grenada at the hands of his army and the inside story of his struggles with Bernard Coard in the Central Committee of their party.

A cable arrives that night from New York. It says, "Come home. *The New York Times* is not sending a toddler to Havana."

Susan attaches herself to me tightly as soon as I appear in Miami, and we spend several days calming down at Amy and Doug's. She does not cry. In her silence, she simply refuses to let go until we are at home in New Jersey again.

Only one other time, while working in the U. S., do I take Susan on assignment. Her babysitter Maria comes along, and we go to Iowa for the Presidential caucuses in February of 1984. I am still an assistant national editor, working with the political reporters, and I think it will be smart to be on the ground there with them. The reporters are all men I know.

It is a miserable experience from start to finish.

At our hotel in Des Moines, Maria and Susan are asked to leave the indoor pool the first day they go swimming. Maria has brown skin, and Susan has dark hair, and I am sure someone thinks they do not belong in an all-white setting. Maria's English is not up to the task of explaining they are guests at the hotel.

Maria is upset, and I am furious when I return to our rooms and find her in tears. I straighten it out with the management, but I cannot persuade Maria to return to the pool. There is snow on the ground, too cold for Maria and Susan. They play in the room and in the hall while I work.

I trail around Des Moines, talking with voters on my own and taking in the scene, but I am not welcomed by my colleagues. I feel as if I have fallen through a time warp, back to the city room in Cincinnati, where the other journalists never invited me to lunch. No invitations for drinks or dinner with the boys in Des Moines. I invite myself several times, but it does not go well. I tell myself it is because I am an editor, but that isn't it. I have seen these reporters' effortless ways with editors who are men. It's a *Boys on the Bus* thing, the Washington political gang transplanted to corn country but still stuck together. I give up. I can't figure it out and don't want to.

I hate being here. I stick it out for a few days. The last straw is a trip I inflict on myself, a visit to a hog farm, one of those industrial setups with thousands of hogs and a herd sire the size of a pickup truck. When the owner walks me into a temperature-controlled building stuffed with hundreds of pigs the same age and size, shoulder to shoulder, the pigs shrink back from us in waves of fear. They're smart, these pigs, and their fright tears out my heart.

I go back to the hotel, pack up Susan and Maria, and head for the airport. I'll edit election stories from my desk in New York.

As it turns out, the guys and the pigs in Des Moines have done me a favor by running me off because one day, back in the newsroom in New York, when the door to Abe Rosenthal's office is open, something moves me to stop in for a chat.

After a few minutes of small talk, I learn from him that the editors on the foreign desk never told anyone Susan was stranded in Miami when I was in Havana. When I planned to fly her down to join me, Abe thought I was being a prima donna, a species Abe despises. He flew into a rage, ordered me home, and vowed I would never get another foreign assignment.

I try to control my own shock at the people I thought had my back while I explain to him what happened. Abe responds by telling me I have just rescued my career. On the spot, he offers me the choice of two foreign assignments: India or London.

"London," I say.

CHAPTER TWENTY-SEVEN:
THE BLACK TAXI

It's August 12, 1984, and my room is on a high floor of the Forum Hotel in Belfast, Northern Ireland. It's a modern hotel, large, and luxurious. Under its old name, the Europa, it was bombed twenty-nine times by the Provisional Irish Republican Army. People called it "the most bombed hotel in the world." I am unaware.

The Europa was intended for the rich and famous. When it opened next door to the Grand Opera House in 1971, the Troubles in Northern Ireland had been underway for three years, so it also welcomed visiting journalists. John Sergeant, formerly with the BBC, called it "a big modern hotel with no normal clients."

The Europa's high visibility as a landmark building and a symbol of investment made it a prime target for the IRA. The presence of so many journalists almost guaranteed maximum publicity for any attack. The hotel windows were blown out so often that replacements for each one were kept ready in a separate warehouse. The bombs were usually detonated in the street, although an IRA unit once walked into the lobby and left a bomb in a box labelled "IRA" on the reception desk. After each blast, the staff swept up and went back to work.

My office in London booked me into the Forum, as it is now called. I know only that it is the unofficial headquarters for foreign journalists here. I saw some television crews in the lobby when I checked in, but no one looked familiar. I waved off the bellman, took my room key, and headed for the elevator.

My room is at the rear of the hotel. It's late at night, and the view from my window is a dark city in the rain. It's still summer, but the room is cold, and there's no way to heat it up. I don't want to be here. Susan is home in London with her nanny. I hope this is a short trip.

The Troubles in Northern Ireland have a low priority at *The New York Times*, so the assignment goes to the junior correspondent in the London bureau. Unfortunately, that's me. I love the poetry of William Butler Yeats but do not remember its political context. As a WASP from the American South, I have grown up with no Irish American friends to remind me.

My family background is British, and after three months in London, I am fast becoming an anglophile. This seems harmless enough. From the moment my plane landed at Heathrow, my welcome to Britain has been both warm and disconcerting.

The New York Times sent a chauffeur in a Rolls Royce to pick me up at the airport. He brought an invitation from my publisher, Arthur O. Sulzberger Sr. – "Mr. Sulzberger" to me – to have lunch with him that day at the Savoy.

Our drive to London was nerve wracking. Susan was exhausted by the overnight flight and pitched a tantrum as soon as we got into the car. She howled and kicked the polished wood paneling until she finally fell asleep. Luckily for me, my mother had come along to help us. She took charge of Susan and our massive pile of luggage after the driver stopped to unload at our temporary flat on Portobello Road. The chauffeur then took me to lunch with Mr. Sulzberger.

Since then, I've found myself strangely *at home* in London. It's an odd sensation for someone accustomed to being an outsider. The *Times* pays most of my living expenses, so – unlike New York – I can live comfortably with Susan on a journalist's modest salary. We have a single-family house in a good neighborhood at the bottom of Highgate Hill. I employ a charwoman and a nanny.

A busy social life has materialized. Invitations, both official and personal, arrive every day to receptions, parties, dances, even to the races at Royal Ascot. I'm oblivious to the scrutiny I face, clueless I am on stage. These new men and women are so warm and charming I fail to realize they may not actually be friends.

My status has changed, and so have the goals for my reporting. Officially, I am a journalist, but I am also an informal ambassador for my newspaper, for my country, and for my profession. The big stories here involve policy. Front page stories come from British government sources, so these officials are vital to us, as are the social occasions where we rub shoulders with them. Local stories, which in the past have opened doors to great investigations, are less desired.

I have worked in the Caribbean and Central America, so I am not a newcomer as a foreign correspondent, but my office has always been in the United States, where journalists do not betray the confidence of other staff members, especially not to the government. I've never given a thought to offhand remarks on any topic, including government wrongdoing, never worried about being overheard in my office.

The rules change abroad. Nothing I say in the London bureau is private: no conversation I have on the telephone, no controversial book or report I want to read. I worried about government surveillance in Cuba. No one cautions me here.

I have been reading the British and Irish mainstream press as I prepare for my assignment in Northern Ireland. Their stories seem to strike a good balance about the situation. I've already been assured the American point of view of the Troubles is nuts, a lot of dangerous, romantic nonsense about a united Ireland. I have also been warned never to write anything that might encourage Americans to get involved. Still, I can't make any sense of it.

At the end of World War I, on April 16, 1922, Winston Churchill, who was then Secretary of State for the colonies, made a historic address to Parliament while trying to win consent for the Anglo-Irish Treaty that created Northern Ireland.

"Every institution, in the world was strained. Great Empires have been overturned. The whole map of Europe has been changed," he said. "The position of countries has been violently altered. The modes of thought of men, the whole outlook on affairs, the grouping of parties, all have

encountered violent and tremendous changes in the deluge of
the world, but as the deluge subsides and the waters fall short,
we see the dreary steeples of Fermanagh and Tyrone emerging
once again. The integrity of their quarrel is one of the few
institutions that has been unaltered in the cataclysm which has
swept the world.

"That says a lot for the persistency with which Irish
men on the one side or the other are able to pursue their
controversies. It says a great deal for the power which Ireland
has, both Nationalist and Orange, to lay their hands upon the
vital strings of British life and politics, and to hold, dominate,
and convulse, year after year, generation after generation, the
politics of this powerful country."

Why are Catholics and Protestants in Northern Ireland
still shooting and blowing each other up over religion?
Churchill did not know, and I have dodged the question and
postponed coming to Belfast. Until now.

Earlier today, in the afternoon, a large crowd gathered
in West Belfast to hear Martin Galvin, an American and the
publicity director of the Northern Irish Aid Committee.
Galvin's group, commonly known as NORAID, raises money
for the families of the Provisional Irish Republican Army, the
paramilitary organization fighting for a united Ireland.
Membership in the IRA is illegal here.

West Belfast is a poor and beleaguered district of the
city. Its residents, most of whom are Catholics, have suffered
great violence during the Troubles. West Belfast is a center of
Irish nationalism as well as supporters of the armed branch of
that group, who called themselves republicans. The rally this
afternoon was to be a peaceful annual commemoration of

internment, which began in August 1971 and ended in late 1975.

During that time, two thousand people were imprisoned without trial and interrogated in ways that constituted some of the worst abuses of the Troubles and gave rise to some of its worst violence in the streets. The Irish government took the cases of fourteen men to the European Court of Human Rights, which ruled that five methods used by the British during their "interrogation in depth" amounted to torture. When the British government appealed, the court modified its ruling to say the interrogation was "inhuman and degrading treatment."

The people who attended this afternoon's rally, including 130 Americans, sat down on the ground to emphasize it was a peaceful event, but Galvin, the speaker, had been banned by the British government from entering Northern Ireland. Galvin, who also has Irish citizenship, appeared anyway.

To arrest Galvin, the police charged the seated audience of men, women, and children, using riot sticks and firing four-inch plastic bullets. One bullet struck and killed John Downes, twenty-three years old, who was sitting with his wife Brenda and their child.

Downes became the fifteenth person to die since these bullets were introduced when Downes himself was a child, eleven years ago. More than 40,000 rounds of these bullets have been fired by the police and army since then, and they will end up killing seventeen people in all, eight of them children.

Now John Downes is dead, Galvin is gone, and British and Irish politicians are demanding investigations. Protesters are organizing a big march tomorrow. For me, there is a local angle – NORAID is based in New York.

I am unprepared. I don't know anyone. I have an address in West Belfast where the march will begin. I have phone numbers for the press officers of the Northern Ireland government in Stormont Castle and the Northern Ireland police force, the Royal Ulster Constabulary. I have no names or contact numbers for NORAID.

I don't want to be here. I want to go home. I turn away from the hotel window, walk to the bed, and pull down the covers. Without taking off my clothes, I crawl in, lie back, and listen to the silence.

In the morning, I buy breakfast and every newspaper I can find. I make the mistake of asking for coffee instead of the incredibly good tea in the hotel dining room, and I order my first "Ulster Fry." Despite its name – for the northern Irish province of Ulster – it is a favorite everywhere in Ireland, dubbed by some "a heart attack on a plate" –a fried egg, cooked tomato, half cooked bacon, and black blood sausage, accompanied by toast properly cooled.

I find good fare in the newspapers. Letitia Fitzpatrick of *The Irish News* reports: "John Downes had been sitting on the wall beside me when he was hit in the chest and mouth." The readers of *The Irish News* are all Roman Catholics who identify as Irish nationalists.

The *Belfast Telegraph* reports Downes was once found guilty of membership in the IRA and possession of a firearm under suspicious circumstances. The *Belfast Telegraph* is the vehicle for the other side of the house, entirely Protestant and unionist. Its readers consider themselves British.

It is a reflex of government press officers, here as in other places, to cast suspicion as soon as possible on the character of victims of police shootings. The truth, if it is otherwise, can come out later when the public has lost interest.

I have no clue about the political leanings of the Belfast newspapers, which have everything to do with what they report. Without knowing these critically crucial differences or what credibility to give their reports, I will quote both newspapers in my story later today.

The protest march has been declared illegal but is going to happen anyway.

This is not looking good.

My nerves take another hit when other reporters in the lobby warn me it's a bad idea to go to West Belfast alone.

I don't even know where West Belfast is.

When I spot a television crew going out the door, I ask if they have room to let me ride along, and they do. I'm glad for the company and relieved to know I'll get to the right place.

This is my first experience with an Irish march, and it is not like American ones I've seen, full of theater but short on distance. It takes place in the rain, and it goes on and on and on. My dress heels are not high, but they are new, and my feet are blistered after a few hundred yards. After the first mile, my feet are bleeding. Most of the Belfast women are wearing spike heels, and they seem indefatigable.

I catch up with Paula, in red high heels, who tells me she normally does not march. This time, things are different. "I saw the brutality of the police on the television," she says.

Just for a moment, I remember the way I felt about seeing the Chicago police beat hundreds of young demonstrators outside the Democratic national convention in 1968.

Marian, also in high heels, has her baby boy in her arms in case there's more violence. "I had him in a pram at the rally yesterday," she says, "but a pram's awkward to run with."

The march seems to go on forever, silent under black flags, up and up the Falls Road, past scarred storefronts, a graveyard, and the bunker that was the local police station. It ends at the spot where Downes died. Lengthy speeches follow, including a statement from Galvin that someone reads aloud, criticizing the police and praising the crowd for risking their lives against "the real men of violence," namely, the authorities.

I get my first look at Gerry Adams, the bearded president of Sinn Fein, the political wing of the Provisional IRA. He looks more like a college professor than a terrorist. He tells us he was standing next to Galvin when the police charged the crowd. Blaming the IRA for Downes' killing, he says, is "like blaming a woman for provoking rape."

When the last speaker is done, I turn around and look for the television crew. They are gone and so are all the other reporters and photographers. The rest of the crowd is quickly melting away. As I make my way back down the Falls Road, children start throwing rocks at passing police vehicles.

To avoid them, I turn into a narrow street and find my way blocked by two barricades of burning furniture. I turn back. I am already lost and feeling conspicuous in my business suit and heels, and now I am caught between the throng of children throwing rocks and several armored police vehicles bearing down on the children and on me.

A man comes from behind me and pulls me out of the way – the children know how and when to scatter – and I find myself standing with the man and his family in the front room of their small row house.

"My children grew up with that," he tells me. "The Protestants won't give an inch, and neither will we. The future looks bleak. Bleak." We talk for a few minutes. I want to stay longer, but I am on deadline and nervous about what I am going to say in my story. The family explains to me how to get back to the hotel.

I walk part of the way back down the Falls Road, then see a black taxi and flag it down. I get in and ask to go to the Forum Hotel. It is not a real taxi. I have no idea what a significant risk I have just taken.

Black taxis as I know them in London do not exist in West Belfast, nor in the Protestant unionist neighborhood of East Belfast. Genuine taxis are afraid to operate in either place. They have been replaced by lookalike black taxis that run up and down the main roads, making point-to-point stops. The drivers are brave, tough men, and passengers know them personally or will not get in.

The men who drive the Falls Road black taxis are Catholics, sympathetic to the nationalist cause and courageous enough to risk attacks by Protestant paramilitaries. Passengers never enter one of these taxis without knowing the driver. For a long time, Catholics were being murdered by a gang of serial killers, the Shankill Butchers, who kidnapped them at random in a black taxi.

The driver for this gang once drove his taxi up and down the Shankill Road in East Belfast in the usual way. But then he joined forces with a member of the illegal Ulster Volunteer Force, a Protestant paramilitary. The two filled his cab with knives and a meat cleaver. Then, with other members of the gang, they cruised the city in search of Catholics to kidnap, torture, and kill, a total of twenty-three men and women between the years 1975 and 1982. The Butchers were finally stopped two years ago, when a victim escaped and identified some of them to the police. The fear of more killers like them lingers in the air.

Thankfully, my taxi driver is not a serial killer, and he does not tell me this is not a real taxi. When I say I'm an American journalist and ask to go to the Forum Hotel, he drives me there, as if he does this every day. I pay him and get out, not knowing anything special has happened.

CHAPTER TWENTY-EIGHT: GETTING IT STRAIGHT

I'm focused on trying to set the day's march in context. I gather up the wire service coverage my office in London has sent by telex. I put in a call to the police, the Royal Ulster Constabulary, who do not have much to say, then call the Northern Ireland Office, the administrative outpost of the British government. Their spokesman is agreeable and helpful. I am happy to have his guidance.

I like the British, and it is easy to accept their self-portrait as the honest brokers between the warring parties in Northern Ireland. In their view, the police are enforcing law and order among terrorists and religious bigots. The buzzword for British policy here under Prime Minister Margaret Thatcher is "normalization." The press office spins the Troubles as a struggle against terrorists, gangsters, and criminals.

I don't know how to contact the warring parties in a hurry. The paramilitaries have no press officers — the internet does not exist — and it is illegal to belong to a paramilitary organization. (They do have agreed-upon ways to claim responsibility for bombings and other attacks, ways known to the authorities but never to me.) The legal arms of these organizations, Sinn Fein for the IRA, and the Ulster Defense Association for the Protestant paramilitaries, have press offices, but they are haphazard operations at best. I do not find them on this trip.

Even so, when I sit down to write, I am not willing to adopt the language of the British tabloids. They call Northern Ireland a place of "mindless violence." My experience with urban riots at home has taught me the participants cannot be dismissed out of hand. Everyone is suffering and has something at stake. No one is mindless.

A small alarm went off in my head today when the press officer cautioned me, as others have in London, that ill-informed Americans with romantic, anachronistic ideas about Northern Ireland have caused untold death and damage with articles the IRA can use as propaganda to raise money and other kinds of support: "A bad newspaper story can do more harm than a bomb."

When someone in the government or the police has done something terrible – such as shoot an innocent person like John Downes – there are important questions about accountability and policy that must be answered. One way to squelch such questions is to raise the alarm that probing state violence will give propaganda to terrorists and encourage more violence.

As I will come to see, the British government, which has an adroit public relations operation with many resources, is at its most masterful in Northern Ireland when it pretends the paramilitaries, especially the IRA, are the only ones who care about propaganda. The British are even more successful when they persuade journalists the government is not engaged in its own propaganda war.

In my first story, I try to cover all bases. On the one hand, I report that the Roman Catholic Archbishop, the Right Rev. Cahal Daly, who is based in Dublin, has called for discontinuing the use of plastic bullets. On the other hand, I dutifully pass along the archbishop's characterization of Galvin's appearance at the rally as a "blatant publicity stunt" designed to support "the murderous purposes of the IRA."

I am so uncertain when I file my story, I am shocked when it makes the front page. My editors praise it effusively. I feel so relieved and validated I have no clue how many fundamental errors of perception and bias I have just passed along to my readers. Not realizing I've blown this story; I send three more dispatches that are just as bad.

As I will discover, I can't fly into Belfast, spend a few days, touch a few bases, and understand what I'm seeing. I know too little to put anything in context.

Foolishly proud of myself for finishing my first reporting assignment in Belfast and making my editors happy, I race for the airport, hoping not to return soon.

In six weeks, the *Marita Ann,* a 50-foot Irish trawler, is captured off County Kerry with a cargo of seven tons of automatic weapons, ammunition, and explosives. Early reports say the weapons came from the United States on a larger vessel and were bound for the IRA.

Sinn Fein, the political arm of the IRA, is its only public face. Three days after the seizure of the *Marita Ann,* Sinn Fein leader Gerry Adams is arrested in a pre-dawn raid. That same day, I fly up to Belfast to see if I could interview him when he gets out. I want to ask him about the *Marita Ann*.

I find him late in the afternoon at the Sinn Fein office on the Falls Road. It is a ramshackle, disconcerting place with a surveillance camera and a cage of wire mesh covering the entrance. When I show up, Adams agrees to see me, and we sit down in a little office. People bring us mugs of tea and ask if we want something to eat. We both say yes, and they bring sandwiches.

"They questioned me for six hours about Martin Galvin," Adams says. "They wanted to know how he got here. They picked up seven other people too."

"All from Sinn Fein?"

"Yes, and they let us go without charges. The police and army stop all of us all the time. They could have brought us in for questioning any time." He looks tired. "That we were arrested in dawn swoops speaks volumes for the police state we live in."

He says nothing about how the police treated him. At this time, I do not know that police interrogations in the North can be horrific, so I don't ask Adams how he was treated. It also does not occur to me that Adams might just want to go home instead of talking to me.

"I heard about your arrest," I say, "and I wondered if it had anything to do with the seizure of the *Marita Ann*."

"No, it was just Galvin," he says. "I don't know anything about the *Marita Ann*."

Then he asks, "What about you? Are you new?"

"I just got to the London Bureau at the *Times*. I'm a single mom, and I have a toddler, a daughter who is two years old. We used to live in New Jersey. We're trying to get used to living in London."

"You should come up here. Spend some time in Northern Ireland with some Sinn Fein families. See what life is like for them."

I am eating my sandwich and staying calm, but there is nothing I want less than the pressure of an extended public relations campaign from the families of terrorists.

I thank Adams and tell him I'll think about it. "I'm busy. I also cover England, Scotland, and Wales. In fact, I'm covering the Tory Party Conference in Brighton, and I'm hoping to take my daughter and her nanny to the conference with me. It might be fun for them."

Adams ends our interview abruptly. I've noticed he hasn't touched his sandwich, which strikes me as odd, since we both said we were hungry. As I leave, I wonder if I have insulted him, by not jumping on his invitation to visit.

Ten days later, the IRA bombs the Tory Party Conference. They target the room above Prime Minister Thatcher's at the Grand Brighton Hotel. She is unhurt, but five people are killed and thirty-one are injured. Susan and I are not there. I'd planned to go, but this was a presumption. The conference is a big story, and my boss, Johnny Apple, covers it instead. He is not hurt. The IRA was aiming at the Prime Minister and her cabinet, not the press.

From all appearances, the Brighton bombing has everything to do with the seizure of the *Marita Ann*. It is the IRA's effort to show it can strike anywhere it wants, even without a massive arsenal of weapons. The IRA communique after the bombing says only, "Today we were unlucky, but remember, we only have to be lucky once. You have to be lucky always. Give Ireland peace, and there will be no war."

Later, at the Sinn Fein *ard fheis*, or annual party conference, in Dublin, Adams calls the Brighton bombing "a blow for democracy."

The bombing does put Northern Ireland at the top of my reporting agenda. I must understand what is going on there. I call Adams and say I will take him up on his offer to stay with a Sinn Fein family in Belfast.

"They just have to be a typical family, not people you can disown later if they say something you don't like. And I would like to stay for a week."

He agrees.

Then I call Andy Tyrie, the head of the Ulster Defense Association (UDA), the Protestant unionist paramilitary organization in the North. I introduce myself and tell him I am going to be spending a week with a Sinn Fein family. I ask for equal time with a trusted UDA family. Same arrangements.

"I'll get back to you," Tyrie says. A few days later, he has a family for me, and I have permission from the *Times* to do the story.

I do not know where such a long feature story will find a place in the newspaper, perhaps the Sunday magazine, but the truth is, I do not see how I can cover Northern Ireland if I can't understand it. Although we speak the same language, the words of the people there do not make sense to me.

I have already seen what a huge adjustment is required to live in another country. I know a stay in a conflict zone like

West Belfast will be daunting enough without Susan. Her nanny Jill gets me off the hook by inviting Susan to stay in Yorkshire with Jill's family and her.

CHAPTER TWENTY-NINE:
PARAMILITARIES AT HOME

The flight to Belfast is brief—less than an hour—but the long journey to the plane at the London airport seems interminable, a maze of security checks and white corridors. I need a stack of IDs, including two driver's licenses, press passes, my passport, and visas. On the street in Belfast, I notice security cameras everywhere. This is not my first encounter with a highly policed state – Cuba is one – but the security presence is more visible in Belfast, with cameras, checkpoints, armored vehicles, soldiers, and policemen everywhere.

West Belfast is a Victorian neighborhood of brick row houses shouldered onto narrow streets. It's November, and it's almost dark by mid-afternoon, as the sun disappears and the gloom of coal fires mixes with mist from the sea.

I find the Wilsons in a tiny row house just off Springfield Road. They are newlyweds and leading members of Sinn Fein. Padraic Wilson, twenty-five years old, and his wife Sal, who is just twenty-one, smile when they open the door. My fears evaporate. Shortly after I arrive, they give me house keys and say I am free to come and go.

The house is tiny, with two rooms upstairs and two downstairs, the kind where generations of working-class Catholics have raised multitudes of children. The only heat comes from a coal fireplace in the parlor. You stay near it if you can at night, then race upstairs and dive under blankets into a freezing bed. I learn the first night to keep my clothes on. For the first time ever, I understand the drawings in children's books of *The Night Before Christmas,* showing a man wearing a night cap to bed. I wear my wool hat.

The noises and whistles of a nearby foundry are the heartbeat of the neighborhood. There are no front yards. Mothers roll their infants onto the sidewalk in prams and park them there, keeping watch through open front doors. Army foot patrols, guns at the ready, scuttle down the sidewalks and around the prams as the mothers ignore them and children mimic them, firing imaginary guns at the passing soldiers.

Padraic and Sal were children when the Troubles began. Both grew up in republican families, and they're veterans of home searches by the Army and police. Both have family members in prison and on the run. Padraic served time in prison for having explosives in the back yard. He's now doing political work for Sinn Fein. Sal tells me this while pouring cups of tea.

We are about to sit down to a dinner of meat and boiled potatoes, served on her best china. There is no room for a table, so we eat on our laps. I've never dined with someone accused of making a bomb, but it's hard to be scared with a lap full of meat and potatoes. I take a mug of tea and ask Padraic about his life and his hopes for the future.

He was seventeen when he first went to prison – he confessed to owning the explosives found in his family's garden, he says. The police who found them demanded a confession or they would arrest him, his father, and his brother.

Prison ended up being his university. It was where he participated in years of "dirty protests," where prisoners trying to win political status refused to dress and live like ordinary criminals. So, they went naked except for blankets.

"I did nothing," Padraic tells me. "I didn't wash my hair. I didn't brush my teeth, didn't bathe, didn't do anything for three years."

During this time, other republican prisoners engaged in two hunger strikes to protest their situation in the prison. The first one, in 1980, ended when a settlement seemed likely. After the government refused to let the prisoners wear their own clothing, a second hunger strike began on March 1, 1981.

Bobby Sands, former commander of the prison for the IRA, was the first, followed by other hunger strikers. Prime Minister Thatcher accused them of a suicide campaign and refused to grant their requests. Sands won an election to Parliament on April 9, but died on the May 5, the sixty-sixth day of his strike. More than 100,000 people lined the roads for his funeral. A popular portrait of Sands hangs in the parlor of Padraic and Sal's home.

Sands was the first of ten hunger strikers from the IRA and the Irish National Liberation Army to die one by one over the summer of 1981. Thatcher did not yield. The last six men called off their strikes on October 3, 1981. The government announced partial concessions, including prisoners' right to

wear their own clothes, but it would not recognize their
political status.

Padraic was released in April 1982. Looking at him two
years later, with his hair cut short, it is hard to imagine him as
a filthy prisoner. He went barefoot on the pavement for so
long, he tells me, he can barely tolerate shoes with hard soles.

After dinner, Sal trades her business clothes for a pair
of overalls, and we head for the Whiterock Community Center
for her evening class in Gaelic. We take a black taxi. The buses
are attack-prone and usually empty. Along the roads, there are
lumps in the asphalt where buses have burned.

In prison, Gaelic has become a way for Republican
prisoners to converse without easily being understood.
Outside the prisons, there is a resurgence of interest in the
language in the North among those who want to maintain
their Irish culture and heritage. The Gaelic class we attend is
standing room only.

Late on my first night, after Sal and I return and go to
bed, I make my way to the unheated bathroom at the back of
the house, off the kitchen, not bothering to turn on the light. I
walk silently, the way mothers of young children do, out of
sheer habit. As I head back to my room through the dark,
Padraic comes in through the back door and takes a long,
sharp breath before he realizes who I am. I laugh aloud
because I am not the only one in the house who is ever afraid.
Once I know this, it is easier to listen to Padraic, and we have
long conversations about the conflict here.

In the following days, there are times I accompany
Padraic and Sal. Other times, I wander around the

neighborhood. The neighbors tell me it can be a dangerous place. When joyriders roar down their streets, burglars break into their homes, and glue sniffers plague their families, they are afraid to call the police. They regard the police as a Protestant sectarian force, as likely to hurt them as to help them. When trouble comes calling, they are on their own.

Padraic hopes Sinn Fein will become a legitimate political force. At the same time, he worries "there's a very good and real chance that I'll go back to jail." In a brief time, both his hopes and his worries will come true.

Danny Morrison, the publicity director of Sinn Fein, has put forward a controversial notion Republicans should campaign with "the Armalite and the ballot box." [Known in Northern Ireland as the Armalite, this weapon is known in the United States as the AR-15 semi-automatic rifle.]

Accordingly, Sinn Fein has launched a campaign in electoral politics. Eventually, this will allow Sinn Fein to participate in negotiations leading to the Good Friday Agreement of 1998 and a power sharing arrangement with the unionist parties. In 2023, Sinn Fein will become the largest vote getter in local government elections in Northern Ireland.

In the interim, Padraic will be arrested in 1991 for possessing a bomb and sentenced to twenty-four years in prison.

While I am working on my story, I happen to overhear other journalists talking about their forays out in the field with IRA active service units. This shocks me. I do not believe reporters should have anything to do with such attacks. Still, part of me wonders if I am too timid, doing interviews by the hearth instead of venturing into the frozen dark where the fighting is taking place. I do not know I am in the middle of things.

Eventually, I will realize the journalists I have overheard are full of hot air – outsiders are never allowed to accompany the IRA. Many years will pass before I understand the chance Padraic took by giving me the keys to his house. In 1999, as part of the peace accords in Northern Ireland, the IRA will agree to surrender its arms. Padraic will be revealed as the commander of the IRA prisoners at Long Kesh, or HM Maze Prison. The government will release him to oversee decommissioning all the IRA's caches of arms, wherever they are hidden. At the time I stayed at his home, and he was working for Sinn Fein, Padraic was probably also a senior member of the IRA.

For my second lesson in family life among Belfast paramilitaries, I travel just a few minutes but worlds away from the Springfield Road, to Glencairn, a low-rise concrete housing development in the heart of Protestant East Belfast.

The last of Glencairn's 1,500 units were still under construction when the Troubles began, and working-class Protestant families fled their homes to come here. They brought along their bitterness and their rage. Glencairn is the birthplace of the North's largest Protestant paramilitary organization, the Ulster Defense Association (UDA). Andy Tyrie, the chairman of the UDA, has arranged for me to stay with his close friends Barry and Marie McWhirter.

The UDA is a legal organization, although some members also belong to two illegal Protestant paramilitaries that have bombed, burned, and shot Catholics and well-known republicans: the Ulster Volunteer Force (UVF) and the Ulster Freedom Fighters. These groups rarely target members of the security forces, however, so the police do not need an armed guard in Glencairn.

Barry and Marie, both thirty-seven years old, have lived for fifteen years in an apartment overlooking the Forthriver road and the city below. I walk through an ugly hallway to reach them, but their apartment is immaculate, with lace curtains, hanging plants, and chalk portraits of Barry and Marie. Barry's handicrafts are on display. He made them in prison, where he served time on a firearms charge after a UVF shooting of a policeman, a rare crime for a loyalist.

Barry works days as a sales rep for a box company. At night, he lends out money for the UDA. People knock on his door at all hours to seek or repay small loans. Most Glencairn residents are unemployed and have no other place to borrow. The UDA charges them twenty-four percent interest.

Marie is ironing Barry's shirts when I arrive.

"Barry's just told me you were coming," she says as she looks me over. "What do you eat?"

She sits me down in her parlor and puts on a kettle for tea. Returning with a tray, she looks much more composed. Her health is frail. She once worked in an office but stopped after heart surgery when she was just twenty-seven.

After I explain I am staying with families in both East and West Belfast, she tells me her mother is Catholic. Her father, who is deceased, was a Protestant. After he died, Marie and her siblings were still raised as Protestants. "If you're born a Protestant, you don't know any other way," Marie says.

When Barry McWhirter comes home, it strikes me that he doesn't just come into a room: he makes an entrance. He is two inches short of six feet tall, but he is built like a football player and works out to keep in shape and to calm what I will come to recognize as a hair trigger temper.

"When you see politicians talking about Catholics and Protestants on TV," he says, "they don't know what they're talking about. It's not a religious war. It's a war between republicans and loyalists."

Shortly after the McWhirters moved to Glencairn, Barry joined the Glencairn Defense Association, a vigilante group. He helped set up the UDA later that year, but at first "there was no military wing." The UDA is now organized as an army of fifteen hundred trained fighters, according to Tyrie. Barry tells me he is not one of them.

He was, however, caught up in an investigation into the shooting of a police constable and later convicted of possessing a firearm under suspicious circumstances. He went to prison in October,1974. He spent three years at Long Kesh under the old rules, as a political prisoner.

"It's an accident of birth you're either a republican or a loyalist because of your family ties," he tells me. "Say my Dad had of been an IRA man and he was caught by the police and jailed, and I come up, and all I'm told is my Da was taken away by the police and they kept him for two or three years, and I start becoming aware and listening to him and attacking a police station for a United Ireland. To me, it's absurd. But I'm only trying to see it from their point of view."

But Barry cannot see life from their point of view because he has not been made to feel how Catholics in the

North are treated like outsiders in their own country. Racism in Northern Ireland is based not on skin color – most people here are white – but on hundreds of years of history.

The native Irish were Catholics, conquered after centuries of struggle with the English and driven off the land. Catholicism was forbidden, the Irish language was discouraged, and Irish place names were changed to English ones.

Protestant settlers were brought from Scotland and given land in the North. When the Irish won independence, the treaty that established the Irish Free State in 1921 excluded the six counties in the North where most people were Protestants. That part became Northern Ireland and remained part of the United Kingdom. As the years passed, the Protestant unionists served and died in vast numbers in the British army.

Today they are still the majority in the North, and they still have the best land, the best housing, and the best jobs. They run local government, the police, and the schools; and they have voices in Parliament. The famed linen industry has always had an all-Protestant workforce. So has Harland and Wolff, the great Belfast shipyard that built the *Titanic*. Many unionists are poor, but their British identity makes them feel superior to marginalized Catholics in much the same way poor whites in the United States have felt their skin color makes them superior to people who are Black or brown.

In Glencairn, the situation of Protestant children and teen-agers is heartbreaking, however. They are caught in a web of unemployment, crime, addiction, and poverty.

"This is a town of no hope," says James Creighton, who is chairman of the Glencairn Community Center as well as a member of the UDA.

When I visit, Creighton and other UDA members are gazing at a youth center gutted by a fire set by a kid who was sniffing glue. There is no roof, and rain is falling onto a tangle of electrical cables. There's no money for repairs, nothing for the kids to do, and they've just found another young glue sniffer half dead of exposure in a vacant apartment nearby. A swarm of boys are hanging around. I invite them to have lunch with me at a Shankill Road restaurant.

Over meat and potatoes and a lot of tea, they tell me they started smoking when they were six years old and have been drinking alcohol since they were ten. They can't get jobs, are all on the dole, and have nothing to do. They are seen as a nuisance at home and on the streets.

"The police say, 'Move on,'" says Eddie. "Move where?"

His words remind me of inner-city Cincinnati and the bitter and explosive chemistry of poverty, youth, and police. The East Belfast boys complain that the police abuse them, curse at them, and cuff them about at random. Riots the summer before, in which Protestants burned shops on the Shankill Road, "were a good thing," they agree.

Echoing complaints I have heard in the States about affirmative action for Black people, the teens tell me, "Catholics get everything, the jobs, the recreation centers." Not one of these boys has ever been in a Catholic neighborhood, nor do they know a single Catholic. The segregation here is just as extreme as it was in the South with

Jim Crow, enforced by separate schools and housing and treatment under the law and by the police and army.

Unlike Padraic, Barry refuses to be photographed for the *Times*. It is out of character for him, but he worries the publicity will be dangerous. He will be hurt anyway before my article appears, and it will have nothing to do with me. He will be shot at home in a robbery. He survives.

When my story about life in Belfast appears in mid-March 1985 on the cover of *The New York Times Magazine* under the title "The Agony of Ulster," I am surprised that my British friends are upset. My article is evenhanded and does not take sides, but that is precisely what is wrong with it. It shows the hard men and women of Belfast as ordinary people with lives distorted by the Troubles. No one who is trying to "spin" the Troubles as the work of criminals or madmen wants to read such a story. [xxvii]

CHAPTER THIRTY:
SHOOT TO KILL

One day, working on a story in Belfast, I hear about a shooting I might have missed if I had been in London. British soldiers ambushed and killed two IRA members riding a motorcycle onto the grounds of a psychiatric hospital in Derry. The Associated Press, citing military sources, reports the soldiers had been told the cyclists intended to kill a hospital employee who also worked part time as a policeman.

The IRA has claimed the dead men but said nothing more. Witnesses heard two bursts of fire. I wonder if the soldiers made any attempt to capture the IRA men before killing them.

In a case such as this, the *Times* wants official statements, reports, and forensic evidence.

In search of these, I go to the police press office, where the man on duty tells me the police report is confidential, and the number of shots fired is none of my business. I'm shocked. At home, journalists get basic police reports right away. But unlike the United States, the British government operates under the Official Secrets Act. All documents are secret unless released by a government minister.

The refusal of the police to tell me anything seems like an insurmountable roadblock. I give up and go home.

It's late November 1984, and Britain is in the 40th week of a miners' strike that speaks to the nation's painful transition from an industrial nation to a center for global finance and service industries. I travel to Rossington, a village in Yorkshire where family savings are gone, there are no strike benefits, and miners are digging bits of coal out of the dirt on the roads to heat their homes. xxviii

Up close, where there is little on the table to eat, the struggle is painful. The strikers tell me the existence of the village itself is at stake. Although the mine here is not on the list to be closed, the heart of the dispute is the prerogative of management – at this time, the government coal board – to close any mine it considers unprofitable, a right the union refuses to grant.

When the miners eventually lose and go back to work, the government will start closing mines as part of Prime Minister Margaret Thatcher's plan to convert the nation's energy supply from domestic to imported coal, and to gas, oil, and nuclear energy.

Currently, Britain has 173 deep pit coal mines. In just ten years, when the coal industry is privatized, it will have just fifteen. The last deep pit coal mine will close for good in 2015. Over the years, hundreds of mining communities, each a small world of its own, will change utterly or die.

As soon as I return to London from South Yorkshire, I am sent out to the streets on an entirely different kind of story. I have orders to shadow Mikhail S. Gorbachev, who is coming to town for the first time. No one in the West has seen him yet, and we are not expecting much. The Cold War is still underway, and my editors expect another frosty Russian Politburo official. He is an important one, however, the second-ranking secretary of the Communist Party. He is next in line to succeed Konstantin U. Chernenko as General Secretary.

I go out to Highgate Cemetery, where Gorbachev and his wife Raisa are expected to visit the grave of Karl Marx. They do not show up. Instead, they go to see the crown jewels in the Tower of London. They do visit the Karl Marx Memorial Library, where Lenin worked, and the British Museum reading room used by Marx. On this tour, Gorbachev jokes, "If people don't like Marxism, they should blame the British Museum."

His genial manner and his smart, pretty wife surprise and delight his British hosts, but my editors in New York ask me if I've been drinking when I file my story about him. Nonetheless, my story leads the next day's Sunday paper. I am relieved when Mrs. Thatcher agrees with the others who have seen him in action. After spending five hours talking with him, she says, "I like Mr. Gorbachev. We can do business together!"

At the Edinburgh airport in Scotland, where I follow along with the rest of the London press corps as Gorbachev continues his visit, Gorbachev stops, brushes his minders aside, and walks over to the press, as friendly as any American

politician. He surprises us by saying he's cutting his visit short.
Marshal Dimitri F. Ustinov, the defense minister, has died, and
Gorbachev is needed at home.

I do not know I am standing next to a man who will
affect the fate of every one of us. When we say, in times of
tragedy, that none of us knew, it's worth remembering we also
may not know when we encounter someone who will be part
of a miracle. In seven years, to the day, Gorbachev will resign
as the last president of the Soviet Union, the leader who will
usher in democracy and help dismantle, at least for a time,
both the Cold War and the threat of a nuclear holocaust with
the West.

As I leave Edinburgh, I am thinking only about myself.
Now I can return to London in time for my daughter's third
birthday party.

As I write my magazine story about life in Belfast, I
decide to take another look at the SAS shootings at the
psychiatric hospital in Derry. Back in Northern Ireland, I go to
see the only person who can tell me how many shots hit the
IRA men, the undertaker who handled their bodies. He says
their bodies were pierced dozens of times.

Two years from now, an inquest will disclose that the
soldiers fired fifty-nine times. They were waiting in an
unmarked car when the IRA men arrived on a motorcycle.
The soldiers rammed it, knocking the passenger off the back
seat. The soldiers shot him as he hit the ground. The
motorcycle hit a curb and threw the driver off. The soldiers
shot him in the back as he lay on the ground.

The major in charge of the SAS unit will testify at the inquest that "if the police had been called, two people might not have been dead." The inquest jury will find that the five soldiers in the unit should have tried to arrest the IRA men, or at least collaborated with the police, but the jury will not recommend prosecution.

Twenty years later, a court will tell one of the widows it is too late to reopen the case. [xxix]

Looking at these shootings in December 1984, I begin to wonder if there are more cases like these and start to ask around. I find a few, and then I find more. Some, like the one at the hospital, have involved the Special Air Service, or SAS, the army special forces units. Other killings were done by undercover units of the police, the Royal Ulster Constabulary, or RUC.

Father Raymond Murray and Father Dennis Faul, two Roman Catholic priests, have been trying to call attention to shootings in County Armagh, on the border with Ireland. Armed republican groups, the IRA and a smaller organization, the Irish National Liberation Army, are active there, and journalists call it "Bandit Country." Two years earlier, undercover police units of the RUC conducted six shootings that were particularly outrageous.

In January and February 1985, with help from Father Murray and from Joe O'Hagan, an old republican, I arrange to meet with families of some of the shooting victims out in the countryside.

Some households may have sheltered fighters and fugitives. I do not know. The men leave the room when a stranger arrives, even though a cup of hot tea and a biscuit are always on offer, along with a seat by the fire. The families want information, and they want justice.

Several families tell me they have just had a visit from a British policeman who is also trying to reinvestigate these cases. The only thing rarer than a visit from a journalist, they say, is a visit from a policeman, and a British one at that. This is how I hear of the work of John Stalker, the deputy chief constable of Greater Manchester, who has been called in to conduct an independent investigation. By coincidence, he begins his investigation at about the same time I start my own.

CHAPTER THIRTY-ONE:
LOVE AND DEATH

I'm going to miss my flight home!

I've just finished interviewing a family in County Tyrone, and it's too late to drive back to Belfast to catch the last flight to London. It's getting dark.

I drive to the nearest large town, Dungannon, but the only hotel is full. They refer me to a local bed and breakfast. It has a room. It's February 19, 1985, Shrove Tuesday. Ciaran Murphy, the proprietor, gives me a cheery greeting and tells me another American is staying at the B&B.

"I'm sure you'll enjoy meeting him!" he says and leaves, promising to return immediately with some Shrove Tuesday pancakes for both of us.

The last thing I want to do is meet an Irish American tourist looking for his roots. My nerves are wrecked. I just want a drink.

But Ciaran reappears instantly with the pancakes, traditionally served plain and cold, and Bill Kelleher, a graduate student from the University of Michigan, who is living at the B&B while doing field work for his Ph.D. in cultural anthropology.

"Nice to meet you," I say, not very graciously although he is friendly and very handsome. "Do you know a place to get a drink and something to eat?"

Bill is on his way to a Gaelic lesson but offers to walk me down the street to a nearby pub for a drink. He never makes it to his Gaelic lesson. Before the evening ends with coffee at his place at the B&B, I am calm enough to realize he is single and fun. As I go upstairs to freeze in my room, wearing my coat, hat, and mittens to bed, I wonder why I never meet nice guys like Bill Kelleher.

The next morning is unusually cold, and frost has formed on the windshield of my rental car. I am scraping it off with the edge of my plastic credit card when Bill comes out and lends me a hand. He writes down the number of the B&B pay phone on a piece of paper and gives it to me, "in case you ever come back to Dungannon."

I wish.

In March, the East Tyrone Coroner announces an inquest into the deaths in 1983 of two IRA men, Brian Campbell and Colm McGirr. The inquest, which will take place in a court in Dungannon, will offer a rare chance to get official information about the shootings and meet the families and any witnesses.

Campbell and McGirr were shot dead by the SAS on a sunny winter Sunday in a field of thistles and rushes near Coalisland, ("Coal Island") thirty-one miles Southwest of Belfast. The official story is that they got out of a car to walk toward a hidden cache of weapons.

Homes of suspected IRA members were being searched so frequently that firearms were often kept in secret locations and picked up just before they were used. These weapons had been used in twenty-two shootings, including the killings of four members of the security forces.

Although their families would later agree that both men were IRA members and were indeed walking toward the weapons, the soldiers had every opportunity to make the hidden guns harmless beforehand and simply arrest the men, who were not armed when they arrived. Instead, the soldiers shot them on sight.

The families claim — and the government denies – this is an instance of an ongoing and illegal shoot-to-kill policy, of execution without trial. Both men, the families say, were previously threatened with assassination by the police and the army.

At this point, I have found thirty-four similar shootings by the police and army in the last two and a half years.

I decide at once to attend the inquest. I call Ciaran Murphy to reserve a room at the B&B. Then I call Bill Kelleher on the pay phone to tell him I'm coming back to town. Bill says he's happy to hear from me.

"I'll have a cup of tea ready for you," he promises.

"I might be late. I have to make a stop first."

Father Murray is visiting Derry, a long drive from Dungannon, most of it over winding, two lane country roads. When I finish talking to him about Campbell and McGirr, it is late. Ciaran Murphy has left the door open for me, but it's 2 a.m. when I arrive at the B&B.

Bill Kelleher meets me with a warm smile and the tea he's promised. He doesn't seem the least upset about my late arrival. His patience and his gentleness impress me. You can't miss his Boston accent either. We drink tea and trade life stories as the night moves on.

His father is a retired Boston firefighter, and Bill grew up in West Roxbury. Like me, Bill is the oldest child. I'm the oldest of six. He's the oldest of five. Like me, he is a voracious reader. Stacks of newspapers and books lean in towers around his rooms. We talk about Ireland. We talk about life. He has dark hair, hazel eyes, and a dark beard. I can't believe he is seven years younger than me. I can't believe how handsome, brilliant, and single he is. He has never married.

Bill is working on his Ph.D. in cultural anthropology at the University of Michigan. He has come to Dungannon to study the workers at the Tyrone Crystal Company, a business started by a local priest. It has a workforce of both Catholics and Protestants – unionists and nationalists – working side by side on the shop floor. Bill is getting to know families "on both sides of the house" in a town where the past lives so powerfully in the present that no one sees the same things in the same light. It's Bill who introduces me to the intricacies of "telling," noticing the superficial things that signify the deep divides between the two sides.

Bill is familiar with the historic landscape and the modern one, but he does not know the troubled one in which I am becoming more deeply enmeshed. I tell him a little about the story I am working on. In the morning, when he decides to walk over to the inquest with me as an innocent bystander, he has no clue his life will change permanently when he walks back out the courthouse door.

We are among the first to arrive. The courtroom for the inquest is small and square, with white walls and oak benches.

Some young broadcast journalists come in, along with the families of the dead men. Soon after, Danny Morrison, the author of "the ballot box and the Armalite" strategy for the IRA, walks in. Morrison is Sinn Fein's publicity director, and he has also been elected to a seat as Mid-Ulster's representative in the Northern Ireland Assembly. He greets the dead men's families warmly and sits with them.

Police officers in riot gear enter the court room, armed and helmeted. They line up shoulder to shoulder along the walls of the room, which seems to shrink with their presence. Even at Mafia trials, I have never felt so threatened.

The coroner comes in to preside, and a small, nervous-looking jury appears and is seated.

The inquest ends almost immediately.

A government lawyer for the Ministry of Defense tells the coroner the army cannot produce the three soldiers who have been called as witnesses. The public defender, appearing on behalf of the slain men, accuses the government of negligence, pointing out they had months of advance notice the inquest would be held, but the coroner responds that adjournment is his only choice.

Everyone gets up to leave.

I try to interview the attorney for the Ministry of Defense, and he refuses even to give me his name. "It's in the record," he says. That record is not open to journalists.

We tumble out into the parking lot, and the crowd includes Bill Kelleher and the families of the dead IRA men. Bill knows Brian McGirr, the brother of one of the dead, Colm McGirr. Bill and I walk over to talk with him. Brian shakes his head and tells us the case will never be investigated properly. "Are you coming over?" he asks.

"Yes, says Bill.

"I'll see you there," Brian says, and Bill and I climb into a car with members of the McGirr family. All around us in the parking lot are police officers.

"If the Special Branch didn't know you before, they certainly will now," I tell Bill.

"No, it won't make any difference. No worries," he says. "I'm not doing anything wrong."

"That doesn't matter," I tell him. "Just being friends with the McGirrs will get you in trouble."

Thirty years later, while archiving thousands of pages of Bill's anthropological notes, I will come across his descriptions of this day, March 14, 1985. He writes: "Perhaps I'm naive, but I do think people have an overly pessimistic view of this place."

From this day forward, the police and army will stop Bill every time they encounter him driving a car in Northern Ireland. His brief foray into the courtroom and his visit to the McGirr home bring him under a permanent cloud of suspicion.

Back in London, the government's pressure on me becomes more overt. My mail at home begins to arrive open. A woman jumps out of her car a few doors away from my house as I am walking down the sidewalk, takes my photograph, then jumps back in her car and drives away. Someone notifies me that I am under investigation for underpayment of taxes for my nanny. (As it turns out, I am overpaying these taxes.)

Starting on the day of the inquest, the McGirr and Campbell families welcome me into their homes, show me photographs of their sons, and tell me stories of their lives. Colm McGirr, a bricklayer, was twenty-three on the day he died. Brian Campbell, an auto mechanic like his father, was nineteen and lived with his parents.

People living near the field where the shootings took place tell me they heard a barrage of shots. They also say the bodies were left on the ground for hours. The McGirrs have spoken to the medical examiner but do not know how many times Colm was shot because official information cannot be released until an inquest.

I wonder why the bodies were left in the field for such a long time and if one or both did not die right away. So, I look for the ambulance crew that went to the scene. There were two men in the ambulance, and I manage to find one of them. He is a unionist, loyal to the government and reluctant to talk to a reporter. Still, he is upset because he wants to save lives.

Eventually, he tells me the ambulance crew was made to wait on the road for ten to fifteen minutes before they were permitted to approach the bodies. He was not certain they were dead and asked to take them to the hospital. He was refused. I include my interview with him in my story in *The New York Times*.

Three months after this story appears, a second inquest is held. The autopsy reports show McGirr was struck by thirteen bullets. He died quickly after four bullets entered the trunk of his body. Two bullets struck Campbell in the back. Death was not immediate.

At this second inquest, the ambulance attendant denies telling me that one of the men seemed to be alive when he examined him. [xxx] The truth is, as I wrote, he was not allowed to approach Brian Campbell until the soldiers knew for certain Campbell was dead. Additional inquest testimony shows they waited ninety more minutes before they allowed a doctor to examine the men. The priest had to wait another half hour.

The families tell me a third IRA man was present on the day of the shootings. He was driving the car for their sons but did not get out. He was shot as he drove away but escaped. There was no official mention of him in news accounts or at the first inquest.

He is a fugitive and very frightened. When I find him, he denies being a member of the IRA, although the IRA says he is. He denies knowing about the arms cache. He says he never saw who fired the shots, only that bullets came from both sides of the road. He was shot nine times as he drove away. It was an ambush, not an arrest.

The official records, witnesses, photographs, and evidence that *The New York Times* insists upon for an investigation such as the one I am working on are almost impossible to get here. I am forced to turn to interviews, also hazardous in a place where a guerilla war is underway, much of it along the border and out in the countryside in remote places.

In these efforts, I am alone – until suddenly I am not, and the hairs on my arms stand on end in fright when armed men in black step into the road in front of my car and wave me to a stop. This happens twice at night on the roads in County Tyrone. Once they are soldiers, and once the police, the very people I am investigating. I am terrified. I'm counting on their not making the connection.

Even worse, these men with guns fear me. I'm an unarmed woman in ordinary clothes, but I could be a local woman with my family held hostage somewhere and carrying a bomb to the nearest town in the trunk of my car. It's dark, and they do not know. My American accent will reassure them I am not a local resident if I can get up the nerve to speak. Thank God I'm driving a rental car.

I lower my window when they motion me and try to catch my breath. My daughter Susan, three years old, is in the back seat. I have taken to bringing her along because I have left her in London for too many days without me.

"Hello, marm, you're by yourself, are ye?"

"Yes, I'm the only adult. That's my daughter in the back seat." I try to keep my voice calm, so Susan, in her booster seat in the back, will not be afraid or start to cry. I force myself not to think about her or the danger these men pose to us.

"Have a look at your license?" I show them my license and my work visa, and they shine the beams of their lights inside my rental car.

"Where are you coming from?"

"Belfast."

"And where are you going?"

"Dungannon."

"And what is the purpose of your trip?"

"I'm a *New York Times* correspondent on assignment."

"Open the boot for us?"

I pull the latch for the trunk and stay in my seat. My suitcase and Susan's things are back there. More lights. They never put away their guns. Eventually they wave me on. I think I have been successful in keeping fear out of my voice, and I never discuss these stops in front of Susan, who does not seem to notice.

A day will come in London, when I am walking along the sidewalk with Susan, when a friendly-looking bobby, unarmed, approaches. She hides behind me.

"Mum, the police!" she shouts.

She too is concealing a tremendous amount of fear.

My first published story about the shoot-to-kill controversy upsets several *Times* senior editors, who say I am spending too much time in Northern Ireland. In a reflection of the long and friendly special relationship between the United States and Great Britain, the *Times* believes the British incapable of dastardly deeds. I am diverted to write features and spot news stories in Britain. I do this easily and well, but my career in London seems to be in danger.

The bureau chief, Johnny Apple, has been kind to me, although I would not say we were friends, and our interests and skills seem to coincide. He enjoys being the *Times* ambassador. He knows everyone who is anyone in power in government or society in London. At the same time, he watches his back in New York. At several points during the summer of 1985, he confides he has orders to replace me but is not going to. He advises me to work harder.

In May1985, there are local elections in Northern Ireland, and Sinn Fein makes big gains at the ballot box, winning fifty-eight government seats and making it hard for British officials to say they will not meet with them. It's an important development I am not allowed to pursue.

As the summer moves on, I'm not the only journalist having trouble with my bosses over Northern Ireland. All the journalists at the BBC and Independent Television News go on strike about it. Their documentary "Real Lives: At the Edge of the Union," presents intimate, at-home profiles of Northern Irish political figures. One is the fiery unionist Gregory Campbell, and another is Martin McGuinness, the Sinn Fein leader reputed to be a former chief of staff of the Irish Republican Army.

The Home Secretary asks the network not to air the show, arguing it will give the IRA "the oxygen of publicity." The BBC governors comply. In protest, the BBC and ITN journalists go on strike and stage a twenty-four-hour blackout of radio and television news broadcasts in Britain and Northern Ireland. Eventually, an amended "Real Lives" will be shown in October, but relations between the BBC and the government will also become more strained. In two years, for the first time ever, the director-general of the BBC will be fired. Northern Ireland is a career graveyard.

The Irish Republic also restricts coverage of the North. Irish broadcast journalists are forbidden to transmit the actual voices of McGuinness or Sinn Fein's Gerry Adams during their reporting. Someone else must read what they had to say.

Apple is replaced as Times bureau chief by Joseph Lelyveld, a veteran journalist, who tells me on arrival I am under a cloud in New York. He asks to see the stories I have filed, both published and unpublished. He reads them and says not to worry. He sees no problems with them. Joe is a fair man and a skilled political strategist who will later become the newspaper's executive editor.

A senior editor with influential friends on both sides of the Atlantic complains unceasingly about my stories from Northern Ireland. "You're a woman, aren't you?" he asks me. "Why don't you cover fashion?"

Over the summer, I'm seeing more of Bill Kelleher and falling in love with him. He comes to London to visit me. Susan likes him, and the three of us go for walks on Hampstead Heath, just down the street from me. I also meet Bill to go dancing in Dublin. We are two people in love, and courting is easier in a country where I am not watched, and Bill is not stopped by the police.

Meanwhile, a British official I've met at a party calls with a surprise invitation to lunch. I am delighted until he makes me an unofficial offer from the government. If I will drop my investigation into the shootings in Northern Ireland, I can have the first look at the Anglo-Irish Agreement that is quietly being negotiated between London and Dublin. It's a big step toward solving the Troubles. The British know how much the *Times* likes being first on big policy stories.

I look at him across the lunch table and laugh.

"Are you crazy? Shoot-to-kill is a real story. No one else is working on it, and the government is killing people. These are death squads, just like Central America. Why would I quit working on this in exchange for a half-hour head start on a story everyone else will have?"

He advises me to take his offer.

I tell him I will pay for my own lunch, and we part ways. I will never see him again.

CHAPTER THIRTY-TWO:
VOICES OF PEACE

An episode just before our wedding does not boost my career at the *Times*. I am sent to Oslo, Norway, on December 10, 1985, to cover the Nobel Peace Prize presentation to the International Physicians for the Prevention of Nuclear War, a group with 135,000 members, based in Massachusetts and headed by two prominent cardiologists, Dr. Bernard Lown, an American, and Dr. Yevgeny I Chazov, a Russian. Dr. Lown is renowned in cardiology as the inventor of the first effective heart defibrillator, coming at a time when heart arrythmia is blamed for half a million deaths a year in the United States. Dr. Chazov's additional accomplishments are important because they are political: he was the personal doctor to the Soviet leader Leonid I. Brezhnev.

Oslo is glowing in the dark that night, lights turning the snow a warm shade of gold. At the dinner before the awards ceremony, Dr. Lown steps away from the table to speak with me for a few minutes about what he is going to say about "the most fundamental of all rights, which preconditions all others, the right to survival," in a world without nuclear war.

"People must come to terms with the fact that the struggle is not between different national destinies, between opposing ideologies, but rather between catastrophe and survival," he says in his prepared speech. "All nations share a linked destiny; nuclear weapons are their shared enemy."[xxxi]

Dr. Chazov's speech is deeply felt and just as eloquent. "True to the Hippocratic oath, we cannot keep silent, knowing what the final epidemic – nuclear war – can bring to the humankind."

"The bell of Hiroshima rings in our hearts," he continues, "not as a funeral knell but as an alarm bell calling out to actions to protect life on our planet."

Standing back in the shadows of that room, their words fill me with both horror and hope. I lived in Japan as a child just after World War II – my father was on General MacArthur's staff. At the time, I was four years old, and I saw the aftermath of the bombing of a great city. Tokyo was blackened and cratered, and former bomb shelters were serving as homes.

As I listen to the speakers, I remember hearing the testimony in Congress of the American Marines ordered to clear the trash from the site of the atomic bombing at Nagasaki. When I saw them as a reporter, they were dying of cancer. They recalled that the metal they gathered was still hot with radiation.

The speeches remind me of the admiral I met at the Defense Nuclear Agency, with his giant posters of mushroom clouds, and the widow of the Army major who was marched into a trench in the Nevada desert to watch such a bomb detonate. It was the beginning of his slow, cruel death from cancer.

"A single modern submarine has approximately eight times the firepower of World War II, sufficient to destroy every major city in the Northern Hemisphere," Dr. Lown is saying. "Why then the stockpiling of 18,000 strategic weapons? In this race, the runners are no longer in control of their limbs." [xxxii]

We are awash in nuclear weapons, still depending on the insane, but aptly named policy of Mutual Assured Destruction (MAD), the belief we and the Soviets will not use our weapons against each other for fear of destroying the planet. Do I trust the admiral with his posters of bombs? Do I trust the Russians?

Sitting in the darkness beyond the bright ceremony, I remember a day when I was six years old, shortly before we left Japan. I went with my family to a garden party at the emperor's palace. My father wore his uniform, and we dressed in our best clothes. There would be refreshments, and this presented a problem, as Americans were not allowed to eat fresh food, which was fertilized with human waste.

On the way, my mother gave me the kinds of instructions you might read in a fairy tale.

"You may not eat or drink anything you are given, no matter how good it looks, and no matter what they say. But *you are forbidden to say you can't eat*. Thank them and say you are not hungry. Do you understand?" Our health was a consideration, but so was respect for our Japanese hosts.

My younger brother Billy was three years old, too little to understand, so I was assigned to watch him. I held his hand, but eventually we were led to tables laden with fruit and good things to eat. I saw peaches and remembered their sweet taste.

After eating from cans for two years, I wanted that fresh peach more than anything, but I told the lady, "Thank you, I'm not hungry," and looked away.

Billy, however, reached out. When I caught his hand, he started to cry. It was clear something was wrong, but the women smiled and beckoned a man who came over and said he'd show us something wonderful.

Our parents had vanished into the crowd of ladies and officers, so we followed the man out of the gardens and toward some buildings where the man told us to wait. Then a white horse was led out of the stables to stand perfect and gleaming in the sunshine. He was stately and quiet, and the man told us he belonged to the emperor.

I had seen the aftermath of war, but a child could not imagine its true horror. Standing before us was the emperor's white horse, the avatar of a dream of power that ignited a war and drowned the Pacific in blood. We were children of the American military who dropped history's first atomic bombs and devastated two cities. We were together in the gardens of the emperor, the physical and symbolic heart of the conflagration, two little children and an old white horse, all of us innocent. It was April 12, 1950. Everything was in bloom, and it was a beautiful day. Peace was beginning.

Two enemies created peace the best way they could. They became friends. The doctors' organization, drawn from two enemy superpowers, is trying to make peace without the prelude of a war. We have not used our atomic and nuclear weapons against each other, but we keep building our arsenals. Why *not* give the Peace Prize to the International Physicians for the Prevention of Nuclear War?

I race back to the hotel to write my story about the Peace Price ceremony and speeches, but before I can send it to New York, the power goes out in the building. Several hours pass. I am not too worried because of the six-hour time difference between Oslo and New York. I am many hours ahead of my deadline.

Meanwhile, to my dismay, my editors have decided to use a sword-rattling wire service report of the ceremony that leads with the controversy around the Russian laureate, Dr. Chazov. Twelve years earlier, he joined in signing a group letter denouncing Andrei D. Sakharov, the Soviet physicist and dissident, who was himself awarded the Nobel Peace Prize. This might be a legitimate sidebar to my story — if it included information about any pressures put to bear on Dr. Chazov to sign it — but it does not deal with the existential threat of nuclear war or the efforts of the physicians from the world's opposing superpowers to stop it.

Except for a few quotes, my story disappears. The published version says almost nothing about the merits of the International Physicians for the Prevention of Nuclear War, an authentic effort that will continue after the end of the Cold War and expand worldwide. At first, I'm incredulous. Then angry. Then ashamed. I have no idea how to apologize for such a distortion published under my byline.

The next day, my editors ask me to stay in Oslo to investigate the decision of the committee to award the prize to the physicians. They suspect mischief. I refuse. I do not know anyone on the Nobel committee, I don't speak Norwegian, and staying in Oslo will mean postponing my wedding, which is only a few days away and in London.

I see such an "investigation" as a nasty piece of Cold War trouble making.

"We have never investigated other Nobel Peace Prize decisions," I tell my editors in New York, "and I do not want to start."

The *Times* sends the Paris bureau chief. He produces nothing new. But he obeys, and I do not.

In January 1986, a month after Bill and I marry and just as we plan to take out a mortgage on a house in the London neighborhood of Muswell Hill, the foreign desk tells me I am being sent home to New York. I am shattered.

Friends of ours in Northern Ireland believe we got off lightly, and this may be true. John Stalker, the deputy chief constable of Greater Manchester who has been investigating six of the shootings, will have his reputation smeared by lies and his career sidetracked, a wrong that will take years to set right. Two Northern Ireland human rights attorneys, Pat Finucane and Rosemary Nelson, will be murdered. My departure is simple and quiet. The Brits don't like me, and that's that. Why didn't I see this coming?

I think back to an intimate breakfast for foreign journalists, where I was seated next to the foreign secretary, Sir Geoffrey Howe. Our conversation was going well until I mentioned the controversy over the strip-searching of IRA women prisoners in the Armagh jail. He dropped his fork, then ignored me for the rest of the meal.

When I call New York to ask why I am being sent home, Warren Hoge, the foreign editor, tells me I am good but not good enough. How does one argue with "not good enough"?

I have a grace period of two or three months, and I want to get the details of an outrageous SAS shooting of an innocent man, Frederick Jackson, a Protestant businessman. I have one piece of information, a newspaper story about the Jackson shooting that includes a photograph of a white car with the rear window shot out. The caption says the car belonged to the victim.

The police have told the media Jackson was caught in the crossfire during a gun battle between the IRA and the SAS. But when I visit the victim's family, they say the bullet-ridden car in the photograph is not Jackson's. He was driving his own car, a different one, when he was shot.

Jackson owned a construction business. Early in the morning of October 19, 1984, he went to a trucking yard near Portadown in County Armagh to check on work his company was doing there. He was just leaving, pulling out of their driveway, the workers tell me, when they saw his car halt and start to roll back. Then they saw Jackson get out of the car and run towards them.

"I've been shot!" he cried and fell to the ground. He'd been shot once in the back.

The windshield on the driver's side of his car was smashed.

The workers called for help, but soldiers appeared and ordered them to put up their hands. When an ambulance arrived, the soldiers made the crew wait for the police. Jackson was dead on arrival at the hospital.

The family wants to know if the delay in getting treatment cost Jackson his life, but they will not be allowed to see his autopsy until a coroner's inquest is held. More than a year after his death, no inquest is scheduled.

The workers tell me they heard no gun battle. And no one at the trucking company knows who owns the white car shown in the newspaper article.

Jackson's family are unionists. They identify as British and support the government. They don't want trouble, and they have not made waves. When I meet with them, they tell me Jackson was just a businessman, not a politician, married with four children, a good man respected in his community. They are bereft, and they want answers. I assure them I'll do my best to find out what happened.

To determine whether Jackson was hit in the crossfire between the SAS and the IRA, as the police say, I need to learn where the battle took place. I feel certain the bullet-ridden car in the photograph was involved, but why did the police lie and say it was Jackson's car? The police and army refuse to talk to me. That leaves me with the IRA. Their driver, who must have been watching the road, will know the location of the shootout. I need to find the driver.

It's February 1986. My time is getting short. I take Susan with me and check into a small hotel in Northern Ireland. I have asked to meet a senior member of Sinn Fein, who comes to the lobby. He walks me upstairs to my room and carries Susan, who has fallen asleep. This person has read my earlier story about shoot-to-kill. When I ask him for help, he asks me why my newspaper is investigating shootings of people who themselves shoot and kill members of the security forces, unarmed when possible.

My answer is the same one I've given my editors. The IRA and the British government are at war. The IRA acknowledges this. The government does not. The state is at war with its own citizens and lying about what it is doing. Sometimes, the victims are in the IRA. Sometimes, as in the case of Frederick Jackson, they are not. The police and army are operating as death squads, and these killings are human rights violations. The government should tell the public it is at war and be governed by public policies, not secret ones.

The person listens to me, seems to think things over, and then leaves with a promise to see what can be done to help me.

It is still early in the evening, although very dark. I put Susan in the car and drive to Aughnacloy, a small town on the border in County Tyrone, where I've gotten to know Bill's friends Paul McCabe, a glass blower at Tyrone Crystal, and his wife Eilish McAnespie, who has run for office for Sinn Fein.

They invite me to join them and other members of the McAnespie family at a cèilidh, an Irish gathering with lots of music and what seems like square dancing. I am laughing like a young girl and dancing with Eilish's younger brother Aidan, a Gaelic football player, twenty-one years old. He was born the year I graduated from college.

It is past midnight when I drive into the hotel parking lot. I am surprised to find a handful of smiling, handsome young men, all British, gathered in the lobby. When I come in with Susan, they greet me like old friends and offer to help me carry Susan up to my room. I thank them and only later wonder if they expected to find the Sinn Fein person there. My room is empty and just as I left it.

A few days later, with Susan back in London with Bill, I have a series of telephone calls and finally find myself in the front room of a small house in a rundown Northern Ireland housing estate. I'm talking with the young man who was driving the van for the IRA on the day of the gun battle with the SAS. We are not at his home. The woman who greets me makes a hasty pot of tea, takes her children, and leaves the house. She does not return while I am there.

I am in a morally difficult position. As a journalist, I want to know whether the SAS deliberately killed Frederick Jackson and whether the army and police lied about how he died. But there are other issues here, the shootings and attempted ambush by the IRA. I do not want to become involved in these after the fact. I need to find out where the gun battle took place and whether Jackson was hit in the crossfire. I do not want to know the names of the IRA men, including the one I am interviewing.

In answer to my questions, the man traces out the complicated route the IRA unit took that day and tells me where the shootout occurred. It was near, but not at, the trucking company where Jackson was killed. Jackson was not struck in a crossfire, nor is it likely he was killed by a lone stray bullet. We talk until I am certain of this. My story appears on March 17, 1986. [xxxiii]

From the evidence at the scene, the victim's brother Alan and other family members wonder whether the undercover soldiers mistook Jackson for an IRA man going to pick up the team of gunmen. This would explain their delay in allowing an innocent man to be taken to the hospital.

Before my story is published, members of the Jackson family, who are still loyal unionists, are considering taking his case to the European Court of Human Rights. After my story appears in the *Times,* the army raids their business. This frightens them. Will their friends suspect them of sympathizing with terrorists? What will happen to their construction business? A rumor can ruin them. When I return to see them, they have decided not to pursue the case in court, and they greet me with fear and rage.

A detailed account of the Jackson shooting will be published in 1990 by Father Murray. [xxxiv] It will draw from statements from the Republican movement on behalf of the IRA and from official police statements on behalf of the SAS made at the inquest in May 1986. The inquest jury will find Jackson was an innocent victim, shot by accident. No soldier will be prosecuted. Frederick Jackson was shot deliberately. The accident was a case of mistaken identity.

My story about Frederick Jackson is the last one I will file from London about the policy of Shoot to Kill, but the shootings will continue.

In February 1988, my young friend Aidan McAnespie, just twenty-three years old, will be shot to death by a British soldier after he walks through the army checkpoint in Aughnacloy, on the border of the Irish Republic, on his way to play Gaelic football in County Monaghan. Aidan will be hit in the back by one of three bullets fired from a machine gun.

His older sister Eilish McCabe will lead a campaign for justice by his family and many friends. They will pursue this for thirty-two years, and she will die of cancer before any sign of success, but a British soldier will finally be convicted of manslaughter in the case, his prison sentence suspended.

As the years pass and military documents are declassified, hundreds of murders will be linked to killers from various Protestant paramilitary groups who have been and will be tipped off, armed, or otherwise helped by members of the police in Northern Ireland and the Northern Ireland-based Ulster Defense Regiment of the British Army. These murders, which date from the 1970s through the 1990s, are still under scrutiny by the press and human rights investigators.

Faced with leaving London, Bill and I do not know what to do. I am pregnant, expecting a baby in December. Bill has not finished the field work for his doctoral thesis and hasn't even started thinking about writing his dissertation. He's not ready for an academic career. He does not think we can live on my income alone in the New York metropolitan area.

"If I have to take a job selling shoes to support us, I'll never get my degree," he tells me. Panic and pain meet in his face. He begs me to quit work at the *Times* and return to Ann Arbor with him. We could live in graduate student housing. I could get a job, and he could finish his Ph.D. and support us by working as a graduate assistant.

"No way," I say. I have worked years to get where I am, at the top of my profession, a foreign correspondent in the London Bureau of *The New York Times*. I am not throwing that away to live on starvation wages as the wife of a graduate student.

I ask the *Times* for maternity leave and compensatory time off. This will add up to a year of paid leave. Bill and I decide to move to Belfast. We'll find a safe neighborhood to live while Bill finishes his field work in Northern Ireland and starts writing his dissertation. I will take care of the children and write. I've always wanted to try writing a novel.

The novelist Derek Miller will tell an interviewer from *Salon* that "writing a novel while raising children is a lot like trying to defuse a bomb while someone is hitting you over the head with a nerf baseball bat while complaining about you." I am a veteran journalist but a newcomer to writing fiction. Miller will succeed far better than I.

There is nothing to rent in Belfast, so Bill and I purchase a Victorian row house near Queen's University. The house is brick, more than a hundred years old, built before electricity or central heating. Bill hires some friends from County Tyrone to install modern wiring and plumbing, a coal furnace, and central heating. He stays in Belfast to oversee the demolition and reconstruction while I go to New York with Susan to work at the *Times* metropolitan desk for the summer.

We sublet a house in Montclair, New Jersey, which means a long commute into the city and long days away from her. Luckily, Susan's former babysitter Maria is free to come live with us again.

This is the summer crack cocaine hits the streets of New York, and the editors ask me to help with the coverage. I can't cover the drug trade on the streets, as I would have done before. With one child and another on the way, I can't take the risk, and I can't spend the time away from Susan.

I do write about the jam-up of drug cases in the criminal courts, more than 84,000 misdemeanor and 5800 felony cases in Manhattan alone. With arraignments twenty-four hours a day, they can't find time to clean the arraignment room. One morning a judge arrives and finds four hundred defendants waiting.

I also survey the condition of the city's 852 playgrounds, using teams of people with score cards I've made up for them. What we find is no surprise: the high-income neighborhoods have the best playgrounds. Playgrounds in poor neighborhoods, especially in Brooklyn and the Bronx, have swings with no seats and slides with stairs that end in empty air – nothing to slide down, just a drop to the ground. A few playground attendants ask the photographer and me to leave because the drug dealers do not like strangers and may cause trouble.

The Recreation Commissioner Henry J. Stern falls asleep during my interview with him. After the story appears, he accuses me of a "military style campaign" against him.

The *Times* is situated at 229 W. 43rd street, a block from the heart of the X-rated porn theater district on 42nd street, at the height of its xxx-rated seediness before the city wipes it clean in a few years. I talk with a handful of women who perform in some of the films and live shows that run day and night. I must be an odd sight walking into these places, as I am very pregnant and look it.

Many of the women tell me their pimps raped them, some when they were teen-aged runaways. They say they were coerced into "acting" for the films. No one says she enjoys the porn business or is getting rich from it. Anyone who watches such a film, they say, is watching a woman being abused, even if she is smiling, even if she appears to be enjoying herself.

But when I propose doing a story about these women, several male editors reject the idea out of hand. All whores are liars, they tell me. Nothing they say is reliable. You can't do a credible story about them, period.

I'm sorry to say I give up on this story. The summer is ending, and I want to take Susan back to Northern Ireland to join Bill in our new home in Belfast at 76 Rugby Road.

We're about to bring another life into the world, a baby girl, and resume our days as a family in a new place. My career as a journalist will be on pause for a few years and then start up in ways I cannot yet imagine.

CHAPTER THIRTY-THREE:
THE THIRD MAN

It's two months since the bombing of the Alfred P. Murrah Federal Building in Oklahoma City on April 19, 1995. I'm driving down a country road near Smithville, Arkansas. My assignment: to see if anyone else was involved in the attack[xxxv]. In the process, I need to take a hard look at the anti-government Patriot movement that inspired the bombers.

This morning I'm heading for the farm where Gordon Kahl, an anti-Semite and tax resister, died twelve years ago in a fiery shootout with U. S. Marshals, the FBI, and the police. Kahl killed two Marshals who came to arrest him on tax charges in North Dakota. He then fled in a stolen police car and traveled a thousand miles east. Five months later, he took refuge at the farm near here, where his death made him a martyr to the white far right.

My route passes through blueberry country. Wildflowers bloom by the side of the road. It's sunny, and I have my car windows rolled down. The air smells sweet and fresh. This is an unlikely setting for violence and horror. But so was Oklahoma City on that lovely Wednesday morning just before the bomb went off. It killed 168 people, including nineteen children and babies. *It's Oklahoma*, people said afterwards in shock, *not Jerusalem or Baghdad*.

In hindsight, there were signs trouble was coming from the far right, but we didn't – couldn't – imagine the horror of the Murrah building, just as we will not imagine the jetliners coming out of a blue morning sky to bring death and devastation from Osama bin Laden on September 11, 2001. At that moment, we will put domestic terrorism on the back burner to launch a twenty-year "war on terror" abroad. As that is ending, we will be blindsided again, by a mob assault on Congress on January 6, 2021.

The sense of grievance among some white people has appeared all along in our polls and elections, but we're a democracy, sure we can handle it. But we don't see everything. Setting out in Arkansas, I have a specific task, to look for links to the bombing of the Murrah Building. Along the way, I will glimpse the roots and depth of the anger building in some parts of the country, but I cannot foresee the times to come.

Now, I only know what everyone else does about the bombing investigation: the FBI has arrested Timothy J. McVeigh and Terry Lynn Nichols. Agents have picked up Terry's brother James Nichols and McVeigh's former Army friend Michael Fortier for questioning. With the bureau's vast resources, it has named only these four. But I wonder: is there anyone else? Families of the bombing victims want to know the same thing: Did the government catch everyone?

So why start with Gordon Kahl, a dead man? Because plots against the Alfred P. Murrah Building have a long history. White supremacists discussed destroying the building with rockets years before McVeigh bombed it. One of those who wanted to attack the building was Richard Snell, who later killed a Jewish businessman and a Black police officer. Snell was executed for his crimes the same day the bomb went off in Oklahoma City. Was this a coincidence? Maybe.

The Patriot movement has many martyrs. Kahl was one of the first. The farm where he died seems like a good place to start looking at what the movement is doing today. One thing I know for certain is that the past lives in the present.

Gordon Kahl was a hero in World War II, a B-25 turret gunner who shot down ten enemy planes. He was still a crack shot when he died at the age of sixty-three. For part of the year, he farmed in North Dakota. In the off season, he worked as an auto mechanic in Los Angeles, where he was indoctrinated into Christian Identity, which teaches that Jews are the offspring of Satan and must be exterminated. He was also a member of Posse Comitatus, an anti-Semitic movement that believes the Internal Revenue Service is a tool of international bankers, a pawn in a Zionist conspiracy to enslave America.

Kahl refused to file his federal income taxes and went to prison for it. He was out on parole when he became an organizer for the Sovereigns movement, which does not recognize the federal government and seeks to form parallel governments and courts based on its idea of English common law.

In 1983, Kahl refused to surrender to two U.S. Marshals who came to arrest him on a tax warrant. A gun battle followed, and Kahl and his son killed both Marshals. Kahl fled from North Dakota to Arkansas and took refuge at the farm of Leonard and Norma Ginter, both members of the United

Sovereigns. When the authorities came to arrest him, Kahl again resisted. A local sheriff died in the shootout, and Kahl was burned so badly his entire remains could not be found at first.

The Ginters served five years in federal prison for conspiracy and harboring a fugitive. Leonard Ginter is now regarded as an elder statesman in the loose-knit anti-government Patriot movement that ranges from weekend militiamen, angry farmers, and tax protesters to terrorists whose weapons of choice are guns and bombs.

"Hail the Victory," the serious ones say in their letters from prison. It's the English translation of "Sieg Heil," one of the most widely used and notorious slogans of Adolph Hitler and the Nazi Party, often accompanied by the Nazi salute. Neo-Nazis in Arkansas. It's hard to put my mind around that one, and yet I'm aware, as I'm driving down the road, I'm about to jump into some deep water I know little about.

The Patriot movement, as it now calls itself, has a history of violence and murder, with its own language and heroes. If I want to know what I'm seeing, I must understand them. The martyrs may well influence the members of the movement who are still alive.

Along with Kahl, at the top of my list of martyrs is Bob Mathews, the leader of the Order, an Aryan Nations offshoot that advocated the violent overthrow of the government. The Order engaged in robberies, bombings, and assassinations modeled on William Pierce's novel, *The Turner Diaries,* the same book McVeigh used as a blueprint for the Oklahoma City bombing. Mathews died in 1984 during a thirty-six-hour standoff and shootout with two hundred law enforcement officers.

Now, all known members of the Order are behind bars. Many wear the number fourteen as a tattoo to signify "fourteen words" of David Lane, another founder of the Order: "We must secure the existence of our people and a future for white children." Lane coined this slogan while serving a sentence of 190 years in federal prison for his role in the 1984 murder of Alan Berg, a Jewish talk show host, by another member of his group.

In the months since the Oklahoma City bombing, small, violent white separatist groups with no apparent ties to each other have appeared, and I have heard about an approach to fighting the government called "leaderless resistance." It has been endorsed by Lane and popularized by Louis Beam, a former Texas Klansman who inspired assaults on Vietnamese fishermen in the Gulf of Mexico. The idea of "leaderless resistance" has spread like a virus through the white underground. Is it just talk? Or is there more to it? Did they help McVeigh?

I'm not optimistic the Ginters will tell a reporter from New York much, but sometimes, even when people say nothing, they do. A certain kind of silence, a look, or a gesture can mean a lot. I hope they will talk to me because they pity the babies McVeigh killed or because it's a suitable time to have their say, or even because they're curious to know why I've come to see them.

"Tell them you were sent by the man who found Kahl's foot," Jimmy Barden, an editor of mine, has suggested. Barden was a local reporter when the shootout at the farm happened, and he came to interview the Ginters afterwards. While he was there, he noticed a burnt foot in the ashes and debris. Investigators had overlooked it.

"The Ginters will remember the foot and the reporter who found it," Jimmy assured me. Such a credential could get me an audience.

A sign at the farm entrance says, "This Is Private Land," "Sovereign Trust #5." Shotgun shells litter the ground, adding emphasis and menace. The Ginters have no listed telephone, so I have not called to ask permission.

The Ginters belong to the United Sovereigns of America, a group that enshrines common law and opposes the "illegal" federal government, the IRS, the monetary system and the "New World Order Conspiracy." They are unknown to the public now, but in less than a year, the Freemen will lead the news in an eighty-one-day standoff with the U.S. Marshals in Montana.

Four days ago, Leonard Ginter and six hundred others from thirty-two states gathered in Wichita to commemorate the anniversary of Kahl's death and meet as a "National Common Law Grand Jury." They concluded that judges and governors were guilty of treason and should be hung.

"If we do about [ten] of them, the rest will straighten out," Ginter told the gathering. "It wouldn't necessarily have to be a judge or a governor. If one governor got it, we wouldn't have any trouble with the rest."

After I pass the farm entrance, the road surface turns from asphalt to rock and gravel. The lane narrows and continues straight down a steep hill, like a chute. Then it then rises another hill to end at a house the size of a mobile home.

The house, made of concrete, is set back into the side of the hill like a bunker. I drive toward it slowly, hoping no one will jump out the front door with a shotgun. Nothing moves. No sounds. No dog. No gun.

I park, get out, and inch my way to the front door with my best smile. I knock. No answer. I wait and knock again. *Nothing.*

Disappointed but relieved, I write a note on my business card and stick it under the door.

The morning is bright and hot – not the weather or time of day for ghosts – but my hair stands on end when I turn around. The remains of another house are strewn on the hill behind me. I missed seeing it when I drove in. The second house is charred black. Its broken concrete walls lie among the dirt and brush like an open grave.

My optimism founders.

This is an evil place. I do not belong here, and I should not have come.

Even my car is wrong, a red Mustang airport rental. It fishtails on the dirt and gravel as I hasten to leave. Its low-slung bottom scrapes the high spots on the ground.

After a few hours, I work up the nerve for a second try at the Ginters, but when I return, the entrance to the property is blocked by a huge tractor trailer cab. On the road to the farm, I had passed the rest of the vehicle, a milk trailer from Wisconsin, parked a few miles back. This time I get out and walk down the hill and up to the house. When I knock, Norma Ginter comes to the door.

"We don't want to talk," she says as her husband comes up behind her.

"If you'd come in 1983 and tried to dig out the truth, that'd be different," he adds.

To acknowledge that history, I mention Jimmy Barden, the man who found Kahl's foot. It makes no difference.

"We don't need the media this time," Mrs. Ginter says. "We'll do it on our own."

"How can I find out more about the organization?" I ask, fishing for anything.

"You'd have to talk with the higher-ups out west," she says.

"Who are they?"

She shuts the door.

I walk back to the car and drive away, taking time to look at the farm gates facing the road. All have "No Trespassing" signs. One says, "Keep Out, Rattlesnakes." Things are not going well. This is the United States, my country, but I'm not welcome.

I think back to a trip to Ireland several years ago. I was driving north from the airport in Shannon after a flight from New York with my daughter Kathleen, who was a baby then, and I was exhausted. After a short while, I stopped at an inn, where I got a warm greeting. I asked for a cup of tea. Only after the tea arrived did I realize I was in the garden of a private home. I was a foreigner, but I was welcome.

If the hostility from the Ginters is any indication, my search for answers is going to be painfully difficult. Any chance of finding the roots of the tragedy in Oklahoma City will depend on knowing as much as possible about what happened before, on, and after that terrible day.

CHAPTER THIRTY-FOUR:
THE OKLAHOMA CITY BOMBING

Wednesday, April 19, 1995, was a beautiful spring morning. More than five hundred people were just starting work at the Alfred P. Murrah Federal Building in Oklahoma City. The Social Security office on the first floor was full, and so was the America's Kids Day care center on the second floor. At 9:02 a.m., a vast explosion ripped off the north face of the building and sent it crashing into the street. Nine floors of concrete pancaked together, ejecting the occupants who were lucky and crushing the rest to death.

A man from the seventh floor found himself on the third floor. A man thrown into a corner of his fifth-floor office turned around and found himself outdoors. Cars parked nearby burst into flames. The blast blew in the windows of buildings for blocks around, cutting the occupants with flying glass. They staggered out to the street, dazed and bleeding. They did not know yet they were the lucky ones.

Shortly after, the catastrophe appeared on network television, the shattered Murrah Building burning and shrouded in a pall of ashes. I was in New York, working as an editor at the *Times*. It was just after 10 a.m., Eastern time, and I was starting my second cup of morning coffee. The scenes on

TV did not look real. I half-expected a reassuring announcement that it was a disaster movie. Then came the first reports that children were inside.

There cannot be children. The world cannot be that cruel.

Millions of Americans watched as firefighters battled the flames and passersby joined police, firefighters, and medics trying to find and help survivors, including people still inside the building. A doctor squeezed through the wreckage, working in a space no wider than his body, to help a woman he finally freed by amputating her leg.

Few were alive under all those tons of steel and concrete. They found Baylee Almon dying one day after her first birthday. A photograph of her tiny body in the arms of Fire Captain Chris Fields became a heartbreaking icon of the rescue efforts, but she did not survive. The rescue dogs dug until their paws bled and then had to be led away.

There is no final tally because rescue workers will suffer mental and physical illnesses, adding to the toll. The original count is 168 people dead, including nineteen babies and children. Five hundred people were injured. Thirty children were orphaned.

Shortly after the attack, one of our editors in New York noticed that the date, April 19, 1995, was the second anniversary of the federal raid on the Branch Davidian compound near Waco, Texas. That raid began with a tear gas attack by tanks and federal agents and ended with a fire and the deaths of seventy-four people, including twenty-five children.

We wondered if the date was a clue to a motive for the bombing, revenge against the federal government by an anti-government group, but we had no evidence.

No one claimed responsibility for the bombing, and as night fell, rumors spread across the country like an epidemic. Many blamed the attack on Middle Eastern terrorists. Such a group had conducted the first attack on the World Trade Center two years earlier, a 1993 bombing that killed six people and injured more than a thousand. Almost immediately, we began hearing reports of attacks on innocent people of Middle Eastern descent in various parts of the nation.

In Oklahoma City, callers flooded local news organizations with stories of dark-haired, dark-skinned people, real and imagined, they saw near the Murrah Building, or at a local motel, or driving a car near the building before the bombing. Some blamed the Iraqis. Others fantasized the federal government bombed its own building to get Congressional support for anti-terrorism legislation.

The rumors, rivers of them on talk radio, were rich and plentiful, and the facts hard to find and harder to confirm. Fortunately for federal investigators, they had a huge asset in local law enforcement and several amazing strokes of good luck.

We did not know it at the time, but a security camera on the Regency Towers, an apartment complex five hundred feet west of the Federal Building, had captured images of a Ryder truck making its way up the street facing the Murrah Building that morning. The truck stopped across from the Regency Towers lobby for twenty-two seconds, then moved on toward the Federal Building.

When the bomb exploded, a huge object came flying back down the street and smashed into the hood and windshield of a red Ford that was parked near the Regency Towers. It was a truck axle, and when two police officers found it, the VIN number could be traced. At 4:45 that afternoon – unknown to the media – an FBI agent walked into the office that had rented that truck in Junction City, Kansas, 280 miles north of Oklahoma City.

The shop employees looked at their copy of the rental contract and recalled the man who came in with a friend to rent the truck. He called himself "Robert Kling," and presented as ID a South Dakota driver's license with the issue date of April 19, 1993, the day of the Waco raid. From the employees' descriptions, an artist drew sketches that were quickly made public. The entire nation started looking for the Oklahoma City bombers, John Doe 1 and John Doe 2.

No one knew John Doe 1 was already in custody. A state police officer had arrested Timothy McVeigh an hour and a half after he blew up the Federal Building. He was stopped on Interstate 35 about sixty miles north of Oklahoma City because his 1977 yellow Mercury had no license plate.

When Patrolman Charlie Hanger pulled him over, McVeigh was wearing a nine-millimeter semiautomatic pistol in a shoulder holster. Hanger arrested him for carrying a concealed weapon without a permit. Although no one thought much about it at the time, McVeigh was also wearing a tee-shirt that said, "Sic Semper Tyrannis," or "Thus Ever to Tyrants," which is what the assassin John Wilkes Booth shouted after he shot President Lincoln. It was visible in McVeigh's first mug shot.

Hanger took McVeigh to the county jail in Perry, Oklahoma. Under normal circumstances, he would have been arraigned that same afternoon or the next day, Thursday, and freed on a $5,000 bond. But the judge was tied up in a messy divorce case. As he waited in jail, a desperate McVeigh called a bail bondsman in Pawnee, Oklahoma.

"I got to get out of here, man, please," he begged, but the bondsman said he could do nothing until a judge set bail. McVeigh spent the night and the next day and night in jail. His bond hearing was set for 9:30 a.m. Friday. The assistant DA had already called the jail on the fourth floor of the courthouse to have McVeigh brought down to the courtroom on the first floor.

At about this time, the FBI called County Sheriff Jerry Cook to ask if a man named Timothy James McVeigh was still in custody. He had used his own name when he checked into a motel in Junction City shortly before the bombing, and the motel manager said he matched the description of John Doe 1.

McVeigh had also given his real name to Trooper Hanger, who routinely entered it into the national crime computer. McVeigh and the officers bringing him to court were stopped at the third floor on their way down. McVeigh was sent back upstairs to a cell of his own. The officers told him the hearing was postponed.

The prosecutor was still waiting in the courtroom. A note arrived, saying McVeigh was the suspected Oklahoma City bomber. The DA later said he thought it was a courthouse joke. By evening, a crowd of hundreds had gathered in front of the courthouse, and TV helicopters hovered overhead.

McVeigh came out of the building under heavy guard at 6 p.m., and people screamed "Murderer!" and "Baby killer! Burn him." McVeigh was tall and skinny, with high cheekbones and a blonde buzz cut. He was young, but he had an expressionless, stony face. It was this face the world came to know, the face I would see day after day in court. Within hours, we knew he was a former army sergeant and the recipient of a Bronze Star. He had served in the first Iraq war and had once been stationed at Fort Riley, next door to Junction City.

Meanwhile, a source in Washington told one of our reporters to check out a Junction City motel. The source said "dream" was part of the name. When our reporter got to the Dreamland Motel, the FBI had already come and gone, taking all the registration records with them. The manager and her son both told the FBI they saw a big yellow Ryder truck parked at the motel while McVeigh was staying there. But the motel manager was very reluctant to talk to the press. The man who had rented out the Ryder truck resisted every request for an interview.

This happened repeatedly with the real witnesses, but others in Junction City were eager to report McVeigh sightings. Some sightings were imaginary; others were publicity stunts. Journalists interviewed the customers at the Club Yesterday, a clerk at a check-cashing business, a hairdresser, a woman who modeled underwear at Fantasee Lingerie, and a disc jockey at the Club Alibi.

As we eventually learned, McVeigh checked into Room 25 of the Dreamland Motel on April 14, five days before the bombing. On the registration slip, he gave his address as a farm in Decker, Michigan, about eighty miles north of Detroit. The press learned about the farm from neighbors when the FBI and the ATF showed up there.

At this point, we learned the Nichols brothers had attended meetings of the Michigan Militia, one of a growing number of armed far-right groups that detested the federal government in general and the ATF in particular, None of us at the *Times* knew much about these groups. They operated on the margins in places we did not cover, and they had not seemed important.

The farm was owned by James Nichols, first described by federal investigators as a potential witness. His brother, Terry Lynn Nichols, lived in Herington, Kansas, a small town just South of Junction City. FBI agents were questioning Terry Nichols at the Herington police station while the search was underway in Michigan.

As we quickly learned, they had seized upon two incidents as proof of government tyranny: the bloody siege at Waco and a siege in Idaho at the home of Randy Weaver, a white supremacist. His wife and teen-aged son were slain, as was a federal marshal, in August 1992.

Just two days after the Oklahoma City bombing, federal investigators showed up in large numbers at the Canyon West Mobile and RV Park on Route 66 in Kingman, Arizona. McVeigh had once lived there. One of the *Times'* best reporters was dispatched in pursuit. He arrived on a Saturday to find the rental office closed. He tracked down the owner of the park, who thought McVeigh had rented an old eight by forty-foot mobile home for $235 a month.

Danny Bundy, a plumber who lived nearby, recalled McVeigh as a belligerent man who hated authority, drank enormous quantities of beer, blasted rock-and-roll on the radio at night and lived with a pregnant girlfriend who had a baby shortly before they left the trailer park in June.

"Him and his girlfriend drove like maniacs through here," Bundy said. Bundy also recalled seeing McVeigh standing at the edge of the trailer park and firing rounds from a semiautomatic weapon into the desert. This was just the behavior we were expecting of McVeigh, so we published what Bundy had to say. The day the story ran, a call came in from a man who identified himself as a former resident of the trailer park.

"The fellow you're describing sounds a lot like me," he said. It was. The neighbor had wrongly identified Tim McVeigh.

McVeigh himself was quiet and had no girlfriends. His drug of choice was methamphetamine. We did not know these details yet, but we did have reporters in McVeigh's hometown, Pendleton NY, near Buffalo. People remembered him as an invisible kid who grew up to be a loner and straight arrow. He joined the army and rose to the rank of sergeant. Afterwards, he immersed himself in far-right politics.

His friends said McVeigh visited Waco and came away hating the federal government. In fact, he was photographed at Waco in March 1993. Later, when he and Terry Nichols were in Michigan, they watched the federal raid on the Branch Davidian compound as it was taking place on TV.

As McVeigh traveled from one place to another, the only constant was his love of guns. People remembered him from gun shows.

In Kingman, the FBI found the third major figure in the bombing, Michael Fortier. He and his wife Lori were McVeigh's neighbors in Arizona and remained his friends. Fortier played a key role in the conspiracy against the federal building, but at the last minute refused to help make the bomb.

"What about all the people?" Fortier had asked McVeigh. McVeigh told him to think about the storm troopers in the movie *Star Wars*, innocent as individuals but guilty of working for the evil empire.

When Fortier became a person of interest to the FBI, they bugged his mobile home and recorded all his conversations and phone calls. Throngs of reporters and photographers surrounded the Fortier trailer during this time, and he came out regularly to denounce the government. Finally, he was arrested and taken away, eventually becoming one of the government's star witnesses at the trials of both McVeigh and Terry Nichols.

At this point, the media, including my newspaper, had a huge ongoing story in far-flung locations: Oklahoma City, Kansas, Michigan, and Arizona. The story kept expanding, to Las Vegas, to Arkansas, to the Philippines. It grew every time a local news organization reported another FBI search. Very few news organizations tried to jump on every lead. The *Times* did.

The government gathered evidence rapidly and quickly put together its scenario for the bombing. McVeigh and

Nichols planned it. To get the money, Nichols stole guns and money from Roger Moore, a gun dealer in Arkansas. Some of the stolen guns – and Moore's bedspread – were found in the Nichols home in Herington, Kansas. Other guns and cash were found in a Las Vegas storage unit. Nichols had gone to the Philippines to marry a mail order bride and left the key with his ex-wife Lana. While he was away, Lana opened the storage unit and took some of the cash.

To make the bomb, McVeigh and Nichols traveled around Kansas and bought two tons of fertilizer – ammonium nitrate – at different farm stores. They kept it in rented storage lockers. McVeigh disguised himself as a biker and went to a track in Dallas, Texas, to buy $3,000 worth of nitromethane racing fuel to make the ammonium nitrate explosive.

They still needed something to ignite the bomb, so McVeigh and Nichols burglarized a quarry in Marion, Kansas, and stole dynamite and blasting caps. They took these to Arizona by car. wrapped them in gift paper and brought them back disguised as Christmas presents.

On the Sunday before the bombing, McVeigh drove to Oklahoma City and parked his getaway car with a sign saying it had just broken down. The sign asked passers-by not to tow it. Then he called Nichols in Kansas to come pick him up.

McVeigh rented a large Ryder Truck in Junction City, Kansas, on the day before the bombing and drove it half an hour South to a state fishing park at Geary Lake, just outside Nichols' home in Herington, Kansas. Witnesses driving by Geary Lake on the highway saw a big yellow truck parked there in the lot.

According to the government, Nichols and McVeigh mixed the bomb themselves, four thousand pounds of ammonium nitrate and fuel in about twenty blue plastic 55-gallon barrels, then stacked them inside the truck to make a "shaped bomb," with the barrels lined up like the letter "v" for maximum impact in the direction of the building. Earlier, McVeigh had shown Fortier's wife Lori how this would work by lining up soup cans on her kitchen floor.

Neither Michael nor Lori Fortier ever warned anyone. And when Tim McVeigh drove his truck bomb 280 miles south from Geary Lake to Oklahoma City, he went alone. No one else helped him. This was his story until the day he was executed at the federal prison in Terre Haute, Indiana.

This was the narrative given at the separate trials of Timothy McVeigh and Terry Nichols. It was a true story. But I am not sure it was the whole story, and that's why I am on the road as a reporter again.

CHAPTER THIRTY-FIVE:
WITH THE RIGHT-WING UNDERGROUND

The inspiration for the bombing came from a novel *The Turner Diaries* by William Pierce, the founder of a group called the National Alliance that was virulently anti-Semitic. In this novel, a white warrior blows up the FBI headquarters with a truck bomb. McVeigh loved this book and recommended it to his friends. What, if anything, did the choice of this novel tell us about the people and philosophies McVeigh admired? Was he collaborating with them? I wonder.

I also wonder, what happened to John Doe 2? After issuing a revised drawing of him wearing a baseball cap, the government said John Doe 2 was a case of mistaken identity. The government said he was, in fact, Private Todd Bunting, who came into the truck rental office the day after McVeigh was there.

When first interviewed by the FBI, however, the employees at the rental agency – who would not speak with journalists – recalled two men, not one, came in to rent the truck.

Meanwhile, the critics of the way the government is managing the investigation are in full cry. Hoppy Heidelberg, a juror on the McVeigh federal grand jury, has told the alternative press he feels the prosecutors are intentionally avoiding John Doe No.2, and he suspects that John Doe 2 is, in fact, a government informant. If this were true, the government had prior knowledge of the bombing. This notion strikes me as outrageous and false.

Others, including a former FBI employee and a retired Air Force general, challenge the government on the nature of the bomb itself, arguing that it must have been placed inside the building to shear the concrete columns. An Oklahoma State Representative, Charles Key, joins the outcry, calling the investigation an "obstruction of justice so blatant that it's been shocking to me." I can't see this line of reasoning either.

The wild ideas are proportionate to the pain, and the government is a handy target. But I do wonder, along with some of the victims' families, if the investigation has been wrapped up too quickly.

As an editor, I have badgered to death most of our reporters by the time Gene Roberts, the great *Philadelphia Inquirer* editor who became managing editor of the *Times,* suggests I leave my editor's chair and go on the road to work on the story myself.

He combines this suggestion with a promise I can cover the trial of McVeigh and Nichols whenever it takes place, even though I have never covered a trial for the *Times.* Meanwhile, I can try to find out two things: were there other conspirators in the bombing, and does the white far right pose a real danger to America?

This assignment comes at the perfect time for my family and me. I had left the *Times* after our year in Northern Ireland to take a visiting professorship at the University of

Illinois at Urbana-Champaign. At the time, I thought we could all live on my salary for a year while my husband finished writing his dissertation for his Ph.D. from the University of Michigan. I had to resign from the *Times* to do this, but I hoped to persuade them to hire me back. I assumed that my husband could find a college teaching job in anthropology in the New York metropolitan area.

How little I knew of the time it takes to write a dissertation! How ridiculously optimistic I was about the academic job market! One year in Illinois stretched into seven, enough time for my husband to finish his degree and join the faculty of the anthropology department at the University of Illinois. By then, the university had given me an associate professorship with tenure in journalism. As I yearned to go back to reporting, my family settled in Illinois.

After seven years of teaching, I was eligible for a sabbatical. While I was working in academia, the British army shot to death my friend Aidan McAnespie, and I wrote an article published in the *Columbia Journalism Review* that criticized the way American newspapers, including my own, covered Northern Ireland.

In the meantime, Joe Lelyveld, my bureau chief in London, had become executive editor of the *Times*. When I asked to return to the newspaper, he said yes, and we agreed to disagree about Ireland.

Now my sabbatical with the university is ending, I do not want to leave New York and resume my life as a journalism professor in Illinois. I want to stay at the *Times*. My husband is desperate to return to our home in Urbana. He loves his students and his work in Illinois and hates life as a house husband in suburban New Jersey. He has inquired about university teaching positions in the New York metropolitan area, and no one is hiring a cultural anthropologist. I can stay in New York, he says, but he is returning to Illinois and taking the kids with him. I am being torn apart. Susan is in eighth grade and Kathleen, born when we lived in Belfast, is a third grader. I do not want to split up our family.

Gene Roberts' offer to let me leave my editing job in New York and work as a reporter based out of our home in Illinois is a godsend. I can keep both my family and my career in journalism. We pack our belongings into two large rental trucks and head west.

I will spend the next seven months trying to talk to white supremacists, traveling from Idaho to Pennsylvania. In the past, it has been easy to speak with underground or anti-government groups because they always wanted to publicize their message, but the situation is different now. White supremacist groups view the American media as an arm of the federal government. We are the *enemy*. They hate *The New York Times* because they imagine it to be a Jewish newspaper.

Their isolation makes it even more daunting to speak with them. They live in rural places, and they are heavily armed. If you want to talk, you must go alone. It helps that I look like a stereotypical WASP. My white skin killed my access to Liberty City during the riots, but it is my passport to the white right. Even so, I don't anticipate all the hostility I encounter. One farm woman runs me off because of my clothes.

"Stockings!" she shouts when she opens her door and looks down on me. "Get out! No city people here!"

Cell phones do not exist, so I arrange to call my editor when I am going to see someone in a dangerous location. I give her the address and promise to call her when I am out and safe.

After my visit to the Ginters, I visit Kurt Saxon, a survivalist and author of *The Poor Man's James Bond*, a staple of the far right. He lives in Alpena, Arkansas in a large house with a tire garden out back. His interests are vegetables and weapons. He invites me to have a seat in the shade of his back porch.

"I describe destructive devices because that's my hobby," he says, handing me a glass of iced tea. "I can't think McVeigh had any need of my book." He shows me a copy of the book *Explosives and Bomb Disposal Guide*. "Every Nazi and Klansman I knew in the 1960s had one of these."

Saxon tells me he was hounded by the press after the bombing in Oklahoma City. He is particularly irate about a story that reported he once blew off his fingers making a bomb.

"If I'd been making a bomb, it wouldn't have exploded," he snaps. "I *know* how to make a bomb. I lost those fingers trying to figure out how to pack explosives into a shotgun shell."

Before giving up on Arkansas, I try Thom Robb, national director of the Knights of the Ku Klux Klan. He lives outside Zinc, a tiny, devastated town of dead vehicles and one-room shacks on dirt and gravel streets. Two creeks flow over the road to Robb's house, an unfinished log cabin with exposed wires and plumbing.

On a summer day, the heat inside the house is breathtaking, so we sit outside the shade until ticks begin falling out of the trees. Then we must move into the sunshine as Robb tells me about his life, his beliefs, and his friends. He tries immediately to distance himself from McVeigh and Nichols.

"I heard that Nichols was married to a Filipino," he says, "so he couldn't be part of an Aryan movement." He does not want to talk about Beam or leaderless cells.

As we speak, Robb's daughter and son-in-law arrive with their children, two- and four-years-old, barefoot, and covered with ticks from the tall grass. Their father was on his way to work and had to bring them in the back entrance because my car was blocking the drive. I have delayed him, and he is furious. When I apologize, he chokes back his anger and is polite, but his distress may be my only glimpse at real life here. He's late for work at a place that appears not to accept excuses if something has gone wrong. Zinc looks like a place where little ever goes right.

Kansas is the same in the towns where the bombing was launched, where McVeigh served in the army, where Nichols lived. Although most journalists describe Kansas and Oklahoma as the "heartland"—as in "How could such a terrible thing happen in the heartland?"—these are also flyover states, where daily life is invisible to people living on the coasts.

The small towns I visit are dying, and the mood is often angry or desperate or both. Many farms have already gone under, and others are folding up. People are living third world lives – a little construction work here, farming there, running errands for someone on another day – not sure where the next meal is coming from.

Nichols was living in Herington, Kansas, and I stop for coffee in a town nearby. When a few locals introduce themselves, I tell them I'm investigating the bombing. I expect the usual sympathy and outrage. Instead, they say, "The only problem is they didn't blow up the White House."

Six months after the bombing, most people figure they know as much of the story as they are ever going to get. There are a few important exceptions. One is J.D. Cash, a businessman who has become a reporter since the bombing and works for the *McCurtain Gazette*. The other is Glenn Wilburn, a certified public accountant who lost his grandsons in the bombing: Chase Smith, who was three years old, and Colton Smith, who was two.

Wilburn, who will die of cancer before the trials begin, is a man on fire. He wants to know everything about the bombing. He and his wife Kathy are not journalists, but they will pull up a seat at their kitchen table for anyone who may have news on the investigation. Kathy serves up food, and Glen looks for any scrap of added information.

J. D. Cash, who will die of cancer in 2007, has a plausible manner with the right wing, an attitude that helps him, and he once tells me he sees no problem making up what he can't prove. But people who will not speak to mainstream reporters will talk to Cash. Now and then, he produces promising leads, including partial copies of McVeigh's telephone records, pieces of the puzzle of McVeigh's travels and connections.

I track down these numbers and find a truck driver, the publisher of a weekly shopper, a dairy farmer, a gun dealer, a professional pool player. If these people remember anything, it is a call from Nichols wanting to buy or sell or rent something: a mobile home, a gun, a fuel meter. Some of the numbers belong to people who are dead, others to people who have left town. The telephone list leads me nowhere.

I start over, looking for people who stayed at the Dreamland Motel in Junction City when McVeigh stayed there before renting the Ryder truck that carried the bomb to Oklahoma City. I also go from door to door in Herington, seeking witnesses, asking one person to introduce me to the next. Slowly, I pick hints of other help to Nichols and McVeigh.

The most tantalizing missing clue is a trailer, one or more.

McVeigh used a trailer to pick up ammonium nitrate from a feed store during a time neither he nor Nichols owned a trailer. I cannot find out who owned or lent them the trailer, but trailers appear in other accounts of the two men.

In Herington, a neighbor recalls seeing a trailer carrying belongings to Nichols house at night, when the neighbor was standing outside smoking a cigarette. The neighbor saw a group of men helping Nichols move in.

Some of the witnesses at the Dreamland Motel saw a Ryder truck there before the bombing. They said it was pulling a trailer carrying something covered up. What was on the trailer? No one knew.

Who supplied the trailer? Where did it go later?

It's possible that McVeigh or Nichols or both borrowed the trailer from someone unaware of what they were planning, a person who never came forward. They might have stolen a trailer or different trailers several times. No one mentions it at their trials. It's a phantom, a loose end.

Years after my work in Kansas, I will meet an FBI agent who worked on the case but never talked to the press. The trailer bothered him more than anything, he will tell me.

"I hunted the entire state of Kansas for that trailer," he will say.

Many people come forward with sightings of John Doe 2, and it's impossible for me to tell which are real and which are imaginary. They've all seen the drawing circulated after the bombing, and their descriptions of a young white man, muscular with dark hair, could be the other bombing suspect or an overactive imagination.

I spend hours and hours with a retired high school coach who lives in Herington and is sure he saw John Doe 2 at a local gas station before the bombing, but his information takes me nowhere. Other local people who believe they were eyewitnesses also turn out to be dead ends for me.

As the days drag on, stress and the environment are having a terrible effect on my health. There are few local restaurants. I find myself grabbing fast food and worrying about my alarming weight gain. I'm fifty-four years old. I do not know yet that my bad diet has teamed up with extreme stress to put my thyroid into a nosedive. I will not recover. I'll be on thyroid pills and weight loss diets for the rest of my life. I overhear J.D. Cash snickering at Glenn and Kathy's

Wilburn's kitchen table in Oklahoma City that I'd make a good mud wrestler. The effortless slim beauty I had for so many years is gone.

When I first began looking into connections between the bombing of the Murrah Building and the white far right, I wondered if there was any connection between the date of the attack and the execution of Richard Wayne Snell, the white supremacist executed for murder that same day. Years earlier, Snell was one of those white supremacists who had discussed the possibility of destroying the Murrah Building, with rockets.

Snell's spiritual adviser was the Rev. David Millar, who presides over a four-hundred- acre settlement called Elohim City in Muldrow, Oklahoma, near the Arkansas state line. After Snell's execution, Millar brought Snell's body back to Elohim City for burial. Millar is an older man – the people who live at Elohim City call him "Grandpa"—who practices an anti-Semitic religion called Christian Identity that regards Jews as diabolical.

Investigators who pulled McVeigh's telephone records after his arrest found a phone call McVeigh made before the bombing to someone at Elohim City. At the time, McVeigh was staying at the Imperial Motel in Kingman, Arizona. Federal prosecutors did not say who McVeigh was trying to call, but there are many possibilities. Elohim City has hosted a range of white separatists deeply involved in violent crime.

Some of them belonged to the Aryan Republican Army, a small group that has robbed twenty-two banks. Did any of their money go to McVeigh? Other visitors to Elohim City before the bombing included Mark Thomas, the head of the

Aryan Nations in Pennsylvania, and Dennis Mahon, a former grand dragon of the White Knights of the Ku Klux Klan. Mahon is friends with Thomas. Did they help McVeigh and Nichols? I want to find out.

Journalists who have ventured out to Elohim City have been turned away. I decide to try instead to speak with Mahon at his house in Tulsa. He was working as an airline mechanic, but that career was ended by publicity about his Klan activities. He's still upset about it. When I knock on his door, I find a middle-aged man drinking whiskey in the middle of the afternoon.

He's surprised to see me, but he invites me in and offers me a chair. He has a handgun on the coffee table. He offers me a glass but seems relieved when I ask for coffee. He needs alcohol today, and I don't see another bottle of liquor anywhere.

These days, he tells me, he is running a Dial-A-Racist hotline and heading up a group called WAR, White Aryan Resistance. His telephone rings constantly. Today the calls are mostly coming from journalists because he's back in the news bigtime. I hear about it from him.

His former girlfriend, Carole Howe, a beautiful and wealthy former debutante, has just been revealed to be an informant for the federal Bureau of Alcohol, Tobacco, and Firearms.

He shows me pictures of them together, smiling, and happy, a gorgeous young woman and an aging neo-Nazi. Their romance strikes me as odd, but who can explain love or rebellion in a young person? When they broke up, Dennis tells me, Carole chose another white supremacist as her new lover.

At that point, however, she became a government informant. The feds dropped Carole as an informant just before they arrested her and her new boyfriend. They charged both with planning to blow up buildings in fifteen cities. Although Carole would later be acquitted at trial, her cover was blown.

Mahon is shaken by the disclosure, badmouthing Carole to the reporters who call as he waits to view his televised interviews with Channel Six, Channel Two, and *Dateline* on NBC. He seems only a little disgruntled when his mother calls. She has seen him on NBC and wants to know what's going on.

"I'm tired of people saying they're friends and turning out to be snitches," he says after he finishes talking with her. "I've always said I'm a terrorist – with my *words*."

Not until she is called as a defense witness at the federal trial of Terry Nichols, two years from now, will Carole Howe reveal she told investigators after the bombing she saw a man resembling McVeigh at Elohim City.

She will also testify she was sitting in Mahon's living room a year before the bombing when the telephone rang. Mahon went to the bedroom to take the call.

"I heard him say 'Tim Tuttle, Tuttle, Tuttle, Tuttle, Tuttle' and then he laughed." She said she did not realize the name "Tim Tuttle" mattered. It was an alias frequently used by McVeigh.

On the afternoon I meet him, Dennis Mahon spins me an elaborate fantasy about the bombing in Oklahoma. It was a "black bag operation using McVeigh and Nichols as fall guys," he says. "Only the government could gain by killing all these kids, and believe you me, the government's capable of doing it."

When I ask Mahon to tell me more about his group, WAR, he gives me a long explanation that begins to interest me when he says: "Our battle is for the future of our race, and we go by the fourteen key words of the Order and David Lane, who's the spokesman of the Order at this time. 'We must secure the existence of our people and a future for white children.' That's what it's all about."

"Does the Order still exist outside the prisons?"

For a moment, he looks disconcerted.

"The Order is a spiritual thing," he says. "Robert Mathews inspired many of us. Some are underground. I'm an above-ground activist soon to be semi-retired. I think the boys who robbed the banks had other ideas. The Order is made up of radical white separatists who are willing to take it to the enemy with unorthodox means."

The whiskey does not seem to affect Mahon, but the coffee is getting to me, and eventually I ask to use the bathroom. Behind the door, when I close it, is a huge assault rifle.

It's a reminder of the sea in which I am swimming. I try not to think about it as I finish the interview.

I leave Mahon's house determined to talk to Mark Thomas, who Mahon says is a good friend. I use Dennis's name when I call Thomas at his home in Macungie, Pennsylvania. Thomas surprises me by saying he's working tomorrow tonight, driving a semi-trailer to the East Coast. If I want to join him for the round trip to Connecticut and back, to keep him awake, he will talk to me. Otherwise, I can forget it.

"I'll do it," I tell him.

I take a flight from Tulsa to Allentown, Pennsylvania, rent a car, and locate the Gulf station near Bethlehem where I am to meet Mark Thomas. He has not arrived. I arrange with the manager to park my car next to the building until the next morning. Thomas promises we'll be back by sunrise. Just after the manager agrees, a huge semi arrives, pulling two trailers.

Thomas is behind the wheel. He's wearing a brown shirt and rimless glasses, and his moustache looks like a larger version of Hitler's. When I climb into the passenger side of the cab, I can see he's wearing an Aryan Nations belt buckle and combat boots laced up high. He has handguns stashed everywhere. Off we go, bumping through the endless construction sites on the interstate.

I begin by asking Thomas about Gordon Kahl. He tells me Kahl's death had an enormous impact on him, but he won't get specific. He does say he has met Leonard Ginter, and he knows David Tate, the most influential living member of the Order. Thomas also accompanied Grandpa Millar to visit Richard Wayne Snell in prison. He was present at Elohim City when the bank robbers were there. All the bank robbers have been arrested, and Thomas asks me if I think anyone else will be indicted.

"I don't know."

For all his connections, which are new to me, Mark Thomas is giving me no clues to a broader conspiracy in the bombing. Indeed, why would he? This interview is a lost cause, although – or perhaps because – Thomas connects the dots in so many ways. His manner is calm and friendly, but I'm getting increasingly scared of him.

When we stop for dinner, we are among the few restaurant patrons who are not Black, and I wonder what the other diners think of Thomas's Nazi regalia – and me. My sense of the unreal grows stronger when the truck Thomas is driving breaks down on the highway.

"Hold the flashlight, will you?"

I am standing on the side of the road, holding a flashlight so Thomas can repair his truck.

If we get sideswiped and killed, what will people say if someone from The New York Times gets wiped out with a guy from the Aryan Nations?

Years later, I will describe this strange interview in a lecture to a group of journalism students. Afterwards, one of them spots my husband waiting in line at an ATM machine at the student union at the University of Illinois.

"Hey, Professor Kelleher," the student will yell in a loud voice, "how did you feel about your wife spending the night with the head of the Aryan Nations?"

It is an exceptionally long night, and the conversation finally turns to religion. Thomas, who identifies as a follower of the Christian Identity religion, holds such extreme beliefs that some of his followers were led to kill their own parents. He claims his religion is based on the Bible.

As a veteran of many years of Sunday school and a graduate of Wake Forest College, which belonged to the Southern Baptists at the time, I am prepared for hours of swapping Biblical citations. Something comes over me –I am only here to interview him, so I don't know why – but I begin to argue with him, telling him his views are not Christian because the gospels teach love – not hate. As I speak, I have the strangest feeling Thomas is actually listening to me. We return to the Gulf station and my car just as the sun is coming up. At this point, I'm thankful to be safe, even if I don't have the information I wanted.

The next time I hear from Mark Thomas will be January 1997, when I answer my phone in the pressroom of the federal court in Denver, where I am covering the bombing trial of Timothy McVeigh. Thomas is in a panic. He tells me his house in Pennsylvania is surrounded by the feds, and he fears "another Waco."

"What should I do?"

I have no idea.

"Put your guns down," I tell him. "Take off your clothes. Put your hands up. And walk out very, very slowly."

He will survive his arrest and plead guilty to charges of being involved in the bank robberies. Later, he will write to me from prison to say he has repented of his anti-Semitism and is trying to start a new life. He asks for books. I will send him some from the Seminary Coop Bookstore in Chicago. As I do not have an account myself, I will send them from my husband's account. My husband is not pleased.

By the time the bombing trials begin, I have not found John Doe 2 and can only report the question of a conspiracy has not been resolved. The government disagrees. The trials center on the witnesses and evidence addressing the guilt of McVeigh and Nichols. The only advantage to the *Times* from all my months and miles on the road — and it will be a huge advantage — is my knowledge of the cast of characters, those who are likely to be witnesses and those who may not.

In the process, I have seen a disturbing facet of American life – white people, especially white men – who feel threatened by modernity, by the withering away of rural towns and country life, and most importantly by the loss of the last thing making them feel important, the white skin they consider the essence of American identity. They feel estranged from a society becoming more diverse, and they do not regard the government as something belonging to them. Some turn to alcohol or embrace new religions. Some choose suicide. Others find power, comfort, and a sense of safety in the gun culture. The ones on the fringe give in to paranoia and violence.

I finally publish everything I can find about John Doe 2, even though I cannot identify him or even confirm his existence. I have promised the families of the victims I would do all I could, for as long as the newspaper would let me. I made those promises one by one to families who wanted only one thing: the truth.

Investigative reporting does not always reveal what you hope to find, but often it discovers other things, large and small, of public importance. Its virtue is that it raises new questions, opens closed doors, and now and then sheds light on the dangers and the dark places in which we live. I never found a third man, but I did find a deep wound in the nation's heartland. This wound will continue to fester for a quarter of a century, nurtured by growing disparities of wealth and opportunity. These grievances will be exploited and distorted on social media until we have the unimaginable, a mob storming the United States Congress on January 6, 2021.

CHAPTER THIRTY-SIX:
THE BOMBING TRIALS

It is clear from the first: McVeigh and Nichols cannot get a fair trial in Oklahoma City. U.S. District Judge Richard Matsch moves the trial to Denver in February 1996 and severs the trials. McVeigh is tried first.

Because it is such a high-profile case and such a heinous crime, the judge issues a gag order to the attorneys. Joseph Hartzler, the lead prosecutor, does not speak to the press until the McVeigh trial is over. Larry Mackey, who is just as tough but more genial, goes on to become to lead prosecutor in the Nichols trial. It's impossible to get any information from him either.

Steven Jones, the lawyer from Enid, Oklahoma, who represents McVeigh, plays the media like a violin. As a friend of his says before the trial, "The most dangerous place in America is between Stephen Jones and a television camera."

Michael Tigar, who represents Nichols, is less flamboyant than Jones but in the end, more successful. His client gets life in prison. McVeigh gets the death penalty.

The magnitude of the crime presents challenges at the trial. There are too many victims to accommodate all of them and their families in the courtroom. Congress passes a special law to show the trial on closed circuit television. Three thousand people qualify to watch from an Oklahoma City auditorium seating two hundred people.

There are more than 25,000 witness interviews, so defense lawyers are still finding surprises a month before trial. The government has tens of thousands of telephone records and seven thousand pounds of physical evidence.

A thousand potential jurors are called to meet with the judge, in groups of several hundred at a time, in a guarded county fairground. The actual jury selection in the McVeigh trial takes three weeks.

News organizations from all over the nation and the world want to cover the trial. The major national media in the U.S. get one courtroom pass each. The same goes for the news media from Denver and Oklahoma: just one pass. Once you enter the courtroom, you may not leave until the session is dismissed.

A vast press room is set up on the first floor, and it is a madhouse most of the time. Most news organizations send a team of reporters who cover the trial in shifts. The *Times* just sends me, and they assign Mindy Sink, a journalist working as a clerk in the Denver bureau, to help me. She conducts interviews for me at the end of the day when I am trying to write. She saves me repeatedly.

I rarely see the bureau chief, Jim Brooke, but he and his wife do invite me to dinner while I am there. The *Times* has rented me an apartment downtown, a short walk from the courthouse. It has a view of the front range of the Rocky Mountains. This is a thrill for me. The landscape at home in Illinois is so flat that our steepest hill is a freeway ramp. I gaze at the mountains as I am getting ready for work or bed, but otherwise have to ignore them.

When I finish writing for the day, I'm talking with editors, reading stories by other journalists, or looking at court documents. No time for drinks or dinner with colleagues. No sources here. On weekends, I fly home.

Denver is on Mountain Time, so court always ends on our first edition deadline. I try to write the top of the story during the break for lunch, but inevitably the key details and testimony come at the end of the day, not the beginning. It is stressful to think and write so quickly, especially for me. Now and then, I can't read my own handwritten notes.

The trials are expected to go on for weeks, but they do not. The McVeigh prosecutors, who consider calling as many as four hundred witnesses, cut their list down to 137, including some who appear for only a few minutes. The prosecution takes eighteen days.

Jones has sent investigators to Europe, Asia, and the Middle East in search of conspiracies by other terrorists, but he is never able to present to the jury his theory that the real criminals are still at large. Judge Match keeps the trial focused on evidence addressing the crime and the defendant. In the end, the defense presents only twenty-four witnesses, and they are done in four days.

The Nichols trial takes just a little longer – ninety-eight witnesses for the prosecution in twenty days. The defense produces ninety-two witnesses in eight days.

Much of the testimony is extremely emotional. At the outset, Judge Matsch warns "This is not theater. This is a trial." He announces he will not tolerate displays of emotion.

Anything used to wipe away tears must be hidden. We can't disguise our red eyes. Sometimes, when we leave the courtroom, the reporters and photographers waiting outside will say, "My God, you all look like you've been to a baby's funeral."

Hartzer opens the prosecution's case against McVeigh with the story of Helena Garrett, who woke up the morning of the bombing to April sunshine and wrestling on the bed with her sixteen-month-old son, Tevin.

"She remembers this morning," Hartzler tells the jury, "because it was the last morning of his life."

His mother took Tevin to the day care center on the second floor of the Federal Building, and he clung to her and cried as she left. Elijah Coverdale, two years old, came over to comfort him and pat him on the back. Mrs. Garrett looked back up at the wall of plate glass windows where the children liked to stand and wave, Hartzler tells the jury, "and it was as if you could reach up and touch the children." He pauses.

"None of the parents of those children ever touched them again."

By the end of the next day, after Mrs. Garrett tells the jury about seeing rescue workers carry dead and dying babies out of the smoking building, at least half of the people on the jury are crying. So are two of the prosecutors, both women, and one of McVeigh's lawyers, also a woman. Rescue workers did not find Tevin for three days.

Over the course of both bombing trials, everyone weeps at one time or another — the jurors, the witnesses, the reporters, the lawyers, the federal agents, Terry Nichols. Two people never cry. One is Judge Matsch. The other is Tim McVeigh.

McVeigh makes several "confessions" to his lawyer and others, to journalists, and to other inmates. Each confession is different in some way. Although he did the bombing, it is not clear he acted alone. He often does not get the details right.

Many of us believe these confessions are efforts to shift all suspicions onto himself. Nonetheless, each "confession" causes a minor tidal wave of angst among the press. *The New York Times* never interviews McVeigh because he insists on the right to "vet" the reporter beforehand. We cannot agree to that. And so, I cannot give my readers Tim McVeigh up close in person. I am relieved not to have to relay another version of his lies, not to have to sit any closer to him. He gives me chills in the courtroom sitting several dozen feet away.

His anger and rage exploded with the bomb in front of the Murrah Building. Now he has retreated inside himself again, a cold and lonely man in a world he has imagined, holding on to an angry, elusive cause for which he wants to die, insulated from the agony he has caused others.

The revolution he hoped to ignite had not occurred, but he wants to die for it anyway, and he will wear the mask of stoicism he has assumed. Other than his lawyers, he has few human connections. He seems estranged from his parents, but he is the most hated man in America, so who really knows? No girlfriends. His sister is the only person we know he loves.

The Roman Catholic priest whose parish includes the federal penitentiary in Terre Haute, Indian, has corresponded with McVeigh and sees something in him. "Even Tim McVeigh is not defined by the worst thing he ever did," the priest says. He's trying to help McVeigh pray in preparation for death.

The *Times* sends me to Terre Haute to cover the execution in June 2001. It will be the first federal execution in thirty-eight years. I agree to go if I do not have to be a witness. I oppose the death penalty and being a witness will seem like participating.

So, I write about the execution from outside the prison walls, where the city offices and libraries are closed. A tattoo parlor has sold thirty dozen tee shirts saying "Die! Die! Die!" The owner is tired of being on television and talking to tourists from as far away as Australia. He says it's a circus, and he wants it over.

Some of the relatives of the dead who wanted execution for McVeigh change their minds during and after the bombing trials and became ardent opponents of the death penalty. For some, the execution of McVeigh will be just one more death. They choose to forgive McVeigh, saying it is the only way they can find peace. One father even goes to visit McVeigh's father to commiserate. It is a victory that cannot be won in the courtroom or the death chamber, a light in the darkness.

At the end of the Nichols trial, we all go home. Or as Julie Delcour, who covered the trial for the *Tulsa Tribune,* will say when I see her years later, "the trial ended, and we all fell off a cliff." Some news organizations send their journalists to counselors afterwards. Most, including mine, do not.

I go on to cover other stories about the white right[xxxvi] and then find myself covering school shootings, including Columbine, and finally 9-11. But for years, the worst nightmares come from Oklahoma City.

At home, I have never spoken about my visits to people with guns. Nonetheless, Kathleen, who is still in elementary school, dreams of someone who appears at our front door with a pea shooter, the worst weapon she can imagine.

After the trials in Denver, I try to assess the damage to my family, but I cannot. I have done my best, flying home to Illinois every weekend to see them, but we are in ruins.

Susan, my older daughter, an artist and a violinist, suffered a breakdown at the beginning. Although she will graduate from high school and then college with high honors, the damage to her soul from the upheaval in our family cannot be calculated.

My younger daughter Kathleen is a top athlete and a girl with a million friends, but her brilliant smile is a disguise, she will say and crush me in later years, "because I wanted you to love me and come back when you went away."

My widowed mother, living alone in Texas, spiraled down into alcohol and dementia while the trials were underway. I went to see her as she moved from her house to independent living to assisted living to nursing care, but she died without knowing me.

I fight with my husband and hug our collie, McDuff. My husband, the dog, and I go to Kathleen's soccer games. We are excited when the custard shop opens for the summer. We change the furniture in our house. The fax machine has been sitting in our dining room for months, spitting out yards of documents from the very people my husband has seen on TV denouncing leaks to the press. My office moves back to a corner of our bedroom, and the fax machine, mostly silent, goes with it.

We stack my white file boxes of paperwork on Oklahoma City into a mountain in our two-car garage. The boxes sit behind snow shovels, wheelbarrows, garden tools, and other out-of-season items. As the pile grows so big we can barely fit one car next to it, the white boxes vanish from view. It will take a family move to upstate New York to force me to recycle most of them.

After all this time and digging, I am not satisfied that I know the whole truth about the Oklahoma City bombing. I do not yet realize the importance of an even bigger discovery, the cancer of despair and hate plaguing sectors of the nation's white population. I do not realize how widespread and dangerous to democracy their grievances will turn out to be.

CHAPTER THIRTY-SEVEN:
THE MOMMY TRAP

After the bombing trial, I cannot get out of the mommy trap at work. Gene Roberts, the managing editor who allowed me to work from home in Illinois, has left the newspaper. The *Times* has a rising star in the Chicago bureau. My editors say they do not need two reporters in Illinois.

"We don't want an Urbana bureau," one says bluntly. They order me to return to the head office on 43rd Street. I long to go there, but I can't move my family.

I travel to New York and explain my situation to one senior editor after another, all men. They do not want reporters scattered everywhere, working from home. It's the end of the 1990s, and the internet is just revving up. The revolution in work caused by the COVID-19 pandemic in 2020 is as unimaginable as the pandemic itself.

My union rep, a woman, understands my predicament but cannot help. My husband won't budge, and I can't bring myself to leave my daughters and return to New York. I do not want to resign from the newspaper. I feel like a firefly caught in a glass jar, my light about to die.

Finally, I negotiate working on contract, taking less pay for the same work. The work, as a utility player, turns out to be different. Sometimes they want help with a spot story, sometimes a difficult problem. After the 9-11 attacks, they will ask me to find out who has been arrested on suspicion of planning to plant a "dirty bomb." No one on the staff knows who it is or where the arrest has taken place.

I will dig around in Florida and tell them the suspect is Jose Padilla, arrested at O'Hare Airport in May 2002. He will be in the Federal court system for years, alleging torture, and will end up at in the Supermax federal prison in Colorado. He will never be charged with planning to build a bomb. Instead, he will be held as an enemy combatant and convicted of conspiracy to murder and fund terrorism.

Most days, like a stringer, I am sent on spot stories at a moment's notice. When my daughters leave for school in the morning, they never know if I will be home or gone when they return. The job is hard on them and on me.

After all these years, I feel I am hanging on by my fingernails. It's not dignified. But I don't want to quit. I'm still in the union but no longer listed as a member of the staff. I'm not burned out emotionally, but you could say I'm scorched. Months of Oklahoma City bombing coverage have burned away a habit of mind that once cushioned me to talk with people in pain.

I discover this when the *Times* sends me to Columbine High School in Littleton, Colorado, where a teacher and fourteen students, including the two teen-aged killers, have been shot dead. I approach a group of students in the school parking lot. They are standing around cars left behind by friends who have been killed or seriously injured. When I see their tears, I can't hold back mine.

"I can't stand this," I tell my editor in New York. "I have kids this age. Send someone else." Never before have I asked to leave a story.

I do the same thing in Shanksville, Pennsylvania, where I am sent to cover the crash of American Airlines Flight 93 on September 11. Most of us don't yet know that the passengers took on the hijackers in an effort that crashed the plane instead of continuing to the hijackers' destination, Washington, D. C.

When I arrive, the crash site is cordoned off. I can't get anywhere near it. Instead, I walk around and interview residents, asking if they saw the plane as it approached. I want a description of how it crashed.

Some say it wobbled at treetop level, then made a sudden dive, nose first, into a field. Others weep and say that body parts landed on their roofs and in their yards, thrown into the air by the blast after the plane went into the ground. As we speak, something dark begins to twist inside me.

Jere Longman, a *Times* sportswriter with many talents, arrives, and we hear that relatives of the passengers are on their way. I call the editors in New York and tell them, "I'm sorry, but I can't talk to any more families of dead people. I must leave before they arrive. I will do anything else you want me to do."

Jere stays and will write a successful book about Flight 93 and the heroism of the passengers who saved the U.S. Capitol, the White House, or Camp David from destruction at the hands of the terrorists.

My editor sends me to Pittsburgh to get on the first plane going to South Florida, where some of the hijackers are thought to have attended flight school. On September 13, when air traffic is allowed again, I board a plane to Fort Lauderdale. The air marshal and I are the only passengers.

Five days later, someone begins sending out letters infected with anthrax, one of which kills an editor at the *Sun* tabloid in Boca Raton. He is elderly, and I interview his neighbors. I can handle the anthrax stories.

I also spend weeks trying to find the flight instructors who worked with the Saudi hijackers who took flying lessons. I find no one in Florida, so I try Phoenix, Arizona, where one of the hijackers, Hani Hanjour, took lessons. My editors want to know what, if anything, FBI agents there suspected about the flight schools beforehand.

My visits to the agents' homes are not welcome. It's as hot as hell walking around, and I dread ringing their doorbells. I do it anyway. To a man, they close the door, if they answer it at all.

I have more luck with the flight instructors. One of them, from Egypt, remembers Hanjour. He tells me Hanjour did not want to learn how to recover the airplane from a stall. He was a terrible pupil, the instructor recalls. "I would not let my family fly with him."

In the wake of the anthrax attacks, my editors also ask me to investigate whether any members of the white far right are using biological weapons. I learn that a Southern California doctor and right-winger who recently committed suicide had stored toxins in his refrigerator, buried weapons in his yard, and met secretly with a South African doctor and poisoner known in his country as "Dr. Death." I write one story but am called off. The nation and the newspaper are focused on Saddam Hussein and his weapons.

I leave the newspaper at the end of 2002, gratified that the staff includes many women and people of color. Members of the staff have felt able to identify openly as lesbian, gay, or transgender. Not all the people in power are white, male, and straight.

The *Times* is undertaking important, challenging investigations, the kind I love, and it will include in its definition of corruption the sin of slavery, evidenced by the magnificent *The 1619 Project* in *The New York Times Magazine.* The *Times* is reflecting and addressing the concerns of the public in ways its best editors have always wanted. As an institution, the newspaper takes on the revolution in digital technology, and it triumphs. I am cheering from the sidelines.

Is journalism a job for a woman? Yes! I was called to do it, and I would do it again. No amount of money could buy such a life. It was a chance to be a witness, to tell the truth and shine a light in the darkness.

It was an opportunity to discover who I really am. I have changed from a sheltered Southern housewife, still a girl, to a woman able to uncover important things and tell others about them. I have witnessed astonishing courage, beauty, and resilience in people I never would have met.

I ran from the family of my birth without knowing you can't run from them. They will come with you. This is clearest when you establish your own family, even one that appears radically different on the surface. All you can do is hold on to what you love in them and make sure your own children know your values. My Southern accent is gone, but I'm still white.

You can't change your skin, but you can change your character.

Newspapers are perishable. They will go out with the trash tomorrow. We value their journalism: telling the public what is going on. In this, the truth is everything. Facts matter. Fairness matters. In the digital age, the truth spreads at the speed of light, but so do half-truths, mistakes, and lies.

We make ourselves through our stories and those of others. Narratives make sense of the world. Narratives change it. As time passes, our worlds will change and disappear. I have been striving to capture and remember matters of public importance with words, sounds, and images. They are by and for everyone. No one can say they are not for a woman.

ACKNOWLEDGEMENTS

For support over the years, I would like to thank my daughters, Susan and Kathleen, and my late husband Bill Kelleher.

Thank you to the women who filed a class action suit against *The New York Times* for better pay and opportunities for women before I was hired.

Thank you to David R. Jones, my mentor at the *Times,* and Leo Hirtl, my first editor in Cincinnati. Thanks to Elizabeth Rion for teaching me journalism and Dr. Edwin G. Wilson of Wake Forest University for never losing faith in me.

For their support and encouragement, I thank Leigh Estabrook, Cindy Carpenter, Cheryl D. Grant, Gus Napier, Tom and Steve Parker, Helene Foley, Bruce McCandless III, Amy Halsey, David Cay Johnston, and my extended family who told me never to give up.

Thanks also to my friends on Lydia Court in Urbana, Illinois, especially Chuck Allison.

Thanks for great edits and suggestions to the members of the Writers Café at OLLI, the Osher Lifelong Learning Institute, at the University of Illinois at Urbana-Champaign.

END NOTES

[i] Rebecca Goodman, "Obituary: Robert Deters Sr. led large west-side S&L." *Cincinnati Enquirer*, April 12, 2003, accessed on Newspapers.com on Jan 3, 2022.

[ii] National Transportation Safety Board, Aircraft Accident Report on Transworld Airlines Inc. Convair 880 N821TW Constance, Kentucky, November 20,1967. Document NTSB AAR6905

[iii] National Transportation Safety Board, Aircraft Accident Report on Transworld Airlines Inc. Convair 880 N821TW Constance, Kentucky, November 20,1967. Document NTSB AAR6905

[iv] See the groundbreaking book by Kim Todd, *Sensational: The Hidden History of America's Girl Stunt Reporters.* New York: Harper Collins, 2021.

[v] Wake Forest was founded by the North Carolina Baptists, and there were years of dispute over the church's views on moral standards and academic freedom. That ended in 1986 when the Baptists voted to sever ties and have a "fraternal" relationship with the University.

[vi] Jim Rohrer, "Strangler Terrorized Cincinnati in 1960s." *Cincinnati Enquirer*, Dec. 6, 2010; "High Court to Hear Appeal

by Laskey," United Press International, June 12, 1968; "Suspected 'Cincinnati Strangler' Serial Killer Dies of Natural Causes in Jail", Fox News, June 12, 2007.

[vii] Jo Thomas, "Chief Negro Need? A Little Soul, Brother." *Cincinnati Post and Times-Star*, June 22, 1967, p.1.

[viii] Jessica Noll, "Former Northern Kentucky Newspaper Editor Vance Trimble Celebrates his 100th birthday." *WCPO Digital*, posted 7:26 pm July 5, 2013, Updated August 7, 2013.

[ix] See Mark Singer, "A Year of Trouble; a City Subverts Itself." U.S. Journal, The *New Yorker*, May 20, 2002; "Cincinnati Officer is Acquitted in Killing That Ignited Arrest" by the *Associated Press, The New York Times*, September 27, 2001.

[x] Lizzie Kane, "Property Management Firm is Sued by Chicago; Accused of Using "Rent-to-Own" Schemes to Prey on South Side Residents." *Chicago Tribune*, August 4, 2023, Section 2, p.1.

[xi] Kerekes was a real person, but I have never revealed his real name.

[xii] Joe Swickard, "Crime Leader Giacalone Dies; Mobster's 2 Images: Fearsome, Dignified." *Detroit Free Press*, Feb 24, 2001, p.1A.

[xiii] Jack L. Goldsmith, *In Hoffa's Shadow: A Stepfather, a Disappearance in Detroit, and My Search for the Truth.* New York: Farrar, Straus and Giroux, 2019.

[xiv] *Elizabeth Boylan (nee Wade), et. al. v. New York Times Co.*, 74 Civ. 4891 (S.D.N.Y., 1978). *See* Nan Robertson, *The Girls in the Balcony*, New York: Random House, 1992, p. 169 ff. for a full account.

[xv] Associated Press, "Reporter Linked to a Senator's Gifts," August 28, 1977; "A 'Heroine' Women Can Do Without."

Washington Post, 1978; Albert R. Hunt, "American Politicians Narrow the Sex Scandal Gap." *The New York Times*, July 5, 2009; Katharine Q. Seelye, "Laura Foreman, Reporter Whose Romance Became a Scandal, Dies at 76." *The New York Times*, July 23, 2021.

xvi Carole Gallagher, *American Ground Zero; The Secret Nuclear War*, Cambridge, MA.: The MIT Press, 1993.

xvii The Dominicans did identify the dead as the U.S pilot and two Dominicans, a Navy officer, and a pediatrician. The injured included the five American crew members and two Dominican physicians.

xviii Christopher Lehmann-Haupt, "Obituary: Aubelin Jolicoeur, 80, 'Mr. Haiti' and Muse of Graham Greene." *The New York Times*, March 8, 2005

xix Jo Thomas, "Haiti Has Little to Show for Millions Received in Aid." *The New York Times*, Sept 27, 1980, p. A2.

xx Jo Thomas, "In Northwestern Haiti, People are Principal Export." *The New York Times*, September 26, 1980, p. A22.

xxi Jo Thomas, "Sadly, the Marooned Haitians Return Home." *The New York Times*, November 17, 1980.

xxii See Rick Bragg, "MISSION TO HAITI: the Troops; the Auschwitz of Haiti for 3 Decades, Gives Up the Secrets of its Dark Past." *The New York Times*, Oct 1, 1994; Alfonso Chardy, "Island in the Grip of Voodoo and Violence." *Sidney Morning Herald*, Sept. 18, 1994, accessed on newspapers.com on January 18, 2020; Dan Coughlin, "Haitian Lament: Killing Me Softly." *The Nation*, March 1, 1999.

xxiii Jo Thomas, "Duvalier Defends Arrests, Warns Haiti Won't Tolerate Interference." *The New York Times*, December 10, 1980, p. A6.

[xxiv] Perry-Castañeda Library Map Collection, University of Texas at Austin, https://maps.lib.utexas.edu/maps/haiti.html, accessed July 12, 2023

[xxv] Douglas Martin, "Orlando Bosch, Cuban Exile, Dies at 84." *The New York Times,* April 27, 2011, https://www.nytimes.com/2011/04/28/us/28bosch.html. Accessed March 16, 2020.

[xxvi] Gwynne Dwyer, "Trump: The Reagan Gambit?" *The Portugal News*, August 17, 2017, https://www.theportugalnews.com/news/trump-the-reagan-gambit/42900 accessed Nov 3, 2010.

[xxvii] Jo Thomas, "The Agony of Ulster." *The New York Times Magazine*, March 10, 1985, Section 6, p.30.

[xxviii] Jo Thomas, "Winter in a British Pit Village: The Spirit is Bitter." *The New York Times*, December 4, 1984, p. A2.

[xxix] *Julie Doherty, Re an Application for Judicial Review* [2004] NIQB 78 https://www.judiciaryni.uk/sites/judiciary/files/decisions/Doherty,%20Re%20an%20application%20for%20Judicial%20Review.pdf Archived 16 July 2011 at the Wayback Machine.

[xxx] Raymond Murray, *The SAS in Ireland.* Cork and Dublin: The Mercier Press Ltd., November 1990, p. 294. Father Murray provides many details from the Campbell/McGirr inquest in this chapter of his book.

[xxxi] Bernard Lown, M.D., "A Prescription for Hope." Nobel Lecture delivered on Dec 11, 1985, in Oslo, Norway. Copyright © The Nobel Foundation, Stockholm, 1985.

xxxii Bernard Lown, M.D., "A Prescription for Hope," Nobel Lecture delivered on Dec 11, 1985, in Oslo, Norway. Copyright © The Nobel Foundation, Stockholm, 1985.

xxxiii Jo Thomas, "In Ulster, the Shoot to Kill Rumors Will Not Die." *The New York Times*, March 17, 1986, p.A2.

xxxiv Raymond Murray, *The SAS in Ireland*. Cork and Dublin: The Mercier Press Limited, November 1990. Pp 315-320.

xxxv Parts of this chapter were published in the *Syracuse Law Review*, Volume 59, Number 3, (2009) pages 459-469, as "The Third Man: A Reporter Investigates the Oklahoma City Bombing," and are used with permission.

xxxvi I was the reporter on the documentary *Brotherhood of Hate* (1999), directed by Pamela Yates and co-produced by SHOWTIME and New York Times Television. *See* https://archive.org/details/yt-1s.com-america-exposed-uncut-chevie-kehoe-480p accessed October 2023

Made in United States
North Haven, CT
12 October 2023

42665995R10259